I0819713

JACK RITTENHOUSE

ALSO BY DAVID FARMER

Siegfried Sassoon: A Memorial Exhibition
Flannery O'Connor: A Descriptive Bibliography
A Trumpet of Our Own: Yellow Bird's Essays on the North American Indian, edited with Rennard Strickland
The Cambridge Edition of the Works of D. H. Lawrence: Women in Love, edited with Lindeth Vasey and John Worthen
Stanley Marcus: A Life with Books
Willard Clark: Printer and Printmaker

JACK RITTENHOUSE

A WESTERN LITERARY LIFE

DAVID R. FARMER

UNIVERSITY OF NEW MEXICO PRESS | ALBUQUERQUE

Printed in the United States of America

ISBN 978-0-8263-6955-0 (cloth)
ISBN 978-0-8263-6956-7 (ePub)

Library of Congress Control Number: 2025054239

Founded in 1889, the University of New Mexico sits on the traditional homelands of the Pueblo of Sandia. The original peoples of New Mexico—Pueblo, Navajo, and Apache—since time immemorial have deep connections to the land and have made significant contributions to the broader community statewide. We honor the land itself and those who remain stewards of this land throughout the generations and also acknowledge our committed relationship to Indigenous peoples. We gratefully recognize our history.

Cover photograph courtesy of the New Mexico State University Library, Archives and Special Collections.
Designed by Felicia Cedillos
Composed in Alegreya

For Carol, always

and

Frank and Joy, Sara Jean, and with fond memories of Gene

Books constitute capital. A library book lasts as long as a house, for hundreds of years. It is not then an article of mere consumption, but fairly of capital, and often in the case of professional men, setting out in life, it is their only capital.

—THOMAS JEFFERSON TO JAMES MADISON, SEPTEMBER 16, 1821

CONTENTS

PREFACE

The day always brightened whenever a new catalog arrived from Jack D. Rittenhouse Bookseller in Albuquerque. Devoted to Western Americana, his offerings promised interesting and important books on the Trans-Mississippi West, its history and development. His notes for each entry were a joy to read, concise, accurate, informative, and penned by someone who knew how to write well. He was widely regarded by historians, librarians, collectors, and publishers as an authority on the West, and rightfully so. He had been involved with books since his high school years, writing, editing, printing, collecting, and publishing them. Few people knew the dimensions of this quiet man's mind: how he had dropped out of college in the Great Depression and ridden the rails with hobos, risen in the echelons of American advertising, operated a private press publishing award-winning books, became editor of western books at the University of New Mexico Press, and later retired into a world of antiquarian bookselling with ease and distinction.

I first knew Jack as a client buying rare books for DeGolyer Library at Southern Methodist University. He then became a generous and informed reader of a lecture I was preparing for an annual meeting of the Santa Fe Trail Association. For a series of profiles on antiquarian booksellers in New Mexico I interviewed him one afternoon more than thirty years ago in his library at home, a comfortable space where he recalled many earlier stages of his life. We were surrounded by some nine thousand books; Jack was in his milieu. Among other things, he remembered with clarity the excitement of reading as a youngster and being drawn to western history, his attraction to printing, the enjoyment of selecting different typefaces for good book design, his survival in New York during the Depression, his trips along Route 66 and the production of his 1946 guide to the "Mother Road" still in print today. Throughout the long interview Jack puffed on his favorite pipe, reaching at times for a book on the shelf that held part of the story he was telling. Clearly enjoying time for reflection, he appeared at the top of his form. I did not realize he was being treated for cancer. My profile was published a month later, and in less than a year he died. With the day-to-day business of running a library, I filed the long interview transcript away, intending someday to write a book about Jack. After retirement and two moves, I uncovered the transcript and began rereading. It reminded me that my own career was enriched by a master printer, editor, writer, and antiquarian bookseller who shared his stories, what he had learned about books, how they are made, and how they can assume a life stretching over centuries. Now it is time to share Jack's story of his life with books.

ACKNOWLEDGMENTS

When I think about the remarkable constellation of people who helped me with this book, I know exactly where to start. It is with the brightest star, my best friend and wife, Carol. The past sixty-four years have included many "best times" in our lives, and we've just lived another one—researching this book together, and with Carol editing the text I wrote. Her keen eye for clear writing steered me through graduate school and made my earlier books better than I could ever have managed on my own, but the past few years with this book have been a golden time as we sat side by side in research libraries (an echo of our undergraduate days) and then I wrote while Carol edited, asking tirelessly if particular sections helped keep the story flowing or got in the way, steering me away from the weeds that always wait beside the path, and moving everything toward a better balance. Our discussions about the shape and tone of this book were deep, long, and untroubled because we shared a goal of making it the best we knew how. I am forever grateful for all of Carol's wise counsel and encouragement throughout the research and writing of this book.

On our numerous Las Cruces trips to consult the Rittenhouse papers at New Mexico State University Library, we could not have asked for a more professional and helpful team in Archives and Special Collections than with Dennis Daily, Department Head, and members of his staff, Teddie Moreno, Elizabeth R. Villa, Jennifer Olguin, and their student assistants, especially Katie Mena. Every time we returned to New Mexico State University, they made us feel even more welcome. Closer to home at the Fray Angelico Chavez History

Library, Heather McClure and Kathleen Dull went out of their way to find books and files essential to Jack's story and also welcome us warmly whenever we came to the library.

With the advent of digitized collections in libraries everywhere, research is facilitated like never before, but inevitably questions arise. I am deeply grateful for the many helpful email responses from the following dedicated librarians: Tomas Jaehn (retired), Dr. Margie Montañez and Jennifer Dawn Eggleston at the Center for Southwest Research and Special Collections, University of New Mexico; Katie Gray, Thomas C. Donnelly Library, New Mexico Highlands University; Maggie Mitts and Cristina Meisner, Research Team, Harry Ransom Center, UT-Austin; Katherine Wolf, Librarian, and Laura Holt, Librarian Emerita, School of Advanced Research (SAR), Santa Fe; Miriam Kolar, Managing Editor, SAR Press; Scott Ellwood and Meghan R. Constantinou, Grolier Club Library; Jose Cisneros, Santan Historical Society, Queen Creek, Arizona; Benna Vaughan, Baylor University Library; Regina Bouley Sweeten, Golden Library, Eastern New Mexico University; Beverly Wigley, Sophienburg Museum and Archives, New Braunfels, Texas; Kathleen Knoth, Director (retired), University of New Mexico Taos Library; Jeffrey Lawson, Duane G. Meyer Library, Missouri State University; Alison Moore, North Baker Research Library, California Historical Society; Katie Salzmann, The Wittliff Collections, Albert B. Alkek Library, Texas State University, and everyone on the Reference Desk at the Santa Fe Public Library! Shortly before his death, Alfred Bush, long retired from the Firestone Library at Princeton, kindly answered inquiries, written in longhand, of course. At DeGolyer Library, Southern Methodist University, I am indebted to Russell Martin, Director, for helping me access many of Jack's antiquarian bookseller catalogs as well as for his enduring encouragement as this project has progressed.

Jack's long involvement in the antiquarian book trade resulted in a legendary status remembered today by those book people still active in Western Americana circles or devoted to the history of the Southwest. I am grateful to the following for sharing their recollections, introducing me to others whom I should contact, and encouraging me to write about a fellow bookman they widely admired: David Margolis and Jean Moss, Michael Heaston, Jan V. Nelson, Ken Huddleston, Lew Buckingham, Al Gonzales, Mike Dawson, Tyler Fletcher, Andre Dumont, Michael Parrish, the late Nicholas Potter, John Randall, and Michael Vinson. Thank you, all!

A dedication to fine printing figures in this biography, and for New Mexico the tradition thrived at the Press at the Palace of the Governors in Santa Fe, a beneficiary of Jack's knowledge and largesse. I am most grateful for the support and encouragement given me by three dedicated printers at the Palace Press, Pam Smith, founding director, and her successors, Tom Leech and James Bourland. These fine printers followed Jack's example and through their work established the Press firmly in the annals of fine printing in the United States. I am also deeply appreciative to Priscilla Spitler, the award-winning fine binder who shared recollections of Jack and some of the special commissions he sent her way. Another printer who apprenticed with Jack was Richard Polese to whom I am grateful for sharing some of the books he helped Jack move through Stagecoach Press in its early years in Santa Fe. I am indebted also to Dan Cronkhite, printer in Yucca Valley, for his recollections of buying (and hauling back to California!) Jack's type collection.

At *New Mexico Magazine* Carmella Jasso patiently answered questions about early contributions to the journal, while Adam Fulton Johnson and Cordelia Snow did the same at the Old Santa Fe Association. I am also grateful to John Kessell and Richard Etulain, former University of New Mexico colleagues of Jack for their helpful responses to inquiries.

Of special note are others who have offered enduring encouragement and support in this book project. I am indebted to Harry Briley for his website devoted to Jack and for answering what must have seemed like an endless string of questions over the past few years. Quotations from Jack D. Rittenhouse's autobiographical memoir *Recollections* are used by permission from the Harry Briley Living Trust

(HBLT) and Harry Briley, editor and custodian of Jack's memoir as published on the website: https://brileyh.weebly.com/rittenhouse-memoir.html. Zang Wood, undoubtedly the first person to start seriously collecting Rittenhouse material during Jack's lifetime, was certainly the most thorough and dedicated in pursuing his interests. His comprehensive collection, now part of the Fray Angélico Chávez History Library, has been essential to this book, and I am most appreciative for his encouragement and support of my work. A Texas-sized thank-you goes to T. Lindsay Baker for generously sharing information on his research and writing about Jack's book on Route 66 and pointing me to a little-known cache of recollections Jack wrote in the last years of his life, cataloged in a way that makes them difficult to unearth. Such friends are what make research so enjoyable! Debra Hutsell, Research Specialist, located scores of book reviews and newspaper articles by a very young Jack Rittenhouse that lay forgotten in newspaper morgues in Indiana. I am indeed grateful to Debra for her tireless work back at microfilm readers, which are still around and much needed when newspaper collections are not digitized.

Finally, I am most grateful to Stephen Hull and his colleagues at the University of New Mexico Press for interest in my work and their careful attention to the manuscript and the making of this book. Publishing is a dizzying, challenge-ridden, technical, and artistic endeavor, and I am deeply grateful to everyone at the Press for their knowledge and professional standards applied to the production of this book. Thank you! Jack would have been proud too!

Whatever missteps remain herein land on my desk alone. I hope they are few and far between, just as they were when Jack was producing books. The entire process leading to this point puts me in awe of Jack when considering the amazing number of books he wrote, edited, and saw through the press during his life with books.

Chapter 1

Building Resilience

The year was marked most of all by my discovery of the town's public library. . . . I was at the library when it opened and read as fast as I could until it closed and then took two other books back to our rooms at the hotel, to read and return when the library opened again.

—JACK D. RITTENHOUSE[1]

ON NOVEMBER 15, 1912, Hazel Giles gave birth to a son in a single room at his maternal grandparent's hotel in Kalamazoo, Michigan. His father, John Anderson, abandoned his family soon after Jack's birth and lost all contact with them. After a few years Hazel met and married Earl Norman Rittenhouse, also recovering from a failed marriage. Many years later the boy learned in stages only a little about his mother's difficult first marriage and how he was named Jack DeVere Rittenhouse.

> On August 18, 1916, Earl Rittenhouse legally adopted me, and my birth certificate shows him as my father. By personal choice, my mother and stepfather never mentioned the origins of my birth. In the summer of 1931, close to age 19, a relative told me about Anderson, and this brought the matter into the open. My parents said they kept it quiet so I would never feel different from my

> brother and sister. They never told my brother and sister about the adoption. I respected their wishes even since their death, but want to set the permanent record straight.[2]

"Childhood memories were sketchy and only partly one's own. Many recollections were things our parents told us later, usually so often that we think of them as our own." Thus, Jack "remembered" the first book given him for Christmas at age three, *Little Black Sambo*. "I was never aware that Sambo was black. I saw so few blacks that I was not conscious that a different race existed." He also received a pair of copper-toed boots that made more of a lasting impression than the book. "I had the idea that the boots were magical, that no depth of water or snow existed from which they would not guard me. I walked into knee high drifts and promptly got both boots full of snow with a chilling disillusion. I sat by the big iron kitchen stove to dry off."[3]

At five, Jack's world expanded when his father took a job in Arizona with an older brother, Charles. The Rittenhouse brothers drilled water wells to supply small irrigation districts in the desert community of Queen Creek south of Phoenix and Mesa. Even with large and powerful water districts already well established, opportunities still existed for entrepreneurs to supply water to smaller communities. The Rittenhouse brothers and others like them tapped into aquifers and installed five-ton Bessemer gas engines to pump the water from wells 300 feet deep.

The Rittenhouse family lived in a two-room, unpainted wood-frame house around which dust began to swirl with no more than a mild breeze. On one side two large, screened windows were protected by hinged doors that the family lowered whenever the dust rose. Jack remembered desert windstorms during which dirt drifted into the house even with the doors and window flaps closed. The setting was minimal: "One room had a stove, table, chairs, and cabinets for dishes and food. The other room had a large bed, a small one, and a cabinet for clothes. There was no running water, gas, lights, telephone, bathroom, or sink. Here we lived for at least a year, while Dad worked. I had no neighbor playmates, but I always amused myself. We had no musical instruments or phonograph. Radio was not yet available for home use."[4] He fondly remembered a pedal car his father made for him "with four wheels from a boy's wagon, pedals that worked a 'crankshaft' to turn the wheels, and a steering wheel. It was hard to operate it in the sand, but some hard surface places existed where it ran fine."[5]

Before Jack turned seven, his mother and father moved to Phoenix so he could start school. Earl built his family a small frame house near the center of town and the newly opened Garfield elementary school. Eight years after Arizona statehood, the city boasted a population of more than twenty-nine thousand. As an adult Jack remembered Phoenix as a city that "grew without the built-in background culture found in Middle Western cities. I liked school very much. The building was new, the teachers good, and the textbooks free."[6] Rather than start in kindergarten, he entered the first grade where he quickly learned to read by studying the phonics system that employed flash cards. He recalled how matching the sounds of spoken words with individual letters or groups of letters made sense to him immediately, allowing him to read more quickly than most other classmates. Reading became an early pleasure, and it sustained him for the rest of his life.

In the summer of 1921 after a deflationary recession, Jack's uncle Charles declared bankruptcy and stayed in Arizona while his parents moved back to Indiana. With jobs scarce Earl Rittenhouse had difficulty finding work in Fort Wayne where the family wanted to settle. In time Jack's father was hired by a company that manufactured gasoline pumps for an emerging network of filling stations servicing the growing number of automobiles in the United States. Occasionally the boy's mother would take in sewing piece work. Keeping a household and putting food on the table was always challenging, and as Jack's parents were getting settled they arranged for his grandparents, Robert and Louise Hassinger, to care for him at their hotel, newly located in Constantine, Michigan, not far from his birthplace.

In a village with a population of 1,200, the Hassinger's owned the Harvey Hotel near the banks of the St. Joseph River.[7] Constantine was conveniently located for salesmen calling on potential clients up and down the state, and the hotel's business was steady. Jack recalled "the year was marked most of all by my discovery of the town's public library. It was open only two evenings a week . . . from perhaps 6:30 to 9 p.m. I was at the library when it opened and read as fast as I could until it closed and then took two other books back to our rooms at the hotel, to read and return when the library opened again."[8]

Young Jack advanced from the first to the fourth grade in two and a half years. Along the way he discovered children's books by Gelett Burgess (1866–1951), an American poet, art critic, and humorist identified with the San Francisco Bay Area literary renaissance in the 1890s. Burgess was the author of nonsense verse, such as "The Purple Cow," and the creator of the Goops—unlikely, baldheaded cartoon-like figures that amused Jack. He also borrowed a book about the Boy Scouts of America, formed two years after he was born. Intrigued by what he read, he decided he would join the Scouts as soon as he turned twelve.

When he was ten Jack moved home to live with his parents in Fort Wayne. Soon they had a small house of their own on the edge of town where they lived for the next eight or ten years. "I recall books from that period," he remembered. "We had a cheap Victorian 'secretary' with a lid that dropped to provide a writing surface, and below that were two shelves perhaps thirty inches wide that housed the family library. While in Arizona, my parents had become great readers of books by Zane Grey, especially *Riders of the Purple Sage* and *Under the Tonto Rim*. My parents still remembered life in Arizona and really preferred life there instead of in Indiana, and the Southwest became a sort of Eden to which I might return. This mystique was further fixed in my mind by the movies of the period, which I saw most Saturday mornings, with all the old cowboy stars, together with Western pulp magazines that were always around the house."[9]

Not all of the reading material at home was Western. Jack recalled his mother, at age thirty, read books by Elinor Glyn, Harold Bell Wright, and romances such as *The Prisoner of Zenda*, "not exactly great literature, but they did let me know that reading was fun. For my eleventh birthday my aunt gave me three books by James Fenimore Cooper: *The Deerslayer*, *The Last of the Mohicans*, and *The Pathfinder*. No one told her or me that these were normally fare for a boy about three years older, so I read them all, more than once." When he moved to junior high school, he began riding the trolley to school located near downtown Fort Wayne. His student pass paid for unlimited rides. At lunchtime he got back on the trolley, rode a few more blocks to the center of town and thence to Woolworth's where his daily allowance of twenty-five cents bought a fifteen-cent hot beef sandwich, leaving a dime to buy a cheap book. Before long his library at home included *The Count of Monte Cristo*, *Treasure Island*, and *The Three Musketeers*.

In his second or third year in high school, he began working as a library page, reshelving books and "reading the shelves" to make certain that everything was in its proper place according to the Dewey decimal system. Late in his life Jack still remembered "that books on economics were under the east windows and books on biography were in the far corner." For several months after classes ended in 1930, Jack worked for the Fort Wayne Public Library, going around town to pick up overdue books from patrons, and allowed to retain the fines, if collected, for his pay. "By now, the world of books and libraries was nothing new to me; books were as natural as breathing, and I took no special notice of them except when an especially good book crossed my trail."[10]

Jack's earlier interest in the Boy Scouts never wavered. On the night before his twelfth birthday he passed his Tenderfoot test and joined Troop 17 in Fort Wayne, Indiana. Active from the autumn of 1924 until spring, 1932, he recalled those years as critical for building his self-esteem and sense of accomplishment. As Jack's father saw the positive influences of scouting on his son, he began taking a leadership role with the troop. He soon organized a new Troop 35 closer to their home and became scoutmaster. The entire family joined scouting: his brother Howard at age twelve, his mother becoming captain of a Girl Scout troop, and his sister, Marie, joining the Girl Scouts. "The troop was my 'gang.' All of its members were from within a radius of three to eight blocks of my home. We had a regular meeting every Friday night, plus a patrol meeting or other project at least one night a week. We had some activity almost every weekend. In our troop there were Lutherans, Catholics, and Protestants."[11]

In 1927, Troop 35 bought a Model T Ford truck for hauling equipment on weekend trips and taking boys to rallies. Jack first learned to drive in that 1919 Model T on country roads—no more homemade pedal cars on the Arizona desert. He also helped print the weekly troop newspaper. On an old Edison mimeograph given to the troop, far from the letterpress printing he would master as an adult, Jack helped produce multiple copies of a modest printed newsletter. "We were also given a typewriter," he recalled, "a very early machine on which the characters struck upward from below, and one could not see what was typed until the roller was lifted. I learned to type on that machine."[12]

Whatever his other Scouting responsibilities, Jack regarded camping as the most important and enjoyable outdoor activity since it required careful planning, good organization, following procedures and routines, leadership, and collaboration. As he advanced in Scouting, he earned twenty-eight merit badges, helping him become familiar with a wide range of occupations. He considered merit badges as a form of career orientation.

In 1928, while he was working in the kitchen at summer camp, he learned about a worldwide Boy Scout Jamboree planned the following summer in England. To attend, each Scout needed to pay five hundred dollars for his own expenses. He knew that amount equaled four months of his dad's salary and held little hope of going. While the Fort Wayne Scout Council had a business donor who would pay all the expenses for one Boy Scout in Troop 35, Jack felt he would be outranked by more senior Scouts. Nonetheless, when troop members voted on who was most deserving, Jack won. The Lincoln National

Life Insurance Company headquartered in Fort Wayne paid his way. Its founder and president, Arthur Fletcher Hall, would later help him with financial support while in college.

The next summer Jack joined 1,300 US Scouts for the two-week Jamboree outside of Liverpool, followed by a two-week tour of England and western Europe with his fellow scouts from Fort Wayne. His vivid recollections of that summer, redolent with details, included the Atlantic crossing on a crowded Cunard ocean liner, making friends with boys from South Africa, Scotland, Australia, and elsewhere, his own duties supervising the cooking for fifty boys, afternoon walks to nearby towns, and a visit to his camp by the Prince of Wales. Early in the voyage, the Cunard staff gave each scout a diary. Jack immediately began making detailed entries of his activities, impressions of his surroundings and the people he met, and reflections on history relating to landmark sites they saw. He sent home four long travel essays, and by age seventeen he became a published writer with his own byline when the *Fort Wayne News Sentinel* ran his contributions.[13] In the walled town of Chester, Jack bought his first antiquarian book, *The Lives and Sayings of the Most Famous of the Ancient Philosophers*, London, 1696. The highlight for Jack was visiting the battlefield of Waterloo where Wellington defeated Napoleon. In his high school history class the previous year, he had prepared a detailed oral report on the 1815 Battle of Waterloo, and when touring the actual site he found "the whole battlefield <u>just as it had been</u> when the battle was fought. Every field, lane, and farmhouse was just the same. The Scouts around me got a second oral report. But the main effect was on me, for this brought history to life more than anything else I saw on the entire trip. And this relation of history to life has remained with me ever since, especially in the American Southwest, where we are still so close to history."[14]

After Jack returned from the Jamboree, he entered his senior year at Central High School in Fort Wayne where he was elected class president.[15] He also became junior assistant scoutmaster of Troop 35, held an after-school job at the public library, and participated in a "small semi-official fraternity." As he prepared for college his interest in active scouting diminished. Still, he always acknowledged the positive impact of scouting throughout his life. When remembering his return from the Jamboree, he wrote, "The boy who got off that train in Fort Wayne was approaching young manhood and far different from the excited twelve-year old who in 1924 had hurried home in the rain with his first Boy Scout Handbook inside his mackinaw, yet, not quite five years had passed."[16]

Two men "diverted" Jack's "stream of life" as he headed to college; both were adult leaders at a Scout summer camp where he had worked as camp adjutant after graduating from high school. Working with Robert Fink, later a professor of classical languages at Kenyon College in Ohio, Jack admired his dedication to majoring in Latin and Greek and his study of German because "many useful books <u>about</u> Latin and Greek were written in German. This impressed me hugely. Imagine going that deep into scholarship!"[17] Fink also recommended books that expanded Jack's appreciation of English fiction. Another Scout leader helped Jack pick a college. When summer Scout camp ended in 1930, Byron McCammon, an elementary school teacher in Fort Wayne, offered Jack a ride to Terre Haute and a tour of the campus at Indiana State Teachers College. Jack decided to stay and try to find work before the fall semester started.

Well-prepared for college, Jack retained much of what he had learned in high school. He had distinguished himself in Scout work, developed social skills, and discovered history and literature that kept drawing him down new paths lined with good books. Even though he excelled in high school, his parents with a marginal income could provide him only occasional and very modest cash support. With no dormitories for men on campus, he found lodging at a rooming house for two dollars per week. With wage-paying jobs impossible to find, he washed dishes and mopped floors for three hours a night at a side-street café in trade for three meals a day and also delivered newspapers. At first paper delivery was a losing proposition. The circulation manager forced him to buy two hundred copies even as his subscription list diminished and nonpayments rose. Later he negotiated a slightly better arrangement to earn a dollar or so a week. One afternoon before classes started Jack rode his bicycle into the countryside to think about what else he could do to afford college. He decided on building and selling ship models, a hobby he took up in high school when reading Homer's *Odyssey*. He did not know of anyone else around Terre Haute who was building ship models from scratch at the time, so he decided to build a scale model of the most famous clipper ship from 1854 that won and held the sailing record from New York to San Francisco for many years, the *Flying Cloud*. As he began, he realized he could make two models simultaneously without much more work by simply cutting two identical pieces at the same time, thus devising a rudimentary production line. He took the finished models back to Fort Wayne and sold them for twenty-five dollars each. Then he called Arthur Fletcher Hall, his insurance company backer, and offered to build a model for him. Hall ordered a model of the USS *Constitution* for seventy-five dollars. Jack's first year in college was funded in large part by model building, finding cheap lodging, working at the café for meals, and making a dollar or two per week with his newspaper route.[18]

The next two years became increasingly harder financially. To reduce expenses, he slept on a cot in the basement of the Boy Scouts headquarters, in a shack without heat, electricity, or running water, and subsequently in an unfurnished house so run down the owner could not rent it. He and a friend kept a pot of stew simmering on the stove as each day they added whatever ingredients they could find, from carrots, to potatoes, or turnips. They slept on the floor, showered and shaved at the gym, used candles for light, studied at the library, and hid their situation from the Dean of Men. "The hard times of the Depression meant less to me than to people older than I, for to me there was no letdown. I had started my economic life in the basement, you might say, and lack of money was as common to me as lack of palm trees [are] to an Eskimo. I had nowhere to go but up." At times he went hungry. On one occasion an English professor stopped him after class and gave him fifty cents; another time a favorite English professor, Edward M. Gifford, came to the door with a sack of groceries.[19] Jack showed his gratitude by giving his professor one of his model boats.

In 1931, after reading extensively about magic, he began building a repertoire of good tricks for making a little money. When his friend Paul Omar joined him, they became "Jack Devere & Paul Omar, Kings of Magic" performing for church youth groups. Jack opened with a talk on "Magic of the Ages," followed by acts titled "Spirit Mathematician," "Cards that Pass in the Night," "Hindu Paper Tearing," and more. Promoting themselves with newspaper ads and bumper stickers, they claimed popularity around their part of the Midwest. However, they never made more than a couple of bucks an evening with their shows.

Jack and Omar's last act, performed at the local summer fair, involved a hypnotized Jack, "buried for a week," and viewed inside his underground coffin illuminated in pale blue light. At the end of the week Omar would "bring Jack back to life." The Kings of Magic kicked off the hypnotism and burial piece with a fanfare. Jack relaxed in the coffin when the fairway was open, reading *Moby-Dick* except when someone paid to look down the viewing tube. At night he slipped out to be with his friends. Torrential rains discouraged most customers. At the end of the week the fairway promoter absconded with the money from ticket sales, and the Kings of Magic went out of business.[20]

Even having to scratch up bits of money for expenses, Jack recalled how much he enjoyed college. There were sunny afternoons when he would set his "old sidewinding Oliver typewriter on some cement blocks out in the yard and write a term paper. Or Roland would play his violin."[21] Jack made friends with ease and relished his courses, especially English and history. He avoided practice teaching classes that were also part of a requirement for education majors because he wanted to take more subject-oriented courses. Jack also joined the Ciceronians, a bookish society. "I remember there were some drama students in the group, some very good musicians who were in the college orchestra, several from the debating team, a few would-be writers, and many talkers—great talkers!"[22]

For the summer of 1932, Jack decided to stay in Terre Haute after meeting Jack Jewett, an older Chi Delta Chi fraternity brother, now a local printer with his press in an old schoolhouse on South Third Street near downtown. With only one newspaper in town and the runup to the election of Franklin Delano Roosevelt under way, Jewett saw an opportunity to print an opposition paper, the *Terre Haute News*, on an old sheet-fed flatbed cylinder press capable of small press runs. His backers wrote the main political articles and Jewett provided the rest. He bought flat sheets already printed on one side with patent medicine ads and stock columns on various subjects of general interest from a syndicated service. Jack contributed some of the other original material in each issue. With an opportunity to write and develop basic skills as a printer, he covered his room and board for the summer.

He started each day at the railroad station where he bought the newspapers arriving on the early trains from Chicago, St. Louis, and Indianapolis. He selected articles and wrote capsulations for typesetting. Paid a quarter of a cent per printed line, he earned roughly thirty cents per column but was not paid in cash. Instead, he was allocated newspaper space for ads that he then had to sell. He could keep whatever he could collect for the ads, usually a dollar or two each week. "I sold advertisements to restaurants and took pay in the form of meal tickets, so I ate well. I sold one ad to a small local tailor, whose business really was chiefly alterations and pressing, and in payment he gave me an old Fashion Park tuxedo, cut down to fit me, with a white pique vest." Jack slept on a cot in the basement of the press except when rumors circulated that someone from the opposition paper might try to vandalize the *Terre Haute News*. Then, he took turns with colleagues sleeping on the large flatbed press upstairs.

Seeking cheap meals, Jack discovered Art's Café which he regarded as "one of the most amazing examples of free enterprise in the

Depression period" in Terre Haute. Art, a hobo, arrived on the scene with about fifteen dollars in his pocket, perhaps from a lucky night of gambling. "On a side street in a run-down part of town, he got use of a store-front room with an old cookstove in back."[23] He cleaned and repainted the place, added a makeshift counter, several old tables and mismatched chairs, and opened his café without a menu. At first Art offered one main dish: fried liver, potatoes, some kind of stuffing or dressing, day-old bread, and coffee. Portions were large and the price fifteen cents.

Taking a liking to Jack, Art coached him at length about how to ride freight trains and survive. He taught Jack how to gauge the speed of a train leaving the railyard and grab onto the front ladder of a rolling gondola; calculate the risk of freight shifting and crushing you once you were in the car; keep from getting locked inside refrigerator cars; avoid the "bulls" (railroad police); and spend nights safely in one of the thousands of hobo camps dotting rail lines across America. Jack didn't know it at the time, but soon he would put every one of Art's careful lessons to good use.[24]

When the semester began again in September, he enrolled for another year, kept working, managed his class readings, papers, and exams, and took part in other college activities, from dates and dances to the poetry club and the debating team. The big bands of Tommy Dorsey, Wayne King, Bob Crosby, and more were on the air and on the road playing one-night stands. When in Indiana they would often play the Trianon Dance Hall in Terre Haute where Jack and friends would take their dates for an evening of dancing. As he learned about iambic pentameter and sonnet structure, he began writing more poetry. By the following year he was published in the student poetry magazine, elected president of the poetry club, and awarded the college poetry prize. The debate society drew him even more. Just as he had taken to reading as a child, Jack found intercollegiate debate offered enjoyment from learning facts, organizing ideas, and developing persuasive verbal skills. In 1932 he made the varsity debating team, which ended its season undefeated. The following year Jack and his team were equally strong, and he received the Jardine medal, given to "the student who has made the best record or rendered the greatest service on the Intercollegiate Debating Team of the school." Jack was the first undergraduate to be so recognized.[25]

Even as he enjoyed college, he began to reassess his experience, the degree requirements, the courses he had taken, those he still needed to finish, and how they fit together to make him a well-educated individual. His journal from the time reveals how closely he read and the detailed analytical notes he kept. He made outlines for key elements in numerous genres of writing and kept other lists of the "50 best" or "100 best" poems, short stories, or novels in various genres. He also wrote plays and essays beyond any class requirements and produced one of his plays in his neighborhood church back home.

As he thought about the past three years, he considered his progress. He had begun college hoping to qualify for an administrative job with the Boy Scouts of America or a teaching position in history. As the Depression deepened and layoffs increased incrementally, he focused more on his changing opportunities. Keenly aware of the strengths and weaknesses among his professors, he abhorred the racists, shunned the intellectually sloppy and lazy, and respected the teaching and mentoring skills of his best professors. Now in his junior year at college he began to have second thoughts about a high school teaching career. He did not like the "fishbowl" aspect of a job that he thought was judged not so much by the quality of work but by societal norms others applied. In addition, he learned his college would soon reduce by three-fourths the number of teaching certificates to be granted each year.

As he began consulting with others about his career possibilities, he turned to English Professor Leslie H. Meeks, one of the most highly regarded faculty members on campus. Jack was struggling to evaluate the continuity and progression in his course of study rather than seeing it as "forty-eight pigeonholes, each stuffed with facts." Meeks suggested studies in ethics, but such courses were unavailable at Indiana State Teachers College. After talking with his parents and their

Methodist minister, he decided to leave college and "see what it was like out in the world."[26]

On one of his last evenings on campus as students were departing for the summer, Jack stopped by the main building where fraternities and sororities had bulletin boards in small spaces and where members met briefly between classes and left messages for one another. He spontaneously drew a coat of arms for his Chi Delta Chi fraternity and affixed it to the top of the board. "After I left college in the fall of 1933, I never went back to Terre Haute except when I was passing through in the early fall of 1944. I had a few minutes between trains, and it was night, but I still went to see the old main building. That was during the 'off' month when no students were on campus. The Chi Delta Chi bulletin board was still in its place, topped by the crest I had drawn—it seemed like a generation earlier. The halls were empty; no one was around."[27] Jack had also moved on.

Chapter 2

Coming of Age on the Road

> I worked that shift until midnight seven nights a week and typed up the daily reports for the night manager. Between two jobs I made enough for us to live on. We were living in an old tenement on West 23rd St., in the Chelsea district, a gloomy place swarming with roaches.
>
> —JACK D. RITTENHOUSE[1]

AS THE GREAT DEPRESSION continued and options for employment disappeared, so did Jack's dream of a college degree. His majors in history and English pointed him toward high school teaching, which he soon rejected as "doing the same thing over and over." Although he had learned how to operate a platen press in off hours at the *Terre Haute News*, he didn't have sufficient credentials or experience to qualify for a job. Back home in Fort Wayne, his deep interest in reading kept leading him to the book review pages in the daily newspapers at the public library. There, he also began reading books about how to land a job. When he made a pitch to the *Journal-Gazette* for writing a book review column, the managing editor turned him down, but Jack was ready. He offered to submit reviews as a local writer and do so for free. All he asked was use of a newsroom typewriter during off-hours, some stationery, and mailing privileges for his outgoing requests for review copies. The newspaper accepted his offer.[2] His new boss also gave Jack some perks such as free theater passes and a street-car pass worth one dollar a week, good for unlimited rides anywhere in the city. Other benefits included an occasional free lunch at the Chamber of Commerce after which Jack wrote stories for the *Journal-Gazette* about their speakers.[3]

For the next few years Jack wrote to publishers on the letterhead of the *Fort Wayne Journal-Gazette*, requesting review copies of books. As the mail arrived, he relished the anticipation of opening another new package of books, a delight he would carry through life. He read the books quickly and wrote his reviews for their final edit in-house. As each new column went to press, Jack bundled up the books he had just reviewed, pulled out his streetcar pass, and headed to the book shops and the public library to sell his review copies for half the price printed on their dust jackets. Living at home, he used his new-found income as pocket money and occasionally bought a book of particular interest at a local bookshop run by a good friend, the retired high school librarian who had hired him several years earlier at his high school library.

At the *Journal-Gazette* in 1934 Jack was drawn to the United Press room with its teletype churning out stories about the rise of totalitarian leaders in Germany, Italy, Russia, and China, as well as the growing threat of war in Europe. As the drumbeat of conflict grew, Jack wrote to the Paris bureau of the United Press, asking if they would hire him as a war correspondent. While the UP had a reputation for hiring reporters with little training or experience, their reply was noncommittal, saying if he were in Paris and war broke out it would consider him for some type of employment. Encouraged, he wrote a brief article for the Fort Wayne newspaper. It read in part,

> Jack Rittenhouse to Leave April 21 for Stay in Europe. . . . He plans to stay at least six months in Paris as a newspaper correspondent, and if circumstances warrant will prolong his stay for two years visiting England, Belgium and Germany. Since last November Mr. Rittenhouse has been book critic for The Journal-Gazette, and

on his travels will write a series of articles dealing with political trends and items of general interest abroad. . . . He will go on a short tour through southern Canada and plans to leave Montreal during the first week in May. He intends to travel alone, vagabonding wherever possible and thus visiting the spots ordinarily least frequented by tourists.[4]

Next, he pitched another new idea to the managing editor of the *Journal-Gazette*—a press card that looked official but carried no promises that the newspaper had hired him. The top line of his "press card" read "OFFICIAL PRESS CORRESPONDENT" and continued with a disclaimer that the *Journal-Gazette* assumed no responsibilities for his acts or financial obligations. Nevertheless, they would "appreciate any courtesies and facilities extended him in obtaining news and information." To make the card appear more official, the editor signed it and a notary public stamped it.

To record his journey he purchased a small Webster Note Book favored by newspaper reporters and pasted on the cover "Travel Notes, Volume I, Diary from April 23 to _____, 1934. Also Addresses, lists of photos Nos. 16-____, Articles."

Inside the front cover he pasted one of his freshly printed cards:

"AROUND THE WORLD ON A DOLLAR"
Jack D. Rittenhouse
(THE ROVING REPORTER)
SPECIAL FEATURE CORRESPONDENT
"Journal-Gazette"—Fort Wayne, Ind., U.S.A.

On the first pages of his diary he noted the political parties in France, his contacts in Paris and their addresses. Thus, Jack's Log of the Wanderlust begins:

Monday, April 23, 1934 (1st Day). The court-house clock showed 8:20 a.m. when I shouldered my pack and climbed aboard the

> Third Street trolley. Shortly before I got off the conductor began a conversation as to my destination, evincing great surprise that I was heading for Paris. With my pack again slung on my back, I walked out to the junction of two main roads; I placed the pack at my feet with the word PARIS prominently showing, and threw my hitch-hiking "thumb" into high gear. I always try a wide grin as accompaniment. It worked. A big orange Kingan meat-truck stopped and I climbed into the cab.[5]

With his new press card, business card, passport, and twenty-five dollars in his pocket, Jack headed to Montreal where, five years earlier, he boarded a steamship bound for England and the Third International Boy Scouts Jamboree. He planned to wrangle a job as a deckhand on any boat headed to Europe, hitchhike to Paris, and knock on the door of the European headquarters of the United Press.

Hitchhiking through Indiana and Michigan, Jack stopped overnight with relatives, starting with his Grandfather Hassinger in Constantine, Michigan. In larger towns he called on newspaper editors trying to interest them in stories he would be sending from abroad. At the *Kalamazoo Gazette* Managing Editor J. K. Walsh said he would be glad to receive Jack's submissions from France and then told him about a similar trip he had made on horseback in South Africa visiting Durban, Natal and Bulawayo before boarding tramp steamers up the west coast of Africa and later in the South Seas. Gregarious and earnest, Jack easily engaged a variety of people in conversations and picked up story leads.

Heading to Plainwell he chatted with a truck driver who gave him the name of Fritzhof G. Erichson, (Commadore of the Yacht Club in Toronto), a good storyteller about "Early Birds," airmen who flew solo prior to 1914. The truck driver also gave Jack "another valuable tip" about Canadian pilot Roy Brown, originally credited with shooting down the German air ace, Manfred von Richthofen (later disproved). At another paper a cordial managing editor responded, "Frankly there was little chance of using any of my material."[6]

By the fifth day on the road, Jack was in Detroit and "thought it would be an excellent idea to spend the night on Canadian soil, so I caught the bus which runs under the tunnel to Windsor. On the way out I had to pass the Immigration authorities." Jack's progress toward the Montreal wharves came to an abrupt halt as Canadian authorities began to question him. He told them he was planning on hitchhiking in Canada and had thirteen dollars for his trip. He was quickly taken to another room where they filled out a detailed form in quadruplicate, explained the Canadian laws against hitchhiking, and the requirement that travelers have adequate funds to cover an emergency in case of an accident. With thirteen dollars in his pocket, Jack was deported from Canada in less than an hour. US Customs officials encouraged him to go back the next day and "ask for Mr. Adams and tell him your story and try to sell them on the idea that you are a newspaper correspondent."[7] Their advice sounded reasonable until Jack sat down to read the deportation form. He could not reapply for admission without a letter from a Canadian minister. For some, this turn of events would have been deeply discouraging. For Jack, it simply meant a change in plans. When he couldn't enter Canada, he decided to hitchhike to New York where he would try to sign onto another steamship bound for Europe or start looking for work, perhaps in a job relating to books.

At the *Detroit Free Press* office he found a "nice chap" who let him use the phone to call transport companies moving new cars from Detroit to New York City. When the Square Deal Trucking Company told him a truck would be leaving the next day, he was waiting at the shipping yard early the following morning. Impressed by how smoothly and carefully the trucks were loaded, he gained the driver's approval, climbed aboard, and started on the road to another adventure along a route leading him to Trenton, New Jersey, and a bridge on the way to Manhattan. During his trip the driver allowed him to take naps in the backseat of one of the new Chrysler Airstreams on its way to a dealership.

As a young man steeped in Revolutionary War history, Jack crossed the Delaware River and was reminded of reading about the Battle of Trenton, that fateful day after Christmas 1776, when George Washington's weary troops won a significant victory against the Hessians. Their win rallied support for the Continental Army and set a course for a new nation. From his seat in a freight truck Jack took in the scene and thought about how the study of history could be part of his future.

On a sunny May afternoon he hitchhiked north from Trenton, New Jersey, and crossed the Hudson. "I stood on the ferry and saw the thrilling . . . skyline unfold before me. All of my weariness vanished." Thoroughly enchanted by New York, he made his way to City Hall Park. "What impressions, what delights, what story-book word-pictures suddenly came real! Battery Park! Sidewalk bootblacks with wooden kit-boxes! Whistling peanut-roasters! Subways! The elevated roaring overhead! Fulton St. Fish Market, with its accompanying odors! Tenements, with washing hanging from the windows! Brooklyn Bridge towering above me! Docks—ferries—liners—tugs! Ship chandlers! Importers shops, filled with all manner of exotic things!"[8]

He inquired about cheap lodging and learned about the Bowery. Walking there he passed more sights: "Sidewalk hawkers! Tough guys! Chinatown! Missions! Flophouses—beds 10¢! Swing-door Saloons! The Bowery—the Bowery!"[9]

At twenty-one, Jack Rittenhouse began exploring one of the great cities of the world. Over the next six months he walked much of Manhattan with more than seven million people squeezed into 22.6 square miles, from the Bowery to Midtown and the Hudson to the East River. New York offered him new opportunities from public libraries open in the evening to ships sailing from its great port toward exotic destinations around the globe. Until he could arrange passage to Europe, he decided to stay for a while and apply for a job, hopefully near the center of American publishing and bookselling.

With the inauguration of President Franklin Delano Roosevelt in 1933, a slow recovery from the Great Depression had begun. New York started clawing its way back from some of its darkest days, thanks to

WPA relief programs. Unemployment still hovered at 21.7 percent, and every day, breadlines on the street fed thousands of people out of work. With severely limited funds, Jack headed into the neighborhood where the breadlines were the longest and accommodations the cheapest. The Bowery that greeted Jack was Skid Row. He began to explore his surroundings: run-down saloons, flophouses, mission houses, and endlessly fascinating street scenes. He recognized his neighborhood depicted in the paintings by Reginald Marsh, prints by John Sloan, and later, writings of William S. Burroughs, Joseph Mitchell, and Jack Kerouac. He began to observe grifters, drifters, and street-side con artists with their shell games and sleight-of-hand tricks, and he wrote about them in articles he sent to his hometown newspaper.

At the Grand Windsor Hotel he rented space for $1.75 a week. "The room proved to be about 6 × 8 feet, one of many partitioned off just as our cabins were partitioned in the hold of the [Cunard liner] we travelled in on our 1929 adventure" to the Boy Scouts Jamboree in England.[10] The desk clerk instructed him never to leave anything of value in his room since there was just a latch on the inside but no lock on the door. Walls surrounding each room did not reach the ceiling, but wire netting at the top usually prevented a thief from climbing over. SROs, single room occupancy spaces for short-term rental to low-income or indigents, kept many people, including Jack, off the streets. Thousands crammed into whatever buildings could hold them, but such conditions didn't matter to Jack. He remained fascinated by the urban scene and its street life. Finally, after hitchhiking 1,136 miles from home and spending nights sitting up in 24-hour diners trying to stay awake on stale coffee, he had arrived.

Each day brought new adventures. With his pack, a few coins in his pocket, and a treasured book of Swinburne's poems he had brought for his trip to Europe, he began his job search visiting the various publishers who had sent him review copies in Fort Wayne. People at Prentice Hall, Viking, and other houses remembered him as the young reviewer whose work appeared regularly in the *Fort Wayne*

Journal-Gazette and were happy to give him new books to review, but none could offer jobs. Still searching for employment, he wrangled a desk and a typewriter at the *New York Sun* office located in a converted department store at 280 Broadway in lower Manhattan. There he wrote his review columns at off-hours when the newsroom wasn't busy, dropped them in the mail, and then headed back to Fourth Avenue to sell his crisp, new review copies on Book Row.

Though new to Jack, for more than fifty years every New Yorker interested in books visited the fabled shops on Book Row south of Fourteenth Street from Union Square to Astor Place. The booksellers "left an indelible mark in the lives of book lovers fortunate enough to have visited them. They left their names in the diaries and journals of bibliophiles, in the letters of collectors, in the archives of libraries, in the memories of readers who journeyed to Book Row America."[11] Those bookshop names resounded with Jack Rittenhouse for the rest of his life.

Soon Jack recognized his book-reviewing routine was not a secure source of income. With no contract at any newspaper and delayed in his plans to reach Paris, he still needed to pay his rent and buy a meal or two a day. Immersed in his new experiences, he wrote a feature article on flophouses in the Bowery and sent it unsolicited to the *Fort Wayne Journal-Gazette*. He hocked his treasured camera and then received a check for three dollars from the *Journal-Gazette* after it published the flophouse feature. At least he had a little money and a place to sleep for a few more nights. He could continue to explore New York while looking for ways to get to Europe. Meanwhile he started walking to "get the 'lay' of the waterfront" and apply for jobs on ships heading to Europe. When he exhausted the obvious possibilities, he bought a *New York Times* and read shipping lists for names of the ships in dock and those preparing to sail.[12] With these lists in hand he spent an afternoon "down along the docks." He saw the *Isle de France*, went on board the tramp steamer *Maaru*, and also boarded the *American Banker* where the chief steward directed him to "Mr. Day" at the employment office on the docks. He met an old sailor who told him that since so many seamen were out of work, they were hiring only men who could show discharge papers from previous jobs aboard ship or with the military.

A few days later Jack walked over the Brooklyn Bridge, saw the Statue of Liberty in the distance, and continued to the Brooklyn Navy Yard. A sailor invited him to come aboard the USS *Wyoming* for a tour. His guide also showed him "other vessels, including eagle boats, cruisers, destroyers, sub-chasers, launches, transports, Coast Guard vessels." Convinced he could not land a traditional deckhand job, Jack soon thought it "folly further to apply at the shipping offices" and turned his attention to a new approach—to "bargain with the publicity directors" of the main lines. He would offer to write publicity in exchange for passage.[13]

"So I started out. The American lines all refused, but the Holland-American man asked me to call back in the afternoon." When Jack went to the offices in Hoboken, he was told to come back in a few days. He reflected, "At least they are not refusing me point blank."[14] Knowing that ocean liners provided well-stocked libraries for their passengers, he wrote to the chief steward of the *Leviathan* asking for a job as library steward. The *Leviathan* did not respond.

Next Jack visited the offices for the German Lines with his publicity offer but received no encouraging responses. That evening he closed his diary entry with his usual determination: "They can't keep me here forever! And so to bed."[15] Drifting off to sleep he thought about a lead picked up on the Hoboken waterfront where he learned of cattle boats leaving from the foot of 6th Street in Jersey City. The next day in Jersey City he discovered the boats were nothing more than ferries hauling cattle to the Manhattan slaughter houses, not vessels bound for foreign ports.

Interspersed with his dogged search for passage to Europe, Jack still called on publishers and patronized the main public library where he read librettos for operas he wanted to see. Over the next few weeks he attended seven performances sitting in the twenty-five cents seats in the second balcony, where he saw *Il Trovatore, La Traviata, Sampson and Delilah*, *Andrea Chenier*, *Norma*, and two operettas by Gilbert and Sullivan. He also checked out books about vagabonding by now-forgotten, free-spirited writers Jim Tully (1886–1946) and Harry A. Franck (1881–1962), men who traveled alone on a shoestring and who wrote widely popular travel adventures. Tully took his readers across America on freight trains, through hobo jungles, and to brothels as he explored the dark underbelly of indigent life in the 1920s and 1930s. His novels, a critical and commercial success, included *Shadows of Men* (1930), *Blood on the Moon* (1931), *Laughter in Hell* (1932), and *Ladies in the Parlor* (1935). Jack checked out one of three autobiographies by Tully, *Circus Parade* (1927), but did not record what he thought of it.

At the library, Harry Franck's first book, *A Vagabond Journey Around the World*, caught Jack's eye.[16] Positive popular response to this book in 1910 encouraged Franck to continue traveling and writing. His publications numbered more than thirty before his death, a remarkable record for a young man who dropped out of the University of Michigan after his freshman year. Franck and Tully fed Jack's dreams of traveling on a shoestring, living in Paris as a world war was brewing, and sending newspaper stories back to America.

In addition to the publishers who already knew of his reviews, he called on twenty-four more in his first ten days in the city, including Macmillan, Scribner, Harpers, Alfred A. Knopf, Viking, and Random House, some of New York's most distinguished publishing houses. Others he visited have now passed from the scene and are only remembered today by dedicated students of publishing history. The purpose of his visits varied. With some he solicited review copies by giving publishers cut sheets of his earlier reviews in the *Terre Haute Journal-Gazette*. At other houses he expanded his general knowledge of the publishing world while initiating contacts that might lead to a job interview. Receptions varied, from "cool" at Covici-Friede to "warmly hospitable" at Scribner. Someone at Harpers was "very cordial showing me all over the plant." At Longmans Green he was invited to the tearoom "whose walls were decorated with a mural showing London in 1829—very quaint and cleverly done."[17]

None of his visits to publishers resulted in anything more than a few fresh review copies. Meanwhile, he was running out of money and growing hungry. After having spent his last dime for a meal, he went back to his room and fell asleep. "I awoke at 6:30, very hungry. The only saleable thing I had was a copy of Swinburne's poems, but the friendly bookseller to whom I offered it named only 5¢ as his price. Such levity! I stalked out of the shop and sat awhile in City Hall Park, reading 'Faustine' which wizardry with words enchanted me so I wrote a few hundred words on the park scene about me." Later, hunger pangs grew more intense. "Finally, pride made me a traitor to beauty—I fled to my room, snatched up the Swinburne, dashed to the 'bookseller' and with what disdain I could muster hurled it before him. With the nickle I bought a tremendous bowl of soup, and [after] eating it went to bed."[18] Unbeknown to Jack, his education in bookselling had just begun with Harry Smolin at a shop on Park Row.

What followed his disheartening transaction was a good lesson for anyone interested in books and how they move through time as market commodities. In Jack the bookseller saw a young man with a good education trying to write and needing to scrape out a very modest living by giving up his only book, his favorite book, for a bowl of soup. Smolin took an interest in Jack, welcomed him to his shop, and encouraged him to spend evenings there. Four days later "the bookstore man took me out to lunch—splendid meal—hung around the shop, waited on a customer or so, helped unload and sort new stock. Paid 50¢." The impecunious vagabond and the knowledgeable bookseller were becoming friends. A few days later Harry Smolin took Jack to lunch once again. In his diary Jack relates what happened next. "Had lunch with Smolin, my bookseller friend, and he offered me $25.00 a month to work for him, albeit I know he does not need another clerk. Learning that my favorite cigarettes are Marlboro's, he bought me a package." Harry Smolin, admiring Jack's knowledge of books and ease with customers, saw a natural bookseller in the making. With his newfound wages, Jack also began to think like a bookseller. He bought back the Swinburne for nineteen cents and resold it two days later for a quarter.[19]

Finally, Jack found an intriguing and welcoming environment in a city that has often been harsh for those with little money. He liked being surrounded by books and magazines, and he enjoyed working for Smolin and hearing the adventurous tales of Harry's assistant, Barney Weinstein.

> Harry Smolin, the proprietor, is a dapper little man of about 40, with wavy hair showing tinges of gray. The real clerk is Barney Weinstein who has been in America 20 years. He tells me occasional experiences he has had with women and of more sanely adventurous [experiences]. Once he was sitting in a railway station in Washington, D.C., when a woman inquired of the time of departure of the next train to Philadelphia. Barney didn't know, and the woman, by adroit questioning discovered that he had no place to stay. Thereupon she dropped her guise and invited him to her apartment. He stayed two weeks and then skipped out with $400 in jewels. I am Barney's assistant, and I do all sorts of work, from waiting on customers to running errands. . . . I like the place because I have always wanted to be a bookseller.[20]

Soon Smolin gave Jack the responsibility to run the shop alone some evenings. When business was slow, he read. "In the corner is a section containing cheap and excellent reprints of the amatory classics. I have read Juvenal, D. H. Lawrence, Lucian, DeQuincy, Voltaire, Defoe, and others." At other times he helped young people. "This evening a little boy came in—a musical prodigy—escorted by his bald-headed, little, old maestro. He bought several 'Etudes,' [a respected magazine about classical music], and as they left I was informed that the lad had already appeared in concerts and that his income supported the maestro as well." Another such visitor was "a 14 year old lad not yet out of knickers. He plunged wildly into the surgical journals. I asked him if he was going to be a doctor. 'I hope so,' was his reply. I let him spend as long as he wished and then sold him a journal at half the shop's price."[21]

The next week Smolin offered him a steady job for a year, but Jack did not want to delay his travels to Europe that long. A few days later Smolin noticed that Jack's shirt was worn. When Jack arrived at work that evening "there was a package hanging by my coat and upon opening it I discovered a fine new shirt, socks, handkerchiefs and underwear—decidedly a generous man, and contrary to all my preconceived and cynical notions about the general lack of Samaritanism in this day and age."[22]

In another surprising development shortly thereafter, Jack noted in his diary, "Things begin on a new scale today. Barney has been dismissed, due to the summer slump in business, and I am now in charge. I receive $10.00 weekly. By spartan living I shall attempt to save about $25.00 each month. In two or three months I can leave on any ship I wish. I spent the day in making a small but elaborate model of a destroyer." Clearly, ocean-bound vessels were on his mind. On June 5th Jack awakened at 4 a.m. to make his way to 96th Street and Riverside Drive where he saw the US Navy Review in New York harbor, an event attended by President Franklin Delano Roosevelt on board the cruiser USS *Indianapolis*. The day before a sixty-mile-long sea parade of warships, battleships, cruisers, and subchasers took seven hours to sail into the formation that Jack viewed at dawn and recorded in his diary as "a magnificent spectacle."[23]

Jack marked four weeks since he left Terre Haute. He was enjoying his employment near Book Row but saw no promise of getting to Europe anytime soon. A letter from the managing editor of the *Journal-Gazette* lifted his spirits with its commendation for the work he was submitting. With an advance of three dollars from Harry Smolin, he rented a better typewriter so he could write his reviews and columns more efficiently.

Jack took advantage of an opportunity to cover the story of a disastrous fire aboard the SS *Morro Castle* when it burned near the Jersey shore. He had missed being hired to work aboard the ship by only a few minutes before its outbound journey, so he framed the story as a hometown boy who barely missed a disaster at sea. "Now this was something of the sort I had set out to write about as a news correspondent."[24] His story ran in the *Journal-Gazette*.[25]

While Jack's routines saw him through the summer, by September he was ready to try something new. He left his job at Park Row Books and Magazines on good terms with his boss and found a room at the "Y" in mid-town for seventy-five cents a night.[26] The William Sloane House with 573 rooms, owned by the YMCA, stood at 356 W. 34th Street near the main post office, Pennsylvania Station, and a few blocks from the Empire State Building. Around the corner he often ate at a "penny restaurant," part of a chain operated by Bernarr MacFadden, the popular American publisher and promoter of physical culture. His favorite meal was "a big dish of thick, boiled cracked wheat (three cents), with a dollop of brown sugar on top (one cent), and some raisin coffee (two cents) made from raisins instead of coffee. For fifteen cents a good meal, especially breakfast, could be had."[27]

Sloane House, close to better subway connections on lines reaching different parts of the city, provided an excellent location for a small one-man "magazine business" of his own not requiring the significant overhead of leased space or the capital needed to stock a bookstore. Jack had learned from Smolin about the value of out-of-date popular magazines. With this information he developed an innovative plan to find and sell desirable used magazines. Riding the subway for a nickel to neighborhoods near Columbia University, Morningside Heights, and Harlem, he sought out janitors in large Upper West Side apartment buildings. He offered to pay them from two to five cents for each magazine on a list he provided them and a little more for higher priced publications like *Fortune*. He convinced them they could pick up a few dollars each week on something their tenants were throwing down the trash chutes. All they had to do was put aside those magazines on Jack's list in good condition and hold them until he returned within a few days.

After Jack made his rounds uptown gathering all the magazines he could carry into two large bundles, he would catch a downtown subway to the second-hand shops on Book Row to make a profit. At times he did this twice a day. Occasionally he would sell magazines to Smolin and fill in for him at Park Row when his former employer needed a little time away on Jewish holidays.

As autumn deepened into winter, Jack found New York weather less and less hospitable. The forty-two-pound magazine bundles he schlepped almost daily from uptown high-rise apartment buildings to Book Row seemed to grow heavier as the weather changed. At every crosswalk he risked being splashed by passing traffic. He picked up some evening jobs starting as a "peanut butcher" working at Madison Square Garden for the World Series Rodeo. A friend at the "Y" coached him on "the names of various ball parks in Saint Louis and Detroit where I had supposedly worked before." He landed the job, but as a newcomer he was assigned to work high up in the balconies. "The method was simple: you went into a locker room and changed into a flimsy white suit, not unlike heavy pajamas. Your clothes were locked up until you settled accounts with the concessionaire at the end of the evening."[28]

"To fill out the week I got a job as a busboy for Bickford's Cafeterias. I was hired at their Forty-second Street place but worked on the late-night shift at a branch in Flatbush, over in Brooklyn. For a week I spent each night clearing tables, running a dishwashing machine, squeezing two gallons of fresh orange juice, and polishing the ample brass plates on the big front doors, Pinafore style." Shortly thereafter he landed a job as a "doorman-barker" at the George M. Cohan Theater showing rerun films on Times Square, just north of the corner of Broadway and 42nd Street. At the heart of Times Square, he was near Minsky's Burlesque and the New Amsterdam where Bob Hope was playing in *Roberta*, a Jerome Kern musical best remembered for introducing the popular song, "Smoke Gets in Your Eyes."

The theater where he worked had once been "a legitimate house, and back of the movie curtain . . . one could climb the spiral stairs to the old dressing rooms. In an old closet I picked up a program for O'Neill's 'Desire Under the Elms,' with Walter Huston as star. But now it was a re-run movie house, playing five-year-old films."[29] Every day Jack worked from four in the afternoon until midnight for twelve dollars a week. The theater provided a doorman's overcoat with lots of braid and a fancy cap.

Soon he gave up his room at the "Y" and teamed with another barker, a French-Canadian named Al Coste, to rent a furnished room at 138 West 46th Street. Located behind Lowe's State Theatre, their building had been a theatrical boarding house when vaudeville was in its prime. A wigmaker still had a shop on the second floor. "Coste and I saw little of other tenants. We had our own group of friends picked up around the square, and they were a cosmopolitan bunch as could be found only around Times Square." Jack's group included a Jewish man who fled Germany and sold vacuum cleaners, a Swede who had no papers but jumped ship to pick up odd jobs in New York, and Americans from other parts of the country. "We often ate together, each one cooking some familiar dish from his home. I recall the wonderful knockwurst mit lentils cooked by the blimp pilot."[30] He was beginning to discover that New York was really a group of villages, each with its own atmosphere, characters, and opportunities. Yet, even with his easy, outgoing nature, his openness to people of all walks of life, and his perseverance in learning more about others, he was losing his enthusiasm for New York as the weather changed.

"When the fall wore on into winter, it was less pleasant working as a doorman. The theatre owner insisted I walk back and forth along the curb, but the passing cars threw slush on my pants legs and shoes, so I invested in a pair of good English riding boots and some whipcord black cavalry pants. . . . I looked a little like a Nazi storm trooper. In 1934 this SS outfit was not too commonly recognized, but some young Jewish fellows knew it well enough and one dark night a bunch of them backed me up against a wall on a dark street and were about to let me have it. I managed to talk my way out of it."[31] His new boots would soon serve him well when hopping on and off freight trains, protecting his pants cuffs from getting snagged in a difficult and potentially dangerous situation.

Having spent his first Thanksgiving and Christmas alone and after working the late shift on New Year's Eve, he watched the celebrations from the sidelines, finding "little novelty left in the job." In mid-January he had lunch with a drifter he met hanging around Times Square. "We were in a Chinese restaurant on Eighth Avenue, looking down at the cars making criss-cross tracks in the filthy slush on the streets below. 'It's mighty nice in New Orleans at this time of year,' Tony said."[32] The more they talked the more interesting it sounded. The next morning they left the city heading south. Jack still carried his pack with the patch, but now it showed only his initials; the word PARIS was gone. After nine months, numerous jobs, and a variety of places to live, he left New York for his next adventure. He had plans to return, but now it was time to travel differently and in a new direction. He still wanted to cross the border into a foreign country, so he headed south.

Jack and his friend knew they should split up because most motorists rarely picked up pairs of hitchhikers. They took a ferry to the Jersey shore, agreed on a cheap hotel where they would meet in Philadelphia, and then parted. This routine worked for several days until Tony fell sick in Roanoke, where they talked it over and agreed to meet in New Orleans. Tony never showed up. Jack's last twelve or fifteen dollars got him to New Orleans with several stops along the way. In Bristol, Tennessee, he found himself out at the edge of town in the dark at a small crossroad filling station where he asked the owner if he could sleep inside by the stove. When the owner replied he did not want to take a chance with a stranger, Jack pulled out his passport to show he wasn't really a stranger. "He had never seen such a document, and as he looked at it I had an idea. I showed him it bore the signature of Cordell Hull, who came from that part of the United States. And there were the words, 'I, the undersigned, Secretary of State of the United States of America, hereby request all whom it may concern to permit safely and freely to pass, and in case of need to give all lawful aid and protection to

Jack DeVere Rittenhouse.' This official document so impressed the man that I spent the night beside the stove. The only time that passport ever did me any good was inside the country."[33]

Throughout his travels Jack was learning valuable lessons not only about how to travel safely as a transient but also about social attitudes and sensitivity with ordinary expressions often taken for granted. In New York Smolin firmly helped him understand it was unacceptable to talk about "Jewing someone down" when settling on the price for a book or anything else, a lesson that stuck for life. In Birmingham he boarded a streetcar bound for the edge of town to hitch another ride. "It was the first time I ever rode in a 'Jim Crow' car, and unknowingly I sat in the back part that was reserved for blacks. Not until I got off did I realize why the passengers, both black and white, had looked at me so strangely."[34]

At Mobile he decided to catch his first freight train along with hobos. "I could not have picked a better place. So many men were going west that the railroad had made a sort of treaty with the bums. Each afternoon at three a train of empty cars stopped beside some vast storage tanks . . . used for bulk molasses. The bums swarmed from the bushes and boarded the train; they were allowed to ride that train without being troubled. In return, they kept off all other westbound trains. Getting on that train required no more hoboing skill than boarding a passenger train. I was in a gondola car with a dozen or more others, and I stood by the chest-high side watching the towns roll by: Pascagoula, Pass Christian, Biloxi. Sixteen years later I was again in Biloxi, riding as a paying passenger on an expense account to a convention."[35]

Jack noticed beside him an old-timer who looked like a professional drifter. When he spoke using an unusual slang phrase, Jack replied in kind, remembering what he learned from his last summer in college working at a carnival in Terre Haute. "I had done some study of the slang they used. It was a secret language, based on thieves' jargon and words from gypsies. There were many variations, the children's common 'pig Latin' is one."[36] When the train pulled up to the next stop the old drifter gave him some wise advice about moving through the trainyards while avoiding the "Bulls."[37]

Jack stayed nearly three months in New Orleans. "Days and nights of intense sightseeing, visiting, talking, . . . were the equivalent of ten months of weekends. Every day, every hour, was a new experience. It was the best time of the year in many ways, leading up to Mardi Gras and just beyond."[38] After a night at the transient center[39] he found lodging for twenty-five cents in an old house in the French Quarter. "It had once been quite a house, built in the Mediterranean style of a hollow square, flush to the front sidewalk but with a large patio within."[40] He stayed in a room with several cots. Under his cot he kept his backpack. In a few days his "Times Square wages were gone" and no jobs were available anywhere around.

Jack's innovative spirit swung into action as he observed artists display their paintings around Jackson Square. With one college art course under his belt, he pawned his camera again and bought illustration boards, some penny postcards of noted New Orleans scenes, and a set of watercolor pencils. In his flophouse patio the next morning, he copied the postcard scenes as enlarged sketches about 9 inches × 12 inches and made cardboard frames for them. On his way to Royal Street in the afternoon, he bought a cheap stool and a beret, set up his easel in front of an empty shop, and went to work putting the "final touches" on his "original" work of art. "And the tourists from Ohio and Iowa and Wisconsin came along the street, with many, especially middle-aged women, stopping to see 'a real artist at work in the French Quarter!' I spoke little, trying to keep my Indiana accent hushed, and sometimes using a bit of college French. My paintings were only a dollar and even at that were overpriced."[41] When he sold three or four of his "paintings," he "knocked off work" and wandered around town. In a day or so, a visiting restaurant owner who had watched Jack work commissioned him to sketch in color the interior of a nearby restaurant for a renovation project in his business back home.

Once more he began finding his village in the city. After Mardi

Gras "a fellow just slightly older than myself came along with a suitcase. He stopped to watch me for a while and then commented that I didn't seem to be drawing any customers. When I said that business was light, he said he could help. Opening the suitcase he extracted a ventriloquist's dummy. As a pair of tourists went past, the dummy started to talk to them; they turned and were soon the center of a small circle of people. In a short time I had sold nearly all of my stock."[42]

The ventriloquist, Ted Valentine, introduced himself, and told Jack he was organizing a cooperative rooming house. Looking for a few more men to join the venture, he invited Jack to rent a room for five dollars a week in a three-story house at the corner of Bourbon and Dumaine Streets in the French Quarter with a bar on the ground floor. Ted lit each room upstairs with a single light bulb hanging on a cord from the ceiling. "The furniture consisted of only an old bedstead and a mattress; each person bought his own bedding, chair, etc., picked up in any salvage shop. The tenants came and went, and often bequeathed things to others when they left. In this way I picked up a small table, a chair, and an artist's easel."[43] There were no group responsibilities, and each man went his separate way in the morning. On some evenings they would gather in one room, pass around a jug of wine, and enjoy a bull session much like at a college fraternity house. No one got drunk; a few smoked marijuana. Jack rented a "fine room" with a bathroom down the hall. The economics of the arrangement were never clear, although he thought the ventriloquist may have rented the entire upstairs for forty or fifty dollars a month. By the time Ted Valentine filled the other rooms with renters, his room was free.

Fifty years later Jack remembered several of the tenants, especially a college art instructor from Minneapolis who spent a few weeks each year in a different part of the country where he would paint. The year before the teacher had painted ships and seascapes in Cape Cod. As an accomplished artist, he could finish four or five paintings each week priced at one hundred dollars each that he sold reasonably well back home.

Jack also found Ted Valentine an intriguing individual. His father "had been a ventriloquist and had taught him the art, and had bequeathed the dummy to him when he died. Ted said he sometimes felt that the spirit of his father still lived in the dummy; neither of us believed this, but sometimes when Ted had enough drinks to blur his speech and became melancholy, he would bring out the dummy and talk to it. Ted's speech would be blurred; the dummy always replied in clear and true tones. It was a strange scene of a man talking to his subconscious as if it were another living person."[44]

Although the house at Bourbon and Dumaine Streets became known as "The Artists' and Writers' Center" among most of its tenants, the atmosphere became troubled when Valentine introduced a friend named Eddie, a recently divorced hard drug addict. Eddie did not have a room at the cooperative but visited often enough that the police came there looking for him when his "ex," also a drug addict, killed someone in a bar. Eddie left town quickly without his luggage; Ted Valentine followed with his dummy, and the Center "dissolved in a day."

Jack soon had another place to stay, thanks to a Russian immigrant named Orest Mykar, whom he had met a few weeks earlier. Orest was trained as a junior officer in the cuirassier guard for the Czar. After the Russian revolution he fled to America where he found a job as a streetcar motorman in Minneapolis and began learning English. In New Orleans Orest was teaching fencing, and Jack paid his rent by building benches and painting the studio walls.[45]

> But it could not last. I had always been aware that this was a trip and not a way of life, and that sometime it must end. I was about ready to go back to Indiana, but my pride wouldn't let me go back after all of my bragging that I would be a war correspondent in Europe at that time, although the fuses were burning short.
>
> Then I thought that perhaps there was a way I could redeem myself in a youthful way. I could go to Mexico, at least to some border town long enough to get my passport stamped. This would

qualify as a foreign country, and if anyone asked me I could say that I changed my mind about going to France and had gone to Mexico instead.[46]

Jack would soon leave the Crescent City to head west, but he had no money for meals while hitchhiking and riding the rails to the border. Ever resourceful, he turned again to art after one of the residents at the Artists' and Writers' Center taught him how to cut silhouettes. Remembering the principles of freehand drawing and perspective from his college art class, he applied the precision and dexterity learned in his model building and began cutting silhouettes. With an eye trained for careful details, he quickly mastered a new skill that could make him a little money practically anywhere he went.

Before leaving New Orleans, he assembled a "thin little box" that fit in the side pocket of his coat and contained some finished examples of his work, a small, well-made pair of scissors, gummed paper for backing, and plain cards. "Any time I needed a meal, I had only to see a child or two playing in a yard, go up to the house, and tell the mother that I would cut her child's silhouette, two for fifty cents, or if she didn't have any change I would do it for a sandwich or any sort of food and a cup of coffee."[47]

As warmer spring days arrived in the south and west, he said goodbye to Orest Mykar and to Dan and Mildred Kelly, other good friends who lived around the corner. Dan was "a most gentle young fellow," a picture framer with a fine precision mortise saw that allowed him to craft beautiful frames. When he was not framing original art on paper or canvas, he would buy old copies of *L'Illustration*, a French magazine with high-quality illustrations tipped in. These plates could stand on their own as attractive framed pieces that sold for a dollar or more.

"When I left, Dan and Mildred came to bring me a present. I still have it: a curious little book on natural phenomena by David Brewster, entitled *Letters on Natural Magic*, published by Harper's in 1870. It is of no great worth as a rare book, but I value the inscription: 'To Jack Rittenhouse from Mildred and Dan Kelly, New Orleans.' Every time I see a hippie today, I think that they are somehow trying to imitate people like Dan and Mildred, feeling that perhaps if they dress that way they will acquire the other qualities. With those two the spirit of gentleness, intellectual curiosity, and happiness worked from the inside outward. They were not rebels in any sense, merely true individualists living their own way of life."[48]

On the road again, Jack made his way across lower Louisiana. At Houma he bought a loaf of bread for a dime, filled his water canteen, and headed out of town where he passed a field of large, green onions. Bread, water, and fresh onions made a satisfying supper. Near dark he walked past a golf course with low-hanging palms, one of which had fronds almost touching the ground. Underneath the tree he found a "tropical igloo" where he spread his trench coat and spent a comfortable night sleeping. It was a better setting than a few nights later in Corsicana, Texas, where supper was simply a loaf of day-old bread and his bed was on the ground beneath a lumber company's loading platform near the railroad tracks. In Fort Worth he found the largest and best transient center of the journey with the residents doing much of the work, including good cooking. Avoiding a scheme at a Big Springs hobo camp to bilk him out of his meagre pocket change, he made his way through Pecos and on to El Paso. At last Jack could get his passport stamped in a foreign country just across the Rio Grande.

He walked over the bridge into Juarez and with his high school Spanish "made the puzzled Mexican border guards understand that I wanted something stamped into my passport to prove that I finally reached a foreign country. They . . . pounded it firmly onto the first page of the passport in the section allotted for visas. 'Abr 11 1935' it read."[49]

The next day on a westbound freight heading to Phoenix, Jack felt the draw of the desert landscape that he had seen as a child and would return to many times with his future wife, Charlotte. The images that tugged at his heart and the scenes he wanted to revisit were out in desert settings. "That particular afternoon was one I never forgot. The railroad snaked its way through sandhills and rock cuts, then out across the desert. I was riding in an empty gondola car in a train so long that the locomotive's cinders did not reach that far back. The sky was a rich blue, and the mid-April sun was warm but not hot. The ocotillo cactus flashed by as the train rocked along. We headed straight into a glorious sunset, and in the early evening the train stopped at Lordsburg. There were signs that cars were being removed or added to the train, indicating that there was time enough to walk over to a grocery. I spent a dime for a loaf of bread and refilled my quart canteen. When I got back on the train, I chose a boxcar for its protection against cool night winds. Another man also climbed in; he was broke, so we shared the small loaf."[50]

Just as dawn was breaking the train slowed down on a curve entering Tucson. Jack spotted an all-night café across the road, jumped off, and ordered a stack of wheat cakes (fifteen cents) and a cup of coffee (five cents). "That trio of wheatcakes remains as richly memorable as the sunset of the night before."[51] Before walking around Tucson in the early morning he cleaned up a bit, brushing his pants with a small brass wire pocket brush, and then washing off his boots at a park hydrant. While his "costume of boots and breeches" did not look like that of a tramp, he was still stopped by a policeman who wanted to ask a few questions. The officer noticed his Boy Scout belt, a perfect entre for Jack to tell him about the 1929 World Jamboree in England and for the policeman to say he was currently a scoutmaster. Before parting he told Jack where he could hop an outbound freight train heading to Phoenix where a visit with his aunt would be his last stop going west. "When I assured her that I planned to stay only overnight, she became warm and welcoming, for she was indeed lonely for any relative."[52]

Jack stayed a couple of days and slept on a cot on the back porch. They visited the mausoleum where his uncle was buried, and he helped with chores around the house. In the evenings he cut silhouettes of several teachers who were renting rooms from his aunt. Although he wanted to go to California, he had heard from hobos that the westbound trains were being stopped at the border and all the hobos were taken off and put on trains heading back east. "I decided that the time of pointless wandering had ended and that I should head back home to Indiana."[53]

His aunt gave him a couple of dollars before he caught a train out of Phoenix to El Paso. In the middle of the night when the train stopped to hitch on cars loaded with freshly picked lettuce, Jack jumped off and picked up several heads of lettuce scattered on the platform. Later, at a hobo jungle on the western edge of Sweetwater, Texas, he spent the night and prepared to make coffee with leftover coffee grounds. He helped dissuade the man building the fire not to do so with journal box waste, an old hobo custom. The waste was shredded rag fibers from the journal box surrounding the axle behind each wheel of a rail car. The box was packed with rags, on top of which a trainman slathered a heavy grease that slowly melted as the axle turned inside the packing. The oily rags burned easily when lit and made a hot flame while also giving off a viscous smoke that soiled hands and faces. It was an easy way to start a cooking fire, but when hobos took rags out of the journal box there was a risk of starting a fire under a freight car. Without its packing and grease for the axle, a "hot box" on fire would soon cause a derailment. "Railroad police were fierce if a hot box were involved, and the hobos themselves, at least in those days, were reasonable enough to feel some human responsibility in the matter, too. So we didn't use journal waste that night."[54]

By noon the next day Jack was hungry once more, thinking "how often hunger enters into any tale of a hobo's odyssey."[55] He walked into Sweetwater and asked for work in the first café he came upon. After the owner gave him a bowl of soup and a piece of pie, he began washing dishes, telling how he had waited tables while in college. His timing was perfect. A charter bus rolled up and the café was quickly packed. Soon Jack was waiting tables, after which the owner gave him a full meal and allowed him to keep the tips.

Back at the tracks he witnessed an act of cruelty he never forgot when a railroad "bull" on top of one of the cars knocked a hobo off by kicking him in the head. Out of Fort Worth he did not have any choice but to board a tank car for a terrible ride. Tank cars did not need to cushion their loads, so they were not equipped with springs. Standing on the platform between cars was tooth jarring. Several nights later he was in Boonville, Missouri, as a cold, late April wind blew out of the north. He recalled his "hobo seminar" when Slim told him about trackside sand houses. Sand was a critical component of the braking systems on locomotives where containers were located above the huge driving wheels. When needed for a faster stop, the engineer would pull a lever releasing a thin bead of sand just ahead of the wheel, creating more friction to stop the locomotive. The sand had to be perfectly dry for this purpose and was kept in a small shack near the tracks in the railroad yard heated by a low-burning coal stove. The doors on sand houses were never locked. Jack found the sand shack by the rails in Boonville. "I stretched out on my own artificial beach and went to sleep."[56]

At St. Louis he had to walk across the bridge into East St. Louis to catch the Pennsylvania RR headed for Indianapolis. On his walk he stopped by a butcher shop to buy twenty cents worth of bologna ends. They were cheap and had a little meat left on them, even though they were a nuisance to eat. With his customary loaf of day-old bread bought off the back of a bread truck and a canteen of water, he rode the gondola through the night as it headed east to Indianapolis, munching away at his cheap meal. Since it would be late when he arrived and the kitchen at the transient center would be closed, he stopped in a bakery to ask for a job and a meal. There was no job, but the baker gave him a whole cherry pie that had been cracked but was still good. At the transient center all the chairs were full, so Jack asked if he could sleep on a table.

> Permission granted, and there I lay when the case worker came to question me. Both of us got a surprise, for he was a graduate of my own college, a couple of years ahead of me, but we recognized each other. When he asked for background information, I gave

> him the highlights of a full year's rambling; he got his money's worth that night.
>
> The next morning I headed northeast on the last lap, a hundred and ten miles from Indianapolis to Fort Wayne. This was familiar ground; I had hitch-hiked it many times in my student days. (Were they really only eighteen months before? I seemed to have placed a generation between myself and college.)[57]

Jack reached home after almost twelve months of travel and a variety of experiences that seemed to energize him. He did not get to Europe, but he had circled through a good part of the United States, from Fort Wayne to the Canadian border, then down to New York, to New Orleans, across Texas to Phoenix, and back home, more than 5,500 miles. Now, settling back in Fort Wayne was a good time to reflect on being twenty-two years old in 1935. Though his parents were struggling through the Depression, each working for minimal wages, they welcomed him home and put three square meals a day on the table.

The past year had been a critical time in Jack's life, a time of disappointment and transition, a time that strengthened his confidence in pursuing what interested him, a time that tested his resilience. In a year when 12,833,000 people were out of work, he adapted, always developing new survival skills as he traveled and gaining a better understanding of the world around him. Soon he would go back to New York and seek work with a book publisher. He was just getting started as a young man on his own, coming home to court a young woman who must have been on his mind while he was on the road.

After returning to Fort Wayne, Jack contacted Beulah Rose Scherrer, a friend from his neighborhood whose parents owned a small grocery store near Jack's home. Both families went to the same church; both young people attended the same high school. They certainly could have dated before Jack left for college, but we don't have any correspondence or diary entries confirming that. However warmly they felt toward one another a few years earlier, it must have been easy for them to reestablish a friendship that soon blossomed amid a whirlwind courtship. On May 31 they became engaged; they were married on June 21. Beulah was ready to travel with Jack and find work in New York, so the impecunious newlyweds made a plan. Jack would catch freight trains heading East and Beulah would follow by bus. He found the trains more crowded than earlier. As the Depression continued, more than 250,000 teenagers were riding in boxcars, panhandling, and living in shantytowns around the country.[58]

> I caught the Pennsylvania east out of Fort Wayne late in the day. There were no empties, and I had to ride outside. This meant the roof of the car, at least after dark. One could hang onto ladders between freight cars, but not for long stretches. There was a strong wind along the top of the train, and I had to devise some way of resting safely and blocking the wind. I lay down on the roof of the boxcar, which sloped gently downward from the running boards along the middle of the roof. With me I carried an extra belt, long and strong, and I looped this through my trousers' belt and through the planks of the running board. I still carried my backpack, and I shifted this so it lay on the roof just beyond my head. This provided both safety and a windbreak, and so I made it into Lima, Ohio, the first division point.[59]

When he arrived in New York for the second time Jack rented a room in Chelsea, waited for Beulah to join him, and picked up odd jobs while researching the publishing houses he wanted to contact for work.[60] He knew summer was a quiet season in book publishing, so he timed his longhand letters of application to well-known houses for September and early October when publishers hired extra staff for the autumn upswing in business.

> I worked during the day at a lettershop firm known as Druggists Addressing Service down near Canal Street, . . . running an Addressograph machine all day. . . . The machines were equipped

> with high-speed drive pulleys, and I sat all day feeding the machine by hand; my top speed was addressing 2,300 an hour, handfed. After five o'clock I got a bit of supper on the way to my evening job which was as an usher at the old City Theatre on Fourteenth St. just off Union Square, near Luchow's restaurant. . . . I worked that shift until midnight seven nights a week, and typed up the daily reports for the night manager. Between the two jobs I made enough for us to live on. We were living in an old tenement on West 23rd St., in the Chelsea district, a gloomy place swarming with roaches.[61]

Lacking credentials and experience, he did not seek the higher-paying jobs. "As my fortunes had never been high . . . , it seemed to me that low-income was the normal way of life."[62] The first response to his many application letters offered a job as #3 mail boy at Alfred A. Knopf paying fifteen dollars a week, five dollars more than a year earlier at Smolin's bookshop. Jack took it.

For a twenty-three-year-old novice interested in book publishing, Knopf was an ideal and heady place to start learning. Founded in 1915, the firm had grown rapidly, shaped by the vision and remarkable taste of Alfred A. Knopf and his wife, Blanche, both of whom traveled the world signing up new authors wherever they found notable writers. Two decades after the firm was founded, Jack became their twenty-first employee. The publisher's list read like a Who's Who of famous writers of the time: Willa Cather, H. L. Mencken, Thomas Mann, Warwick Deeping, and Joseph Hergesheimer among many others. The company's mailing list, numbering twenty-three thousand names, was growing thanks to a reply card laid into every copy of every book Knopf printed. With this card anyone could ask to be added to the mailing list. One of Jack's duties was maintaining and updating this critical part of the Knopf book promotion.

At Knopf, Jack thrived.

> My work was interesting from the start. Each morning I arrived

> a half-hour before the rest of the staff. Hanging from the doorknob on the rear office door was a mail sack, usually half-full. I opened the bag, sorted out any letters marked "personal," and ran the rest through an envelope opener. Then I sorted the letters into wire baskets for Mr. Knopf, Mrs. Knopf, Orders, Payments, Editorial, and so on. The tray of orders was given top priority and went to the billing department. Then Mr. Knopf's letters went to his secretary. The mail was the best possible education. I saw proposals from W. A. Dwiggins on [book] design, from Georg Salter on [designs for dust jackets], from Vail-Ballou on the price of binding, from the Book of the Month Club on proposals, and from authors everywhere. There were letters from Thomas Mann, H. L. Mencken, Willa Cather, Carl Van Vechten, Warwick Deeping, and all the greats of the book season of 1935–36.
>
> Sometimes I saw these authors in the office, Willa Cather, looking like a Helen Hokinson matron out of *The New Yorker*; and Langston Hughes, slim and athletic; and H. L. Mencken. Once I rode down in the elevator with H. L. Mencken, who . . . talked about the value of book advertising and book reviews. . . . Mencken said that they did a little good but the real impetus came from people talking about a book.[63]

While Jack never sat in editorial meetings or met with book designers or the production or marketing teams, he had a sense of what was going on upstairs by studying the contents of all the letters he was opening and sorting. "I soon saw that being an editor was not for me; Alfred and/or Blanche Knopf made the real editorial decisions; the copy editors seemed to be people who sat studiously at desks all day long, moving seldom. The real action was in the advertising and promotion department, then consisting chiefly of Sidney Jacobs. Action was in the air around him all the time; he was always moving swiftly, waving proofs or printed pieces. I started a notebook of my own on publishers: advertising, listing, organizing, and charting all of the functions."[64]

Sometimes he ran errands for Mr. Knopf. As Christmas 1935 approached, Jack rode with Knopf's chauffeur to deliver gifts to the New York apartments of prominent writers, but he only met the maids who came to the door to accept packages, not the notable figures who lived there. He also remembered a "steady flow" of books arriving from European publishers. When the office shelves were overflowing, Mr. Knopf asked Jack to box the books and take them to the shop owned by Phillip C. Duschnes. With this first glimpse of antiquarian bookselling, just stepping into a distinguished shop on behalf of his employer made a lasting impression. Jack liked what he saw and remembered it decades later.

Most of all Jack was drawn to books and book production, and he was earning enough to move to another apartment. "Fifteen dollars a week was not bad. We lived in two furnished rooms on West 46th Street, at $7.50 a week, and cooked over a gas plate in a tiny kitchenette. New York was vital and exciting then: there were no muggings on the streets."[65]

By the end of spring he wanted to learn more. Asking if there were a path for advancement at Knopf, he was told no. Determined to regroup and move forward, Jack and Beulah returned home to Indiana and a little log cottage beside Big Long Lake that they would soon buy from her father for $300.[66] With his marriage and work at a major publishing house in New York, the lure of vagabonding in Europe dimmed. Jack was already thinking about another season in New York working for a publisher, but in the meantime, he had a full summer to read voraciously and write his review columns for the newspaper. He still raised a little money selling review copies at secondhand bookshops in Fort Wayne, but he also kept some for a growing library collection in his cabin by the lake.

As autumn approached Jack and Beulah were ready for another season in New York. On Labor Day 1936, he hopped a freight train on the Pennsylvania RR once again for his last free trip back East, while Beulah traveled by bus. Experienced at picking up odd jobs, he would make just enough for cheap rent and inexpensive meals until he could find a job with another publisher. With each of his previous stays in the Big Apple he had learned more and earned a little more money in an arena that in time he would occupy with distinction—the world of books.

For his next outreach to publishers Jack decided to send a typed letter that he reproduced attractively and signed in ink. Showing a flair for advertising, he opened with a statement intended to grab the reader's attention: "PAPERMEN, printers, publishers, poets! William Rittenhouse founded the first paper mill in the United States in 1690 and ever since that time each generation had seen the name Rittenhouse connected with publishing in some way. I am only a leaf from the old tree, but books are my career." Following this lead Jack gave his qualifications, including his work at Alfred A. Knopf Inc. as a "general assistant." He emphasized his ability to undertake tasks in several departments. "I can lay out and letter posters, write ad copy, am familiar with much of the work of the production department. I am an expert addressograph operator and mail clerk, can handle general correspondence, read and check manuscripts and proof and handle routine office tasks."[67] He sought a minimum salary of twenty-five dollars a week and offered to work "hours unlimited."

Goldsmith's at 77 Nassau Street, the largest stationery and office supply company at the time, produced one hundred copies for him. He sent ninety-three copies of his letter to publishing houses around the city. The earliest positive responses were from Prentice Hall and Hillman-Curl. Prentice Hall offered him a job writing sales letters for books. Hillman-Curl needed an advertising manager. He chose the more complicated and challenging job at the recently established Hillman-Curl Company, which was barely a year old.

Alex Hillman was already experienced in publishing before going into business with Sam Curl. Hillman had joined the Eastern Book Corporation in the 1920s. Some of its partners were convicted pornographers and others produced pirated editions of well-known writers such as Samuel Roth's edition of D. H. Lawrence's *Lady Chatterley's Lover*. While Hillman avoided illegal publishing activities with his new partner, he chose another lucrative field for some of his books—pulp fiction packaged in lurid covers with suggestive titles. Sam Curl had been an editor in the publishing division of Brantano's Books, a venerable New York City bookshop.

When Hillman and Curl interviewed Jack Rittenhouse, they asked what he knew about book advertising. He produced the charts and notes made the year before at Alfred A. Knopf while observing the head of advertising, Sidney Jacobs. Hillman-Curl hired Jack for twenty-two dollars per week, not the twenty-five dollars he anticipated. Nevertheless, that was seven dollars a week more than he earned at Knopf.

Late in life when Jack began writing notes about his experiences with books and publishing, he recalled vividly how Hillman-Curl scrambled to stay in business during the Depression. "Alex Hillman was a businessman with literary leanings; in later years he took over *Pageant* magazine and also became interested in the high-level auction business. The literary man was Sam Curl, a man of wide reading, who liked to play chess, and who kept a Siamese cat in his Greenwich Village apartment. The staff, for the most part, regarded Sam with affection and respect; whatever their attitude was toward Hillman, there was always a little fear present."[68]

Without a strong backlist such as the one Knopf generated in twenty years of careful and distinguished publishing and without a single bestseller, Hillman-Curl maximized their profit with four separate imprints, each with a different focus. The main imprint for better books that carried the owners' names had a hard time attracting and paying well-established writers, but there was also Arcadia House, which published the latest romances with marketing pitched toward rental libraries that were popular at the time. Arcadia books rented for twenty-five cents a week and "could pass the strictest censoring," Jack recalled. "They were vapid and inconsequential, and there was another new crop each month for rental libraries who wanted to offer 'the latest.'" Jack remembered another series, the Godwin imprint, as "a little different," meaning they were moving closer to something licentious. "They were not exactly spicy but came as close to it as permissible. Today, they would be innocuous. Their most daring venture was the use of asterisks," and the cover art featured busty young women dressed in clinging satin.[69] Hillman paid the artists $100 for each different cover painted in full color, an equivalent of more than $1,800 today. Authors earned a flat fee without any royalty. Rarity Press produced books appealing to "masculine tastes" and drew upon works by Pierre de Louys, Rabelais, Balzac, Boccaccio, De Maupassant, and others, all out of copyright.

At Hillman-Curl the Rarity Press imprint picked up older British printings no longer under copyright, cut them apart, made sets of engravings and electrotypes, printed the new Rarity edition, bound the books in wine-red cloth, stamped them with a little imitation gold, and featured them in full-page ads in men's magazines. The pitch was a forbidden book for ten dollars rather than the European price at forty dollars. After a short life for each title, the company sold the plates to another publisher for its own line of "forbidden" books.

By the time Jack began working at Hillman-Curl, he knew enough about publishing to understand how the owners were watching the market and structuring their business. "Hillman was a calculating businessman when it came to analyzing the market. It appeared at times that he might be actually publishing books to be remaindered and could make a profit on a book remaindered at twenty-five cents. The first step was to reduce author expense, done by having authors on monthly contract. The next requirement was standard length, so the books could run about 224 pages, including front matter, and thus print in seven signatures with sixteen pages on a side. After the type was set, a staff editor could trim the long books or, at times, write a little to extend the short books. Cloth was contracted for by the carload or other large quantity, all the same grade but varying in color. Typographic design was undistinguished.

"Once the new book appeared, there was a predictable sale to rental libraries and to book wholesalers, and after a market life of a few months, the book was offered to a remainder wholesaler at a price that allowed a small profit per copy. Pennies counted in those days, and each month there was a small harvest as a new lot moved into the remainder market. Never was the quantity larger than what the remainder people preferred. It was a shrewd, successful business, a manufacturing rather than a publishing operation except for the Hillman-Curl books."[70]

Jack's responsibilities at Hillman-Curl included reviewing and approving all invoices the company received, sending out review copies, and preparing and mailing lists and catalogs. Without a large budget for advertising, the firm could only occasionally place ads in *Publishers Weekly*.

Meanwhile, Jack, eager to learn more about publishing, joined the BMG (Book and Magazine Guild), a trade union where he took classes on various aspects of book production and sales. He also studied advertising, not yet knowing how important that subject would become in the next phase of his life. His text was a copy of *Modern Advertising* by Kenneth M. Goode. He also learned all he could about copywriting, typography, and printing. Yet, he still needed a jolt of recognition that there were more profitable ways for him to make a living. That fresh insight came at the end of his time with Hillman-Curl.

From his observations on how Sidney Jacobs promoted books for Knopf in 1935, and his BMG classes on publishing, he thought he might be ready to write a Hillman-Curl ad for one of the infrequent placements in *Publishers Weekly*. He showed an idea to his boss. Unimpressed, Hillman told him to take it to an outside agency. Disappointed at the time, Jack was primed to view the ad agency invoice as a new opportunity. When it arrived, it was the inspiration needed to make another change in his career. As he authorized payment for the agency bill of $120, he thought about his weekly check for $22. "I was on the wrong side of the desk, or in the wrong business."[71]

> I was, nonetheless, absorbing by osmosis much of the tradition of publishing. We were . . . near 60 Fifth Avenue. Just north of

> us was the main office of Prentice Hall, in their own tall, narrow building. Below us was the Macmillan Building, looking for all the world like a temple or a bank. Between Macmillan and H-C (we had only a floor or part of a floor) lay the antiquarian bookshop of Dauber & Pine. Across the street was a mail order remainder house that served libraries. We had no regular coffee breaks in those days but could get away occasionally for a cup, and one of the men I met then was Ed Delafield, handling sales. I also heard gossip about the Macmillan people, who had just acquired a Civil War, pro-Southern novel that they felt might be a really good seller—perhaps as much as twenty-thousand copies, tops. It was called GONE WITH THE WIND.[72]

Returning home to Fort Wayne with a modest grounding in book publishing and its routines for promotion, Jack moved into ad agency work at age twenty-five. He landed a job with the Louis Wade Agency. For the next twenty-three years in several parts of the country he applied his keen mind and boundless energy to this new line of work where he mastered the art and craft of organizing projects, writing copy, selecting typefaces, designing layout, planning production methods, and assembling all the specs for letterpress printing. These were skills he honed to perfection for the rest of his life as he moved up in advertising and then into publishing. He thought about print on paper as the logical conclusion of a process that began with research and writing, and he was as comfortable in the press room as he was in a library surrounded by books.

Chapter 3

Facing Headwinds

This was my real initiation into the working aspects of typesetting, engravings, electrotypes, paper selection, and printing. . . , at a point in time when these mechanical methods were beginning to change. The best engraver's proofs were still pulled on the old Washington-style handpress.

—JACK D. RITTENHOUSE[1]

IN 1937 JACK AND Beulah returned to Fort Wayne where he was determined to break into the advertising business. "I walked into the [Louis E. Wade] offices and was readily granted an interview. I told Lou that I wanted to get into agency work and offered to work for nothing for three months to show what I could do. The idea interested him, and . . . he could not accept me for nothing but would pay me fifteen dollars a week. After six weeks, he raised me to about twenty-five dollars a week and paid me back wages."[2]

Wade's two principal accounts were Century Distilleries and Allied Mills. Century produced spirits, while Allied produced calf feed, chicken feed, and mink and fox feed, along with a companion business, incubators for baby chicks. In the Midwest with Prohibition over, spirits and animal feed products were highly competitive businesses depending on print-based advertising for their success. Jack began working closely with Wade writing copy for advertising.

After about eight months Wade asked Jack to fill in for the production manager who was leaving for another job. "This was my real initiation into the working aspects of typesetting, engravings, electrotypes, paper selection, and printing."[3] Much of the work was set on a Linotype machine. It was an exciting time for anyone interested in printing because methods were beginning to move toward offset lithography and away from hot metal, giving Jack the opportunity to learn more about printing methods he had previously observed at newspaper presses in Indiana. At the same time, he saw engraver's proofs still being pulled on a vintage Washington-style handpress.

At the Wade Agency Jack worked with two or three account executives, a staff artist, the media department, and the bookkeeper. He and his boss traveled to Denver, Milwaukee, Chicago, and Saint Louis once or twice a year as members of a regional agency network to discuss new developments in their field. Through these meetings Jack began to form a network of colleagues with shared interests and experiences who could help him solve tough problems or even locate another job in the future.

He also gained in-depth knowledge of a new way to organize ad agency work, the Ellis Plan, for increased profitability. Lynn Ellis, "a top account executive once with McCann-Erickson [who] handled work on the Standard Oil account" developed a way agencies could increase profitability by systematically tracking workflow, timing, and dollars. Until Ellis introduced his management methods, most ad agencies operated as studios in which the staff were the artists and the owner, the conductor. Jack admired Ellis as "a professorial type who was passionately interested in management methods. He saw that only by the institution of forms, systems, and standard practices could the advertising agency business be converted from a 'studio' operation into a real business."[4] Louis Wade had just implemented the plan in his agency, and Jack embraced it immediately. Such a systematic and carefully developed approach to the business of advertising reflected the way Jack worked from research and writing to planning a trip or laying out and printing ad copy. When he first encountered the Ellis Plan, he spent sixty nights cramming on its texts. "I had to learn about bookkeeping, accounting, time studies, and the structure and functions of corporate work. Much of this stayed with me when I went back into publishing."[5] Even though he would change employers several times for various reasons over the next years, he carried with him a deep commitment to implementing Ellis's systematic approach to the business of advertising.

"After a year with Lou Wade, disaster struck and initiated me into the chancy life of an advertising man. The government laid a heavy tax on each gallon of liquor, and the Century Distilleries decided to cut their advertising budget by enough to absorb the tax. It was to be only a temporary measure, but Lou Wade received a telephone message that cut his annual receipts by $50,000 overnight."[6] Wade had to cut staff, and he began with his two most recent hires. Jack was one of them.

Along with his intuitive grasp of the Ellis Plan, Jack realized the growing need for sales training manuals and presentations. Few agencies were focused on sales training as he began assembling files of magazine articles on the subject, with particular focus on preparation of training kits for companies seeking to increase the productivity of sales staff. "In a new field, it did not take much knowledge and experience to run ahead of the pack and become known as a specialist."[7] Seeking a new job, he put together a methodical sales presentation for himself, caught the Pennsylvania train to Chicago, checked in at the YMCA, put the finishing touches on his presentation, and called on a half dozen agencies in the next two days. At the end of his second day, he accepted a job as a copywriter with the Jesse Gorov Agency in the Furniture Mart near the Lake Front. Jack convinced Gorov on the benefits of the Ellis Plan, and his new boss asked him to set up new "source files of creative material, procedures for systematizing the flow of internal work and handling service to accounts. He wanted me to set up systematic procedures for servicing all clients as my first task; I started on that."[8]

Within eight weeks of hiring Jack, Jesse Gorov fell ill and was unable to work for three months. His wife came to the office immediately and asked what could be done. Jack told her about the new account-handling system that he had just installed and how he thought it would help them "hold the line" during her husband's absence. "So I moved into the big office and took over. Of course, his own secretary was the most competent of any of us in keeping things going. But I handled all contacts, and some of the clients expressed wonder how I could know so much about their operations, as they had never met me before."[9] Jack more than held the line for the agency. They did not lose a single account and even added a couple of new clients before Gorov regained his health and returned. At that time, Jack went back to copywriting.

At twenty-six in the autumn of 1938 and too young to be partnership material, he moved to another job in Chicago with Mason Barlow and Associates. The owner offered him a fifty/fifty split on all their projects. When his partner failed to bring in new accounts, Jack realized their partnership was little more than "enthusiasm and talk." After his experience with Barlow, he started a short and challenging run with his own Mercury Advertising Agency. The ups and downs were numerous, but he did attract one good account, a Fort Wayne builder, George Poag, who developed small subdivisions in various parts of the city. For Poag he wrote a set of training materials that ultimately helped sell more new homes than any other builder in Indiana, but Jack was unable to attract other accounts to grow his business. While he eked out another year of hand-to-mouth existence, filling in here and there with local consumer surveys and other small ad-related jobs on the East Coast, he was still barely getting by. His most consistent success came from agencies in Madison and Chicago seeking help to install Ellis Plan methods.

In less than three years Jack had earned recognition in the advertising field for his knowledge of the Ellis Plan and ways to implement it. A growing list of satisfied clients and a certificate for "the best contribution to advertising agency operation" heralded his success. He decided to take his Ellis Plan experience on the road to agencies beyond the Midwest. For such a venture he needed reliable transportation. It was time to buy a car. With only a modest amount of savings, he bought an odd-looking used 1939 American Bantam two-door coupe. Not much of a car as far as its size and engine were concerned, it was affordable. As the first economy car built in this country, new Bantam models ranged in price from $399 to $575. "This little car could carry two, with a compartment behind the seat to hold the equivalent of two transfer file cases. It had four cylinders, a standard transmission with floor-mounted gearshift, and mechanical (not hydraulic) brakes. . . . The best mileage I got was 55 miles per gallon on the road. I owned it from 1940 until 1946 and put over 100,000 miles on it. . . . This car effected a change in my future."[10]

He decided to "spend January and February of 1941 traveling through the West working with agencies that wanted personal consultation on Ellis methods. . . . I easily lined up a tour, charging fees of $50 to $100 per day, sometimes more when several agencies joined in a seminar session. I went first to Fort Worth, Texas, then on to El Paso, to San Diego, Los Angeles, San Francisco, Portland, and Seattle, and then went back to Los Angeles for repeat sessions. In those days, gas, motels, and meals were low in cost; often they were included as part of my fee. I didn't make a great deal of money, but enjoyed myself hugely and got a little ahead financially."[11]

Somewhere along Route 66 he had an idea for a book about the ribbon of road he was driving, a road with endless allure to travelers, a road already gaining its own unique legendary status as the "Mother Road" across America. With his book idea taking shape, it was not far removed from the manuals he was writing for his advertising clients, but with the impending war, he needed to keep working as best he could in the advertising business. He was having a "hugely" good time in 1941 on his first long road trip, enjoying the freedom to head West where he always wanted to travel. At the same time as he made money along the way he also made lasting professional contacts he would draw upon in the future. Laid out in multiple ring binders, the Ellis approach often required considerable tailoring to specific organizations, a process for which Jack was well prepared and one with which he could earn some money.

Having successfully completed his circuit of prospective agencies, Jack returned to the Martin Agency in Huntington Park in Los Angeles where Ted Martin offered him an attractive proposal.

> He would provide me office space in the same building, a monthly retainer if I produced certain sales manuals for his clients, and other inducements. At that time, several agencies around the country formed an association for the purpose of exchanging material on how they produced sales manuals. The group was simply known as the "Exchange," and I was asked to be its executive secretary, with most of the dues being allotted to me for my work.
>
> I accepted the ideas from Martin and the Exchange, had my office records shipped out from Fort Wayne, and ended the Mercury Advertising Agency. I operated simply as Jack D. Rittenhouse. Nearly all of Ted Martin's clients were manufacturers of equipment used in oil well drilling or in oil well servicing. One of the first sales kits I did was for the McCullough Tool Company. I also worked on catalogs for such firms as Baker Oil Tools, Hamer Valves, Byron Jackson pumps, and others. I continued to build a collection of sales manuals for industries of all types. It was not a phenomenal success, but it was becoming a stable income.[12]

By November 1941, Jack resigned from the Martin Agency and the Exchange to join Company B, Sixth Regiment, of the California State Guard. At twenty-nine, he regarded this service as part of his civic duty. "No one had urged or suggested that I do this; it was wholly my own idea. No one invited me in."[13] "I went back to my office and simply locked the door and had the telephone disconnected. Later I moved out all of my papers. The State Guard had no funds to pay us any salary or wages. For several weeks my family existed only on a collection taken up in the building where I worked, with most of the money coming from one man. It would be at least three months before we got any State Guard pay."[14]

Japan bombed Pearl Harbor a month after Jack's entry into the Guard. City officials requested his unit post sentries around the municipal water tower in Huntington Beach twenty-four hours a day. When the challenge of providing meals for the men became evident, he was made mess sergeant in charge of feeding several hundred men, utilizing well-practiced routines learned while working in the kitchen at scout camp and later at restaurants while in college. Allocated fifty cents per man per day, he drove the regimental truck to the LA Farmer's Market early in the mornings for fresh vegetables. Potatoes were three dollars for a hundred-pound sack. He and his men bought canned goods, flour, and seasonings at wholesale prices, and he ensured the entire meal process ran smoothly. Even with the truck they did not have enough vehicles to move supplies, so he painted his Bantam military regulation olive green and pressed it into service for supplying the kitchen. He remembered one afternoon when "several exuberant men lifted it atop a concrete picnic table. I was called to see it and simply told them that supper would be served when it had been lifted down. Supper was served on time."[15]

In the spring of 1942 the Bantam saw service in a more serious way when Jack's guard unit was ordered by train up to the Benicia Arsenal northeast of San Francisco to help patrol the Embarcadero, the Oakland Bay Bridge, and several reservoirs and dams in the nearby hills. "When we were ready to move out, the train had no cars to carry trucks. The only car we could take along was my little Bantam, because it could be manhandled into a standard baggage car."[16] With its new regulation paint job it looked rather official despite its size. To increase its carrying capacity Jack built a wooden footlocker sized to fit precisely on the back of the Bantam above the spare tire.

Among his diverse Guard unit he found few opportunities to talk with anyone about books. Some of the men had left Oklahoma during the Dust Bowl. He found they held many prejudices against Blacks and Hispanics, but in contrast, the company also had a few Hispanic men with ROTC training who were "alert, sharp, and disciplined." Another group, ages forty to fifty, were "winos," who "made very poor soldiers." Still others "were erratic, alternating between stretches of real brilliance, only to sink suddenly into near-insanity. We dealt with these men very circumspectly, for they were capable of anything when irrational. This type of man was generally unemployable in industry, and they found a haven in the State Guard, where they had steady food, clothing, regular discipline, and a sense of doing something worth-while. They were not bad soldiers, but they had to be watched."[17] Soon, he met "a new officer friend, a Lt. Davidson, who had been in the British Army. We often talked about books. Once I told him of reading Robert Briffault's *Europa*, a novel. He said, 'That is all true you know; he modeled most of his characters around real people and events.'"[18]

In addition to befriending at least one officer with whom he could discuss books, he also found some old military pamphlets of interest left behind when a National Guard unit moved out of the building where he worked. "In particular, I enjoyed reading one on logistics. Basically, this is the science of moving men and materials and supplies around so they all came together at the place and time where they were exactly needed. No shortages, no delays, no surpluses. This does not happen only in the military but in any business, so it was something I could apply in business as well."[19] Among other useful books he found at the armory were a manual for mess management, an "Officer's Guide," and "government-issued manuals on the duty of the soldier, on scouting and patrolling, and on the revolver."[20]

From November of 1941 to September 1942, Jack rose quickly in the ranks of the California State Guard from private, to private first class, to staff sergeant. When his company moved from Huntington Park to join the full regiment in Compton, he became regimental sergeant major, a rank reserved for only one soldier per regiment. With his higher rank he also was issued a pass allowing him to go into town when off duty. Near the end of summer in 1942 he was promoted to a rank of second lieutenant and attached to the staff at regimental headquarters. The promotion raised his pay "in the neighborhood of $60 to $80 a month" but was inadequate for a married man with a family to support. Boredom set in as threats of a Japanese invasion receded. Feeling like little more than a watchman when on duty with the California State Guard, he resigned his commission, informed his draft board of his change in status, and went to work at Timm Aircraft Corporation in Van Nuys. "I wanted to get into the plant as a systems control man, because I was acquainted with preparation of written standard practices, flow charts, etc. But they did not need such people. Instead, I was hired as a woodworker. . . ! The firm built light plywood training planes for the Navy, the planes in which new, young pilots made all of their first flights. My experience building ship models had enabled me to work wood within a tolerance of 1/100th of an inch."[21]

After a few months he realized his woodworking skills "were not good enough to keep up with the cabinetmakers who worked with me." He also felt his draft number might come up soon and did not want to leave Beulah and his son, David, almost four years old, stranded in California.[22] Since they had no furniture, they shipped a few household goods, loaded up the Bantam with the rest, and headed out on Route 66. Jack remembered two things about November 8, the day they reached Chicago: "Gasoline rationing began, and the U.S. troops made their first landings in North Africa."[23] With no job and wartime rationing expanding, Jack and his family found a cheap apartment and split the rental with Beulah's sister and brother-in-law while he searched for temporary work.

Over the next year Jack moved from job to job, while his parents in Indiana expressed concern that "he could not settle down." At the end of 1942, in Chicago he found work at the huge post office in Union Station where he and others handled thousands of parcels during the holidays. He worked "on the outside platform where incoming railroad trains were unloaded of packages. Each night, all night, through the Christmas rush, I and others on my team opened cars, took out parcels, and threw them onto a conveyor belt into the Post Office.

After the Christmas rush, many of us were laid off."[24] Tedious work and low wages convinced him to take an evening course in aircraft sheet metal fabrication with hopes of a job at the Pullman Company making aircraft wings for warplanes. By the time he finished the course, the Pullman plant had phased out wing fabrication to increase their manufacturing of the M4 Sherman tank and munitions.

His marriage, already showing signs of strain, soon ended. "It was at this time that Beulah and I were divorced. It was an amicable affair, and I had known for a few years that it was inevitable. We had been developing divergent tastes in many ways for a long time. I now reached a critical point in my life. It was . . . 1944, and I was approaching the age of 32 years. I had moved into one room on Rush Street, just below Chicago Avenue, on [the] near north side. I lived alone, with few possessions: the aging Bantam car, a typewriter, my clothes, a few tools, and a radio. The cabin at Big Long Lake I left to B.; my library there I left for David; I had no bank account that I recall."[25]

Chapter 4

Charting His Course

So many people had never been over [Route] 66—they wouldn't know where the desert begins, how to get over the mountains, or anything. Friends thought I was kind of nutty, but I thought Easterners could use this book. So I did it.

—JACK D. RITTENHOUSE[1]

GOOD FORTUNE SMILED ON Jack Rittenhouse when he was around printing presses. In Indiana he was drawn to them as a high school student, and in college he began hanging out at the local Terre Haute newspaper when he discovered the satisfaction of watching his book reviews come off the press and head out to the newsstands where readers would see what he had written. As he learned the basics of pressroom operations, he liked what he saw in the systematic approach to careful setup, inking, and adjustments on complicated machinery that produced what he loved seeing—words on paper produced by inked metal type. In his first year in New York in 1934, he had toured the *New York Times* to see the vast composing and press rooms turning out one of the major newspapers in America. In Chicago he took a class on printing clean, readable, well-designed pages.

Later when the editor of the weekly *Chicago Union* newspaper was drafted into World War II, Jack, needing a job, helped out temporarily. There, in the pressroom, he met a bright and attractive young woman, Charlotte High, whom he would soon marry and who would become his close companion for life. On a September Sunday in 1944, the newlyweds headed to Los Angeles on Route 66. Neither one had a job waiting for them. They were on their honeymoon and would find work later after reaching California. It was Charlotte's first adventure on the "Mother Road" and Jack's third time driving its entire length. Both were intrigued by the sights along the way. She began keeping notes on details, the kind of information suitable for the guidebook to Route 66 that he would publish two years later.

"We drove from St. Louis to Victorville, California in Betsy, our 1939 Bantam," Charlotte wrote. Her notes on their journey opened each new day with the mileage on the odometer. They were enjoying their first road trip, exploring sights along the way and documenting the experience. Their American Bantam was the right car for this journey: compact, economical, and small enough to be slightly quirky but very affordable to drive. When they reached Rolla, Missouri, the newlyweds "arrived at [Charlotte's] Granddad's. . . . Kate, Granddad's wife, just does not know how to cook. We had to go out and get cantaloupe and coffee after dinner." Charlotte logged a major milestone for them when Betsy's odometer rolled up 50,000 miles "4 miles south of Miami, Oklahoma."[2]

Heading west beyond Albuquerque, Charlotte reminded Jack he had told her if she wanted to "climb a mountain" just to let him know when she picked one out. Near Laguna Pueblo she spotted what was really a mesa.

> We stopped the car and climbed the relatively low mesa. At the top we found the ruins of a small early village: a few low walls of stone. It was our first ruin, not anything spectacular, but impressive to us because it was our first such experience. That evening we stopped in the town of Grants, New Mexico. There was a small Indian curio shop open, so we went in. The owner was an interesting man, Mike Croteau, who had been in the Southwest since 1911. He told us that if we knew more about archaeology, we would

know what we saw at an Indian ruin. Later that year, when we were in Los Angeles, we took an evening course in archaeology (anthropology) at the University of Southern California, under Ruth D. Simpson. . . . It started our interest, which grew over the years.[3]

As Jack and Charlotte drove farther west, she noted her first sightings of "cowpunchers," cactus, adobe houses with flat roofs, volcanic cones, precontact native ruins, sheep crossing the road near Acoma Pueblo, Navajo hogans, trading posts, and ghost towns left in the dust of faded mining booms from earlier times. "Between Kingman and Topock, we took one mountain road which fulfilled all qualifications for a mountain road. It twitched, writhed, twisted, and turned. It rose and fell all 10 miles in length. It seemed like Betsy was not going to make it, but she tugged it out. Considering this, it is not surprising that she tired out a little before Los Angeles. The surprising thing is that she went as far as she did."[4]

At Topok, Arizona, on the Colorado River, they crossed the Old Trails Bridge, a landmark arched structure leading into California. Closed today due to a rerouting of US 66, it can be seen in two notable twentieth-century movies, *The Grapes of Wrath* (1940) and *Easy Rider* (1969). Nearing the end of their trip the travelers took time to explore the ghost town of Calico and hike up Odessa Canyon to an abandoned silver mine. After lunch and a game of pinball at the Old Trails Inn in Barstow, this part of Jack and Charlotte's trip soon ended. "Betsy's timing gear was defective, finally breaking down completely at Victorville, and the rarefied mountain air cut down gasoline mileage."[5] Jack and Charlotte rearranged their baggage so they could carry it more easily, left the car for repairs with a lieutenant and his wife living in an abandoned filling station, and hitchhiked to the railroad station to wait for the next train. At 7:30 a.m. the next day they stepped into Union Station in Los Angeles, ready to freshen up and find a place to live.

Jack and Charlotte's honeymoon trip in the Bantam gave more life to his idea for a guidebook to Route 66. By 1944 it was a true highway paved its entire length between Chicago and LA. Gone were the days when automobiles crossed the desert on wood planks to prevent getting stuck in sand. Car radios and even air conditioners were available to improve the journey. New drive-in restaurants and outdoor movie theaters along America's roadways heralded the age of the automobile. Before long there would be more than thirty thousand motor courts spread across the country. Jack kept up with these developments. He assumed that as the war ended, gasoline and tire rationing would end, along with the 35-mph wartime speed limit. A recovering peacetime economy would mean more people on the move, driving east and west along Route 66 for business and pleasure.

Heading west Jack and Charlotte sensed an endless allure to Route 66 for travelers. It was already gaining its own legendary, historical, and fictional status as the "Mother Road" across America, a central motif in a widely read novel in 1939, John Steinbeck's *The Grapes of Wrath*, winner of both the National Book Award and a Pulitzer Prize. The following year a Hollywood film version of the book starring Henry Fonda and directed by John Ford popularized the route even more. While Jack didn't have a title for his book, he had a good fix on the concept: give readers a smallish, handy-sized book with short entries on towns and cities along Route 66 from Chicago to Los Angeles, all 2,400 miles; divide the journey into sections useful for travelers getting on and off the route for shorter trips, but also make it essential for others driving the entire length; show mileage in two directions in a guide that could be used for eastbound or westbound travel; name and briefly describe the towns; give population numbers; note the garages, gas stations, motels, hotels, and cafes without making recommendations; note road conditions; provide call letters for radio stations along the way;[6] and, most important, include notes of historical interest.

Once they reached California, he wanted a job that would allow him and Charlotte to set up housekeeping and still provide time to finish gathering everything needed to start writing his book. They settled in a housekeeping room on Flower Street in midtown LA where Charlotte wrote, "The luck of Rittenhouse holds, and Mr./Mrs. Jack Rittenhouse are at home in a real nice place." Jack was back in LA to reestablish contacts in ad agencies that he had visited on his last trip West. At the old Theo M. Martin Agency, he found Martin had retired and the number two person, Lester C. Nielson, had become head of the firm. Jack's timing was good; Nielson was seeking additional employees to write and edit technical handbooks for the Air Force. Manuals were one of Jack's growing specializations. He accepted a job to produce a manual for "repair of an electrical relay that controlled a standby generator on a B-29 bomber. This relay was built by a Los Angeles firm and furnished to the aircraft manufacturer ready to install. By requirements of the time, each such sub-contractor had to provide an instruction sheet or sheets that would help the ground crews remove the component, take it apart, repair it, and put it back together again if the plane was in some remote theater of war. When the war ended, my handbook department switched to production of catalogs; the largest I handled was a 1,500-page wholesale hardware supply catalog."[7] Jack was where he wanted to be—in the American West, not far from desert landscapes, and working on projects at which he could excel.

By spring of 1945 Jack and Charlotte were ready to buy their first house on West 59th Place with a small living room, one bedroom, bath, kitchen, and garage. The cost was $3,500, and they raised the requisite 10 percent down payment mainly with the sale of Charlotte's war bonds. They were homeowners at last, even if it was a 400-square foot dwelling. There would soon be room for their first postwar appliances, an electric refrigerator and a radio. In the autumn they were able to take a one-week vacation trip to Death Valley where they became "devotees of the desert," a landscape they came to love. "We had bought the available travel guides to Death Valley and all of the detailed U.S. topographic maps of the area. On one map we found the location of a place called Surveyors' Well, several hundred yards off the main road on a trail you would easily pass if you didn't know what was there. Under a small tree's shade was an old hand pump. We worked the handle and out gushed a stream of pure, cool water. We pitched our Army pup tent, and that night the full moon rose over the Funeral Range to the east, bathing the land in a light actually bright enough to allow us to read a newspaper."[8] After visiting Death Valley Scotty's "Castle" and enjoying Thanksgiving dinner in the Amargosa Hotel at Death Valley Junction, they headed home, enchanted by the desert and the rich history of their surroundings.

Meanwhile, Jack continued research for his new book by poring over the American Guide Series, a major publishing effort produced by the Federal Writers' Project. He focused on guides to states through which Route 66 ran: Illinois, Missouri, Kansas, Oklahoma, Texas, New Mexico, Arizona, and California. Each WPA guide had earned a solid reputation as a respected source of information for its time. Written by a team of authors native to each state, the guides covered natural history, archeology, history, agriculture, education, newspapers, radio, and folklore, among other subjects. Jack mined these books for historical, cultural, and other facts for his manuscript.

By early 1946 Jack had worked at the Nielson Agency for seventeen months, his longest employment anywhere to date. He liked his work but found his boss very difficult. When he initiated discussions with Darwin H. Clark, Clark offered him an attractive job at his ad agency. To buy time for completing his Route 66 book, Jack negotiated his start date thirty days after leaving Nielson. Now he had a month to expedite his guidebook project. "So many people had never been over 66—they wouldn't know where the desert begins, how to get over the mountains, or anything. Friends thought I was kind of nutty, but I thought Easterners could use this book. So I did it."[9]

To set to work on the Route 66 book, Jack needed to drive the entire route one more time from LA to Chicago, taking notes all along the way. The Heinn Company in Milwaukee provided just the financing he needed when they asked him to write a detailed booklet on how to prepare and produce extensive product catalogs with large press runs such as the one he had done for Republic Supply Company over the past year. Heinn manufactured the post binders Jack used for the Republic project. Now the company wanted a how-to booklet for using its binders effectively. While Neilson did not want employees to accept outside jobs, Clark had no problem with the arrangement, leaving Jack free to work with Heinn on his own time.

This lucky break came just before the month-long road trip to finish researching his new book. Heinn had followed Jack's work closely when Republic ordered around three thousand of their post binders. The company knew they could sell more binders with a booklet explaining some of the intricacies of planning, printing, and binding similarly large projects, and Jack was the best qualified to write what Heinn needed. He bid the job at $750, Heinn agreed, and Jack soon delivered his manuscript, clearing the way to hit the road in his little American Bantam one more time.[10]

He bought a stack of writing pads, tucked his portable Corona typewriter behind the seat, and gassed up Betsy for another adventure that would lead to his first book.[11] For the next thirty days, as he drove the entire Route 66 to Chicago and back, he made extensive notes all along the way. "I drove all day long—from sunrise to sunset. I'd stop for the day when it got so dark I couldn't see to make any notes. I made my notes on yellow pads I kept right beside me on the car seat. There weren't tape recorders then for me to use. In the evening I'd get a room at a tourist court and type my notes from the day while I could still read all my scrawling. I'd mail them back to Charlotte in Los Angeles. If I heard certain things or interesting stories in certain towns, then I'd try to find somebody to talk to in order to verify the story."[12] All along the way he was checking mileage, the spelling of names, and noting call letters and frequencies for radio stations, road conditions, historic sites, and more.

After a thirty-day, five-thousand-mile trip, Jack was home to start work for the Darwin Clark Agency during the day and spend evenings and weekends writing the text and designing his first book. As the sole writer, layout designer, and publisher, he had much to do. He drew thirty-one maps, specified the type, had it set by linotype, and then corrected proofs. He prepared all the pasteups needed for the lithographer to print three thousand copies. "I pasted up the pages in imposition, so each lithograph negative could hold four pages and needed no further stripping. This cut that phase of costs by three-fourths. I wrote up a description of this procedure for *National Lithographer* magazine and received a check for the article. I also devised the cover, specified the binding as a side-stitched paperback with a drawn-on glued cover and printed about three thousand copies, paying all costs as I went and producing the book within my budget of $750.00."[13] Throughout the book he used thirty small stock cuts available at the time from type foundries with images such as a bronc rider, a man with a plow, a covered wagon, a stagecoach with two men in the box on top and a team of four horses, some generic urban scenes, and two different cuts of men panning for gold.

For drivers on cross-country trips, Jack included additional tips: things to take on the trip such as extra water, a proper jack and a board to place under it when in soft dirt, dates for Pueblo dances, "Some facts about Navajo rugs," "Grand Canyon Information," and a short list of books of interest including *The Grapes of Wrath* by John Steinbeck, *The Saga of Billy the Kid* by Walter Noble Burns, *Laughing Boy* by Oliver LaFarge, and *The Shepherd of the Hills* by Harold Bell Wright. For radio stations he gave the call letters and kilocycle frequencies on the way west; however, beyond Albuquerque car radios fell silent because there were few US broadcasting stations in the 1940s for the next eight hundred miles.[14]

With World War II having just ended, Jack identified sites relating to the long conflict—training camps, bombing ranges, airfields, prisoner of war camps—all of which would be familiar to soldiers who trained in the west before being posted to Europe or the Pacific. Along with features we no longer see, such as airplane beacons, Jack included many notes of historical interest: where Washington Irving camped when traveling out west before writing *A Tour on the Prairies*; the entrance to Fort Reno established in 1876; a note on Belle Star; the

Goodnight cattle trail blazed in 1866; trails relating to the gold rush of 1849. At the Arizona–California border he identified the Desert Training Center where General Patton prepared ninety thousand US troops for desert warfare in North Africa.

Many motor courts identified in the guide had names reminiscent of an earlier and more innocent time. Sprinkled with hyphens and wordplay the names of popular places to stay included Camp-On-A-Way, Hav-A-Nap, Trav-L-Odge, Pig-in-Pen Log Cabin, Park-O-Tell, or, simply, Tha Best. One can still imagine seeing these names beckoning weary motorists with softly flashing neon lights.

As he moved the book toward production, Jack allocated twenty-two pages for ads. His letters and printed flyers offered ad space, saying there would be ten thousand copies printed in the first edition.[15] An early two-page promo flyer provided details about the guide and the rates for full-page, half-page, or ads inside the cover. The publication date was set for September 17, 1946. Response for ad placement was poor. The only ad in the book is a full page for Missouri "in the heart of America" paid for by the Missouri State Department of Resources and Development.

With his book on the press Jack, drawing on his advertising experience, sent another mailer seeking orders. It was headed, "Here's what you've been wishing for . . . PROFITS," along with another pitch that the book SELLS ON SIGHT. "One glance at the complete contents of this new Guide Book, and any tourist will reach for his billfold. Dollars are loose when tourists are on the road, and you deserve your share."[16]

When the book was printed and delivered, he implemented his marketing plan. From his LA to Chicago round trip in March he now had a large collection of business cards from motor courts, cafes, curio shops, and newsstands to which he mailed publication announcements and special offers. He also wrote letters in several versions for subsequent mailings. If the first letter did not bring an order for books, he sent a follow-up. One early promotion letter reads: "This guidebook meets a need never before filled so completely. It describes the route from Chicago to Los Angeles over this famous 'Will Rogers Highway' with exact detail, given in mile-by-mile directions with speedometer mileage readings. It tells where steep grades are met, distances between towns, where each historic spot is passed. It tells about each of 182 cities and towns: its accommodations, altitude, population, industry and history. It describes gala events in various towns and warns if these events fill lodgings. It names garages which may be called in case of trouble, and gives other helps. Between towns, it gives the location of every roadside filling station, café and camp on the entire trip!"[17]

All through the spring, summer, and autumn he and Charlotte had devoted their evenings and weekends to the book while working out of their small, rented house at 1416 West Fifty-Ninth Place in Los Angeles. Their first focus was editing and production work for the book, followed by typing and sending letters, taking orders, wrapping and mailing packages of books, and finally sending follow-up letters. Promotion pieces alone required much time to write, format, and print. Over the next months he created and distributed at least seventeen different forms of letters, notices, pitches, and flyers. By autumn Jack wrote to hospitality and shop managers that the *Guide Book* was being sold in 37 cities and towns along Route 66. That left 145 to go if he wanted to place it in every community named in his guide.

The process was slow and never completely successful. The following year when he was considering a second printing, Mainstreet Publishing in Tulsa, Oklahoma, issued their own guide to Route 66 retailing for sixty cents. "It didn't have half the information," Jack said. "But it had enough. That was the end of my travel book career."[18] Sixteen years later, after moving to Houston with his Stagecoach Press, Jack was still offering his Route 66 guide for sale. His guide never became the financial success that he hoped for until forty years later when America rediscovered the old Route 66. Hundreds of books about it were soon in print. Aware of this new market interest, the University of New Mexico Press reprinted an exact facsimile of Jack's guide in 1989 that remains in print today. In its preface Jack explained how his 1946 edition was researched and printed in an edition of three thousand copies and sold "for a dollar each, doing business by mail to bookshops, newsstands, cafes, and tourist courts (no one then called them motels) along US 66. And I learned the hard way that a self-publishing author usually has a fool for a distributor. I never reached my full market."[19] He was depending on owners and employees of tourist courts and curio shops to help sell his book as they struggled to serve an ever-increasing customer base.

Time has proven that with a well-known publisher, a large distribution network, and the right timing Jack's guidebook was poised to find a consistent market. It is setting a notable record—over three-quarters of a century in print. Fifty years after its first publication he reflected on the book project that grew out of his driving trips along Route 66. "Getting that Library of Congress number on your card was like seeing your epitaph on bronze in Westminster Abbey," he said. "This is going to be forever. I am immortal. It was my first book and I've got to admit—it was a pleasure, a kick. I never felt the same about anything else I wrote. I've had more satisfaction out of other books since."[20]

With the publication of his guidebook and his work with the Clark Agency, Jack had launched dual careers. His guide to Route 66 was well received by those who bought it, and his fulltime job with the Darwin H. Clark Company provided the scope and variety of research and writing he enjoyed. Clark's company had clients in three areas of advertising: oil field service firms, financial businesses, and an assortment of smaller and specialized fields from cosmetics to instruments. There were clients who wanted company publications known as house organs for both internal and external distribution. Annual reports were also part of the mix. Jack's first steady assignment was staff writer with a magazine the agency produced for Lane-Wells, a large technical oil field services company with major offices in Los Angeles, Houston, and Oklahoma City and forty-eight field branches scattered over every western state with significant oil production. With the Lane-Wells account he was responsible for *Tomorrow's*

Tools—Today!, a quarterly publication distributed to eight thousand people in the oil industry. Each issue contained a variety of news items about the company, short articles on technical advances and services written by company employees, and three or four short human-interest pieces. While Darwin H. Clark was listed as the editor, Jack wrote multiple nontechnical and historical pieces, short and long, for each issue. Some carried his name, and others were unsigned or published under a pseudonym. Because his contributions were so numerous Jack and his boss thought it best that his name not appear too frequently. He did sign most pieces devoted to historic subjects.

In the issue for the first quarter of 1949, he wrote and signed a piece on the history of the crossbow, one of a series of his articles on ancient weapons. In the same issue there was an unsigned piece he, no doubt, wrote on Switzerland "famed for cheese and Alps, for clocks, chalets and democracy." Also in this issue Jack introduced the character of "Permian Pete" writing under the pseudonym of David Kimsey, the first and middle names of his first-born son. At the foot of the page he announced, "This is the first of an original series of adventures about a new oil country character, Permian Pete. If you know of any similar problems Pete might tackle, mention them to us."[21] Jack enjoyed writing the sixteen episodes featuring Permian Pete. When he started the series, he was already thinking about how his tall tales could be gathered in a little book. After Lane-Wells's management learned how popular Permian Pete had become with their readers, they requested that the Clark Agency produce a book of the tall tales for a Christmas keepsake in 1951. It was economical and easy for Jack to create this book because type was already set, and the cartoons of Pete and his cohorts were drawn and in the files. Each tale was imposed for a right-hand page, with its associated drawing left of the fold. Three thousand quarto-sized copies were printed by lithographic offset with half the run bound in a heavy paper cover and the other half with paper over binder's board. All were given away by Lane-Wells. The Southern California Industrial Editors Association recognized the book with first honors for a public relations piece in

1951. "We took many awards at [local and national] levels with 'T.T.T.' Even on overall excellence, we once scored a rating of 98%, which was as high as ratings ever went."[22] The Permian Pete book gave Jack more experience and confidence in bookmaking and started him thinking about owning a press on which he could print books under his own imprint.

Writing articles and notes on subjects of interest for readers working in "the oil patch," Jack needed to learn more about the industry. He began collecting books on petroleum history, building a research library at home to shorten his time spent in the Los Angeles Public Library. From his growing book collection, he found information on forgotten oil-well drilling methods, early rotary drills, early pumps, railroads, and more for his "T. T. T." articles. Since 1940 he also kept clipping files on diverse topics relevant to his writing interests, such as early bicycles, hot air balloons, Spanish gold explorations, the passing of old-fashioned cigar stores, old advertising cards, cattle brands, fine English porcelain, or oil-field food.[23]

As he settled comfortably into his new job with Clark, he had time to explore the Los Angeles book scene on weekends. He discovered the remarkable scope of rare and out-of-print bookshops around LA and began making friends in the book trade. "The stores were like clubhouses for the owners' patrons and friends, hangouts for writers and artists," Victoria Daily, an antiquarian bookseller, wrote. "They were places where ideas were discussed and argued, the conversations often enlivened by illegal hooch, especially during prohibition."[24] By the 1930s there were more than twenty bookshops near downtown and more than sixty in greater LA. "The presence of the Huntington and Clark Libraries, opened in 1928 and 1934 respectively, helped to create an intellectual climate conducive to antiquarian bookselling. Also, starting in the late 1920s there was a remarkable confluence of talented individuals interested in the production, selling, and reading of books. Printers Saul Marks, Ward Ritchie, William Cheney, Richard Hoffman, Grant Dahlstrom and others started operations in Los Angeles at this time. The Zamorano Club for book collectors, founded in 1928, came to include Elmer Belt, Carl I. Wheat, Robert Cowan, Henry Wagner, and Leslie Bliss among its members."[25] As Jack began exploring the LA book scene, he met and become friends with most of these bibliophiles. Conducting research in the Huntington Library as well as the William Andrews Clark Library, he moved with ease among book people in LA. One of his favorite shops was Dawsons, well established and filled with interesting books. It was a treasured haunt of collectors and writers who always felt welcome. Browsing for books there in the 1940s, he met brothers Glen and Muir Dawson who ran the firm their father founded in 1905. The shop specialized in rare books relating to California and the West and ran its own publishing program for small, well-designed books on early travel in California, including Baja California.

Another favorite shop for Jack was Zeitlin & Ver Brugge, the Red Barn on La Cienega. Jake Zeitlin was a magnet for book collectors as well as creative people in photography, writing, printing, art, and music. Carrying his guitar and a rucksack, he had hitchhiked from Fort Worth, Texas, to Los Angeles in 1925 and settled in Echo Park, the locus of a flourishing bohemian scene. From there he developed a circle of remarkable friendships from Aldous Huxley to Robinson Jeffers and Frieda Lawrence. The books and prints Zeitlin stocked drew Jack, but he and Jake also found a common bond from their earlier years when both had hitchhiked and camped with hobos, Jake coming across the Southwest and Jack riding the trains and sleeping in hobo jungles from New York to New Orleans and on to Arizona in the depth of the Great Depression. Their backgrounds along with their mutual interest in writing and books led to a lifelong friendship.

After a short time Jack met another mover and shaker in the world of books, the legendary director of libraries at UCLA, Lawrence Clark Powell. Larry Powell had already distinguished himself as an engaging lecturer, writer, and librarian unafraid to speak his mind in support of reading and the role of libraries as the cornerstone of every community. He became head of the main library at UCLA in 1944, the same year Jack and Charlotte settled in LA. Writing eloquently about authors and their books, collecting, the importance of libraries, and travels with books, he made friends with prominent writers and artists associated with the Southwest, including Erna Ferguson, Haniel Long, Jack Schaefer, Paul Horgan, Ed Abby, Frank Waters, and Maynard Dixon. In addition, he wrote engaging essays about Aldous Huxley, Gertrude Stein, Henry Miller, and M. F. K. Fisher, all of whom he knew well. Larry Powell and Jack bonded around their love of books and fine printing.

Jack's circle of book people widened even more as he and his new friends exchanged ideas and shared information about favorite writers and books, new and old. Through his work with the Clark Agency he met fine printers such as Grant Dahlstrom and Ward Ritchie, quickly becoming friends around their mutual interest in the history of typography and fine printing. Expanding his knowledge and appreciation for the history and art of typography, the importance of beautifully made paper, and the lasting value of well-made books, he began to talk with friends about ideas for new books that he might publish. He already understood the importance of building momentum in publishing by closely following one successful title with another. When he asked Glen Dawson if he thought a book about horse-drawn vehicles in America could sell, the experienced bookseller told him there might be "a certain demand, not great but good."[26] That was all the encouragement Jack needed to start work on his second book, *American Horse-Drawn Vehicles*.

What drew him to this subject reveals much about how he chose and researched new topics. In early summer 1947 he recalled his youthful enjoyment of building ship models from scratch and decided to build a scale model of a wagon or a carriage. "So I went to the Los Angeles Public Library and found several books about carriages, but all of the photographic illustrations had the undercarriage obscured in shadow, not available as a guide to modelling. I asked at the reference desk if there was a book such as 'carriage builder's handy compendium' or some such book that showed the details I wanted. They said they neither had nor knew of such a book, although later I learned that there were a few such books available through antiquarians."[27]

Glen Dawson's cautious encouragement sent him back to the downtown library for another evening compiling a detailed list of American companies building buggies and carriages in the late nineteen and early twentieth centuries. The key source for this information was *Thomas' Register of American Manufacturers* first published in 1898 and expanded to thirty-four volumes before the end of the twentieth century when it became an Internet publication. "Thomas," as it was known at library reference desks throughout the country, offered sourcing information on industrial products and services. Jack brought home a list of fifty-five companies that built wheeled vehicles pulled by animals in a harness. "I wrote a letter explaining my interest in old catalogs and drawings of carriages, and copy-edited this to get it down to the fewest words, because I would have to retype this same letter fifty-five times."[28] One-third of his letters were quickly returned and marked "out of business," and another third generated responses that the company no longer made wagons and had nothing to send. "But the remaining letters brought a flood of free treasure: old catalogs, circulars, photographic prints, and drawings."[29]

Jack also began filling out his collection on wagons by placing ads for books he wanted to buy in *AB* (*Antiquarian Bookman*). As a new spinoff from *Publishers Weekly*, *AB* met the needs of a flourishing mail-order market beginning to develop for out-of-print, secondhand, and antiquarian books.[30] Jack's ad in *AB*, among the new magazine's first on January 17, 1948, listed four titles he wanted to purchase on coaches, carriages, and coach building, as well as "Old and Rare Magazines on Wagon and Carriage Building." At this time, there was little or no interest in printed ephemera, let alone material relating to wagons and carriages. Yet, ever since the founding of the American colonies up to the beginning of the twentieth century, wagons had carried goods to market all over the nation.

With little competition from others for ephemera, he soon assembled an enviable collection of original printed material on American wagons and coaches. "The most battered catalogs were cut up to furnish prints; the more valuable ones were photocopied. In a few months I had gathered my material and laid out the book. During a two weeks' vacation I wrote the text for each picture, specified the type and had it set, and prepared the pasteups of all the pages, paying costs as I went. The book, which was kept in print by reprint houses for twenty years was a sort of picture dictionary showing all types of buggies, carriages, and wagons, with all illustrations reproduced original size."[31]

With a new book being planned, a new addition to the family also arrived on Christmas Day 1947, when Jack and Charlotte's son Douglas was born. The baby suffered brain damage at birth, and later required a special facility for his residence, care, and schooling, which the family would arrange at the Austin State School, a ninety-five-acre facility for the mentally disabled. Throughout their lives, Jack and Charlotte set aside Christmas vacation to spend with Douglas. Their annual family tradition included a trip to the Texas Coast, returning to favorite restaurants and other sites, staying at the same motel, decorating a small Christmas tree with the same ornaments each year, and exchanging presents on their son's birthday.[32]

Since Jack did not have the capital to move his book through the entire printing process at one time, he made special arrangements with a lithographer and a bookbinder to produce high quality results at minimal costs. One of his key associates, Jack Dillon, owned a small lithograph shop working for Clark Agency clients. To minimize costs Dillon offered to copy old halftone wagon illustrations dot for dot with a new fine-grain Kodak developer and prepare offset negatives at slow times during the weeks ahead. Jack proposed that Dillon

> do nothing until I could guarantee receipts from sales. I would prepare and mail a circular at my own expense, using his building as my return address. We would go first after library orders, where payment would be certain. When the orders equaled his cost, we would start platemaking and printing. Books would be

> stored at his shop, from where I would do the mailing, and all receipts would come to his address, and the first receipts would all go to him until his costs were paid. If the circular brought no replies, the whole project would simply be cancelled. Then I made a somewhat similar arrangement with Earle Gray, a giant of a man who was known as one of the best bookbinders in the West.[33]

Unable to afford his own copy of the directory of American libraries, he took bundles of circulars to the public library each night where he addressed mailers to libraries around the country, preparing to send "a few thousand." At this point "a strange hitch occurred." Some librarian back East passed the circular along to the most knowledgeable man on carriages in the United States, Col. Paul H. Downing, who wrote Jack "a blast of a letter, calling me an upstart who rushed in where experts feared to tread, pointing to many errors in my book circular . . . and mentioning that he was in the process of doing a lifetime, multi-volume work on the subject that I was rashly pre-empting."[34] Jack's letter of "moderation and almost apology" mollified Downing who responded with an offer to help in any way he could, including research in his library at home on Staten Island. Jack sent specimen pages on which the colonel made useful suggestions. They remained friends for life.

As library orders arrived, he pasted up their letterheads to show how many were ordering the book and used the image for testimonials. Soon they had enough orders to start production. Earle Gray suggested a lithographed image on the front cover, which was difficult in 1948 when the binder's cloth required hand cleaning before it would accept an image in the press. One thousand copies were printed and bound, priced at $7.50, and offered to libraries at half price, postpaid. On July 20, 1948, Jack picked up his first copies of *American Horse-Drawn Vehicles* from the bindery and began fulfilling orders for his new book.[35] His second book exceeded expectations in sales and recognition, winning an award for its design in the Western Books competition sponsored by the Rounce & Coffin Club, and producing consistent sales.[36] When the book sold out in a couple of years, Jack sold the negatives and the copyright. The first reprint was issued by Bonanza Books in 1949; a second reprint was issued two years later by Floyd Clymer, the Los Angeles publisher of books on automobiles and other wheeled vehicles.

With *American Horse-Drawn Vehicles* published in 1948, Jack established himself as a new and discerning publisher who understood how to reach a niche market interested in his books. He had even begun collecting vintage type, but the one thing he did not have was his own printing press. It was time to fill the gap.

Chapter 5

Into a World of Books

The manners, the enthusiasm, and the intellectual sparkle of the members of the Zamorano Club went a long way to smooth away some of the rough spots on a Hoosier boy.

—JACK D. RITTENHOUSE[1]

JACK'S "WAGON BOOK" LAUNCHED his reputation as a designer, publisher, and emerging bookseller in Los Angeles book circles and beyond. It soon won a significant design award and generated orders from libraries, individual collectors, and booksellers. In addition, he found interest growing and readers asking how to find books listed in the bibliography at the end of *American Horse-Drawn Vehicles*. As inquiries continued, he began building lists of collectors and book dealers with specific interests, a critical component to any bookseller's success. Clearly, he had introduced an engaging topic largely unexplored by other writers and booksellers, a topic that sparked a demand for more information.

> When people wrote, I sold the research copies I had bought for use. Other people offered to sell books, and as I had many multiple orders, I bought these books and resold them. . . . Within two years I was buying books from Italy, from England, and from rare

> book dealers, and was selling them to collectors, using mimeographed catalogs or lists. I had no real competition in this special field; I knew which libraries had bought my book and therefore had special collections, and I was learning about the individuals around the country who were interested in this field. So I began an antiquarian book business.[2]

He started in September 1949, with his *Advance List No. 1* devoted to books, magazines, pamphlets, and old catalogs issued from 1837 to 1948. This first bookseller's list brought orders from 20th Century Fox, the University of Michigan, and a number of serious collectors, including Ivan L. Collins in Oregon who built miniatures of horse-drawn vehicles.[3] After filling the Collins order for eighteen items, Jack wrote him about sending out the list, saying he "was buying a large two-storey place in Sierra Madre and had to convert everything to cash."[4] The gross receipts on his first catalog came to $92.22, a little over $1,000 in today's values, applied to the purchase of Jack and Charlotte's new house.

His smooth transition from book publisher to book dealer impressed his friends in Los Angeles book circles. They began to recognize Jack as a serious fellow bookman. Muir Dawson recommended him for membership in the newly organized ABAA (Antiquarian Booksellers Association of America), an affiliation he treasured and maintained for the rest of his life. Since its founding the ABAA set standards for conducting business, describing books with detailed accuracy, and following ethical guidelines for antiquarian booksellers. Its standards continue to instill confidence in the book trade.[5] "At that time [the Southern California Chapter] admitted such part-time dealers as myself. . . . I attended meetings and came to know the bookmen from the professional side rather than as a customer. It was a wonderful education."[6]

Jack's recognition by the Rounce & Coffin Club for good design of *American Horse-Drawn Vehicles* further attested to his reputation for thoughtful typography and attractive printing. Ward Ritchie, whose work as a fine printer starting in the 1920s made him a major figure in a Golden Age of printing in Southern California, sponsored Jack for membership in the Zamorano Club in 1949. Founded in 1928 and still active today, it is the oldest organization of bibliophiles and manuscript collectors in the southern part of the state. In the 1940s and '50s membership was limited to around fifty, and admission was by invitation only. Though booksellers were not admitted to the Zamorano Club at that time, Jack, primarily known as an author, designer, and publisher of well-made books, was eligible.

As his reputation grew, he was hitting his stride in book and printing circles, attending the Wednesday luncheons at the University Club where the Zamorano met in its own room. "The big round table would hold about a dozen men, usually sufficient. There was no luncheon program; there was only good food and good conversation; anyone could bring a guest; prominent people in the book world were invited, such as Alfred A. Knopf, whom I had not seen in more than a dozen years. The membership itself was an amazing group."[7]

Among the men around the Zamorano lunch table, Henry Raup Wagner was probably the eldest and the most honored for his 170 publications about Spanish exploration of Mexico and the American Southwest. His scholarship was impeccable. Many of his publications are still consulted and referenced by those studying the West. Frederick Webb Hodge, director of the Southwest Museum in LA, had formerly held positions at the Smithsonian and the Bureau of Ethnology where he had edited the authoritative *Handbook of American Indians*. W. W. Robinson, founding president of the Friends of the UCLA Library, wrote extensively on Southern California history exhibiting his thorough knowledge of local history and land development. He was also founding president of the Friends of the UCLA Libraries. Edwin Carpenter, a bibliographer at the Huntington Library, shared with Jack a deep interest in hand printing presses still in use in California and the Western states. Another member, Lawrence Clark Powell, recently named head of the university library at UCLA, was beginning to lecture and write eloquently about Southwestern writers and their books. In his element sitting at the lunch table with these members, Jack shared their enjoyment of books and collecting. He recalled it was a "joy to participate in these Wednesday luncheons, which began promptly at twelve and ended by one-thirty." Anyone could speak on any subject, but no one was allowed to dominate the conversation. Having read widely throughout his college years and into adulthood, Jack's recall of authors and books was remarkable. His growing knowledge of typography and printing also served him well at Zamorano gatherings. Most at the table had good stories to tell, and they were seasoned raconteurs. One day a member spoke about Candelario's, a historic curio shop in Santa Fe, where he visited and noticed a trap door in the floor. The trap door prompted some musing about how it concealed treasures in the basement. Remembering these discussions some years later, Jack visited Santa Fe and stopped by Candelario's to make his own interesting book discovery there.

In addition to weekly lunches, the club held a monthly dinner, announced with a well-designed letterpress card in a matching envelope. After expenses were paid the balance, most years, was "enough to commission a fine press printer to print a book that was given free to each member; none were ever sold. Each was a gem. . . . The manners, the enthusiasm, and the intellectual sparkle of the members of the Zamorano Club went a long way to smooth away some of the rough spots on a Hoosier boy. More than anything else, the club sharpened my interest in books about the Southwest, while the papers at the monthly dinners broadened my knowledge of early printing."[8]

As Jack was introduced around the Zamorano Club, he soon learned that, traditionally, each new member produced a printed keepsake for colleagues in the organization. He had located a Gally's Universal press for sale and asked Ward Ritchie if it would be suitable for printing books, pamphlets, and broadsides. The master printer assured him of the Gally's ability to turn out fine letterpress work. A slower, platen press, it was often sidelined in shops that updated their equipment to more efficient cylinder presses. Nevertheless, it was perfectly suited for the printing Jack wanted to do.[9]

"In 1949 I bought a [Gally's Universal] printing press and wanted to take it apart for cleaning." Recalling the manuals he had produced for the Air Force, he decided to disassemble the press, clean all the parts, and reassemble it using the "exploded view" technique for all the moving parts, how they fit together, and how they worked. "I put the press in the middle of the garage floor, took off the first nut on the right side, and laid it against the right wall of the garage. Then I took off the washer and laid it between the nut and the press. When I was all finished, the parts lay on the floor to the right and left and front and back, in the order which they had been removed. To reassemble the press, all I had to do was start with the nearest piece and work my way to the outermost part."[10] When he finished he not only had a clean and smoothly running press, he knew precisely how each part needed to be adjusted to keep everything in top running condition.[11] It would take him two years to find the time and material to produce his Zamorano keepsake, but at last he had a reliable press suitable for printing books.

The last half of the 1940s was an engaging, productive, and very busy time for Jack in Los Angeles. At Darwin H. Clark Company, his publication projects for several major clients required him to write articles of general interest, often from a historical point of view, based on books and pamphlets that he was collecting as well as his extensive clipping files on topics of interest. Each week he stopped by bookshops where he found new material for his growing library. He also met collectors while visiting with book people active in the Rounce & Coffin Club as well as the Zamorano Club. Associating with fellow book collectors often proved the highlight of his hunt for books of interest. He remembered times when he was "always in the rare book shops around town. . . . I often went to Jake Zeitlin's 'Big Red Barn' out near Hollywood, and once while I was there I saw J. Frank Dobie for the first time. I also went often to the shop of Nick Kovach, who dealt in back-number technical journals for libraries."[12] The Clark Agency ran ads in these specialized technical journals, and the publishers sent them regularly to Jack's office. He traded back runs of these journals for early issues of *Scientific*

American printed between 1850 and 1880, a reliable source for writing his historical articles.

Before heading home he would often stop by the Pickwick Book Shop where Louis Epstein dealt in old and new books. Jack regarded Epstein as one of the great antiquarian "bookmen of that time and region." As they became friends Jack learned the story of how Epstein had bought the Spanish Colonial Churrigueresque building at 6743 Hollywood Boulevard and filled it with books. The Pickwick, in an earlier location, had rented five thousand books to a movie studio for dressing one of its film sets. When asked his charge for this unusual service, Epstein just pulled a number out of the air—five cents per book per day. He wrote the rental agreement, all the parties signed it, and he packed the books to be trucked away to a movie set on the studio's back lot. "Time passed, and the books were never returned. Epstein called a few times but was given the run-around. About a year later a truck pulled up in front of his shop and dropped off the 5,000 books that had been used as set props. The studio sent him a check for a 30-day rental. After some phone calls protesting that they owed him $250 per day for 365 days, the studio said, 'no way, we only needed them for 30 days. Sorry that we forgot to send them back on time, go pound sand.' Epstein phoned his lawyer instead." The attorney won his case, and the studio paid nearly $100,000. When Epstein called to collect the money, his lawyer refused to give it to him, saying, "If I give you this money, you'll just spend it foolishly buying more books and having a good time. So here's the deal: you go find a building to buy and I will release the money into escrow, that way at least you will own your own store."[13] Following his lawyer's advice, in 1938 Epstein bought the building on Hollywood Boulevard where Jack spent many happy hours visiting and shopping for books, as did F. Scott Fitzgerald, Raymond Chandler, William Faulkner, Humphrey Bogart, and Marlene Dietrich.

Jack also visited frequently with Harry Dale who ran a shop in a half-basement on Sixth Street, not far from the Clark Agency offices. As they became friends Jack dropped by after work to help Harry unpack, price, and arrange books. After Dale was uncharacteristically absent for a few days, the bookseller showed up looking haggard and unshaven. To Jack, he looked ill until Harry explained he had "struck a rich lode and had been mining it without letup." The lode was an enormous collection of sheet music weighing several tons, bought for next to nothing from another dealer who wanted to unload it. Harry was having second thoughts and "wondering what irrational impulse had caused him to buy this junk, when he saw that one piece of sheet music bore the legend, 'words by Mary Baker Eddy,' a Christian Science item. Another piece of music had the imprint of a midwestern town's printer, and Harry knew that it probably was one of the first imprints from that location. Why not sell them as collectors' pieces and imprints, rather than to musicians?"[14] Harry began assembling batches and quoting them to likely academic libraries. Orders started arriving, yet his mountains of sheet music were not diminishing very fast, so Harry offered Jack all he wanted for a penny per item. Already a savvy bookseller, Jack turned down the offer. His interests lay elsewhere. Nevertheless, he learned from his friend's experience. "It demonstrated one important lesson in creative selling: get away from the ordinary and try to see a new facet in a product; don't sell music as music; sell it for some other desirable aspect—by locale, by subject, by author, by printer."[15]

Jack's work also led him to unusual collectors beyond the realm of exclusive book clubs. By 1949 as Director of Publications, Darwin H. Clark Advertising Agency, he contracted with W. Everett Miller, a well-known designer and illustrator, to produce artwork for a publication Jack was designing. Miller had bought a copy of the wagon book, so he was already familiar with some of Jack's interests and work. Jack, too, would have known of Miller's reputation for custom coach work on automobiles only Hollywood stars could afford. He had designed gorgeous, unique cars for Rudolph Valentino, Tom Mix, Douglas Fairbanks, Mary Pickford, Mae West, and Clark Gable, among others. Over a fifty-year career he designed more than one thousand different vehicles, products, and advertisements for more than one hundred clients.

His longstanding interest in automobiles led him to form an enormous collection of photographs, drawings, and printed material on cars, a collection so large it had its own building.

The pace of Miller's collecting increased when he was working on a car design for Tom Mix. He told Jack that he "found he had no reference works on stagecoaches and had to make a long search. He resolved then to remedy this, so everywhere he went he picked up anything on any phase of transportation, especially land vehicles, as long as it was something he did not already have and cost no more than fifty cents." By the time Jack and Everett met, the collection filled many rows of filing cabinets housing information on more than three thousand different makes of American autos. Soon Everett became an internationally known independent research consultant on transportation. At the time of his death in 1983, his 'Library of Vehicles' "weighed in at 15 tons, and included 3,500 books, 25,000 catalogs, 7,000 periodicals, and 250,000 clippings covering any and all types of transport, albeit motorized or not."[16] Everett Miller was Jack's ideal of a dedicated collector. He admired Miller for his concentrated, long-term, affordable, in-depth collecting on a tightly focused subject others had overlooked.[17]

The year 1949 was filled with good developments for Jack. He joined the Southern California Industrial Editors Association (SCIEA), an organization of about forty men and women who edited house magazines for local companies. Before long he was elected president of the chapter. His professional colleagues in SCIEA were "lively people" who worked for notable companies around Los Angeles. One of his new friends edited the in-house magazine for 20th Century Fox Studios where he toured Jack and Charlotte through the back lot and behind the sound stages. Another colleague managed the account for Western Air Lines headquartered at Los Angeles International Airport. Jack arranged with him to hold an Editors Association meeting aboard a new Western Air Lines plane "as it circled over Los Angeles for an hour late one day, to observe the smog conditions and hear a speaker on the subject. I gaveled the meeting to order in the sky."[18]

The SCIEA, part of a national organization, recognized one of Jack's business publications with a rating of 98 percent for overall quality. On the local level, he also won awards each year recognizing his innovative solutions to the design and production of printed material at the Darwin Clark Company. Readers of the *Baroid News Bulletin*, designed and produced by Jack, appreciated his articles. His general interest pieces balanced the more technical pieces written by specialists. As a division of the National Lead Company, Baroid's key products were "materials used in the mud-like fluid that is pumped down the hollow drill stem while drilling an oil well." The material, pumped down and flowing back up around the outside of the stem, carried rock chips loosened by the drill bit at the bottom. "This business was neither simple nor cheap. The descending drill encountered many types of formation: solid or porous, or into gas pockets that threatened to blow the well, or into formation of minerals that acted adversely with the materials in the drilling mud. On a very deep well, the cost of mud materials could run to $200,000 or more. Baroid had a wide range of products to meet these conditions and had field engineers to prescribe the proper mixtures. It was necessary to inform the oil well drillers about these products and their proper use."[19]

During the first year of Clark's advertising consultancy with Baroid, the company kept its bulletin production in house. Soon Clark asked Jack to analyze the bulletin and offer suggestions for improvements. He recommended Baroid retain the original format and technical articles but expand the general interest pieces as an inducement for readers to engage and save articles with a travel or historical interest. The company, grounded in sound engineering and management, was also home to stories reflecting "oil patch" folklore and traditions, a rich source that Jack recommended tapping for their publication. Baroid liked his proposal, including ideas for articles that appealed to him—incidents in the history of the American West, steam cars, black light, first oil leases, ghost towns, cable cars, circus life, the history of drilling mud, and much more. Over the next two decades he wrote more than 190 stories and articles for Baroid.

After the first year Baroid moved all of its advertising work to the Clark Company, including the editorial, design, and production for its *Bulletin*, which Jack managed. At Clark, everyone regarded him as the best qualified person to spec type, select paper, and lay out any printing job of more than four pages. He also had the discretion and authority to take agency production work to "such fine printers in Southern California as Grant Dahlstrom's Castle Press and also Ward Ritchie."[20]

Applying what he learned from the Ellis plan, Jack continued designing parts of projects so they could be reused for other applications, thereby saving money. For example, the Baroid Division had wanted a technical handbook for several years "but never seemed to be able to get their work organized to produce a book of two or three hundred pages." Jack realized the 6-inch × 9-inch format for the *Bulletin* was also suitable for a handbook. He decided to include in each monthly issue a section of the handbook Baroid wanted. Once each issue was initially printed, his team set aside the production designs and negatives. In four years, he had all the copy for a multichapter technical handbook. Using his saved negatives, he produced their handbook at a fraction of the cost had they started from scratch. He used the same approach later when Baroid wanted a separate twenty-three-page booklet, *The History of Drilling Mud*.

Following his enjoyment of tall tales and facetious hijinks, he created a "facsimile reprint of an 1865 burlesque prospectus on an outlandish, hypothetical oil company" from an original broadside stock certificate (fictional) in his personal collection.[21] Titled, "Oil Humor in 1865," the facsimile appeared in the June 1950 issue of the *Baroid News Bulletin*. He prepared a keepsake, printing the title page and covers at home, and inserting extra copies of the press run along with his imprint for the Stagecoach Press, Sierra Madre, California. The keepsake carried a titlepage reading, *Prospectus of the Munchausen, Philosopher's Stone & Gull Creek Oil Company, 1865*. The colophon reads: "Sixty copies were printed by Jack D. Rittenhouse for his friends among the bookmen of Southern California." With his fourth Stagecoach Press book, he was experiencing the most intellectually stimulating and enjoyable period of his life to date.

Darwin Clark, considering Jack a key member of his senior team, offered him round-trip air fare to the association's conference in Canada. For Jack, driving was more appealing than flying, so he applied the air fare money for gasoline, using vacation time for part of the trip. "This way, Charlotte and Douglas could go along; they stayed in Saint Louis with her parents. I picked up David in Indiana and took him to Toronto. By this time we owned a 1940 Plymouth sedan and no longer had the Bantam."[22]

At the end of May, Jack was back home and writing a new friend, Paul Klosterman, president, treasurer, and manager of the Huntingburg Wagon Works in Huntingburg, Indiana. Even though his wagon book had already been published, Jack remained deeply interested in documentation on early wagon manufacturing and eagerly visited manufacturing shops that were still open.

> I finally returned from my trip two nights ago, having driven over 6,000 miles. I saw plenty of sights from Niagara Falls to the Grand Canyon, but to me the most interesting of all was the visit I had to your plant. The pair of wheels and hubs excited much curiosity along the way, and I saw many Huntingburg wagons when I was on a side trip up in the Navajo reservation. To top it all, your parcel of old catalogs was awaiting me upon return. This material was exactly what I had been seeking, and should be very useful to me in answering queries from universities, museums, collectors, etc., and possibly in a future companion book on other vehicles.[23]

Jack closed his cordial letter with a note about the preserved fruits he was sending from California as a thank-you gift. He also suggested the idea for a book about the wagon-making industry based on the Huntingburg Wagon Works. He stated his hope for an extended visit when he could bring his press camera and plenty of lights for a spread that he thought LIFE magazine might like to publish.

Jack then wrote Miss Tillie M. Foertsch, the secretary at the Huntingburg Wagon Works who had put together the "splendid parcel of old catalogs, folders and photos."[24] She had written him to express interest in his "carriage book," saying, "Practically all my life has been spent in the horse drawn vehicle work. I began at the age of 15 at the Carriage Department and later on, after a short period at business school, started working in the office. I have almost reached the half way mark in years so you can see that most of my life has been spent among buggies and wagons and I do appreciate your work on the book."

Miss Foertsch also sent Jack a copy of an intriguing pencil drawing of a hearse sketched by Porter Coats Jr., in Rowletts, Kentucky. She noted that Mr. Coats was hoping to have a Huntingburg Wagon Works' hearse for his "last ride" and had been sending the company a drawing every year for fifteen years, even though they knew he had "no means to buy much of anything." Over the years, his naïve drawings of wagons included drivers "most often pictured with high hats and the horses are always lively and stepping high. . . . I have always wished that I could meet the old man. Thought you might enjoy the story and a copy of his drawing."[25]

Jack responded with a cordial letter conveying one of the last remaining copies of his book. He mentioned how the book prompted "numerous requests for information on various types of vehicles, harnesses, etc., from museums, universities, libraries and collectors. Many requests are for information on subjects unknown to me—for instance, the University of Chicago wanted to know the origin of an Oregon Trail freight wagon known as the 'esponshay.' I tracked this down to the original maker, Louis Espenschied, whose name was mis-spelled to give the wagon its title. Confirmation came from a small old folder I had, so you can see that even an insignificant piece of advertising material can have some historical and scholarly value."[26]

On October 10, 1949, Jack and Charlotte started "escrow proceedings to buy the house at 223 W. San Gabriel Ct., for $10,500."[27] Twelve days later they completed the transaction and moved into a two-story "staunch old house . . . built of redwood," which became their "treasured" home in Sierra Madre with room in the basement to set up his newly acquired Gally's Universal press (1872) and cases of type. The house sat on a wooded lot with tall palm, macadamia, and avocado trees not far from the foot of the mountain and the Huntington Library where Jack secured a scholar's card allowing him research privileges.

About twelve blocks square, Sierra Madre attracted creative people. A near neighbor made specialized human dummies in his basement for use at Mojave Desert sites testing rocket-propelled planes set on rails. Jack and Charlotte's best friends included Bob and Margaret Nash. Bob, a high-tech engineer, worked for a defense research lab. He and his wife lived with his mother who ran an antique business in their home. Bob's hobbies matched Jack's: letterpress printing, book collecting, and building ship models. Another friend, an older man named Ransom Matthews, was curator of mechanical collections at LA County Museum. He would occasionally bring over "old-time gadgets such as a table fan powered by a caloric or hot-air [motor]. Set it on a table, give the blades a spin, and it ran without any electric or other power."[28] Devices like this intrigued Jack and no doubt delighted his two-year old son, Douglas.

The drawbacks to living in Sierra Madre were the encroaching smog and the twenty-two-mile commute to and from Jack's office downtown. By 1950, LA's population had grown to 1,957,692.[29] It had 1,712,545 automobiles, 152,001 trucks, and 119,885 motorcycles registered in the county.[30] Jack occasionally rode the Red Cars of the Pacific Electric Railway Company, a privately owned, countywide, light rail system that included a line from Sierra Madre to the center of LA. Most often he drove to work, twenty-eight minutes in the morning and forty-five minutes home along the recently built parkway through Arroyo Seco Canyon and into downtown. When completed in 1940 the Parkway was designated an alignment of Route 66, the first stretch of the Mother Road running over a modern, limited-access highway, a development not lost on Jack. The drive to Sierra Madre in late afternoon traffic required constant vigilance at the wheel. "I usually had to sit quietly for a while after reaching home. It was not pleasant."[31] In 1950 the smog rose slowly above their home during the day and disappeared at night, so at least the morning views over the San Gabriel Valley were clear and crisp.

Jack and Charlotte felt very much at home living in Sierra Madre. It had the feel of a small town, innovative in its approach to solving community problems. Residents and their elected leadership held open town meetings in the tradition of New England villages. He recalled how the township addressed the growing need for a nursery school for prekindergarten children through public meetings, the formation of citizen committees, rummage and bake sales, architects drawing plans pro bono, and the city donating cleared land on which the local National Guard unit had held demolition exercises. Local contractors oversaw the construction with local men and women providing the labor. Everyone involved in the project earned credit for their child's attendance at the new school. Charlotte spent significant time on the project, and when the new Sierra Madre Nursery School opened, young Douglas Rittenhouse was one of the first students to enroll.

In late winter 1950 Jack's twelve-year old son, David, who had been living with his mother in Chicago, came to live with his father and stepmother to finish the school year in Sierra Madre. That summer Jack and Charlotte took David and Douglas on a "good vacation" even if it was on a "skimpy budget." He recalled later, "We bought a surplus Army tent, wall type, about 8 × 10 feet, and a couple of cots. We borrowed a small Coleman stove and hand axe. We still had the pup tent, and somewhere we got a couple of surplus folding cots. We were gone a week or more." After visiting Charlotte's Uncle Bert, they drove "up through the Mother Lode country and made camp at . . . Calaveras Big Trees grove. Each day we headed out in some direction to see other places. We had to make this entire trip on only fifty dollars. . . . We had a good time."[32]

With autumn approaching, "David was given the choice of staying on in Sierra Madre or going back with his mother. He chose to return east. It was probably the best choice all around, but after he was gone I went upstairs to his empty room and cried. Except at funerals, it was the first time I can recall that I ever cried as an adult."[33]

After David's departure at the end of the summer, Jack was fortunate to have his ad agency work and printing press to occupy his mind. As soon as he had restored his Galley's Universal printing press in the basement of their home in Sierra Madre, he began working on several projects, including his only type specimen book, *A Showing of Type Faces Antique and Modern Offered at The Stagecoach Press*. In twelve pages he set and printed examples of the type he had already collected, along with cuts and printing ornaments (sometimes referred to as *dingbats*). Printers operating their own private presses have always enjoyed producing specimen books such as the one Jack created to document their options for type selection based on how the type face and font size appears on the printed page. Jack was proud of the type he had acquired for his third Stagecoach Press publication of which he printed forty copies. He gave them to fellow printers, including William Cheney, who shared an interest in the history of typography, especially eighteenth- and nineteenth-century type once used throughout America. Cheney had already given Jack one of his specimen books, and instead of inscribing his gift to Cheney, Jack set his inscription in type and printed a unique and amusing small broadside for his friend. Although he continued to collect type over the next decade, he did not set and print another specimen book. (See figure 13 for inscription.)

At last, Jack had the time and equipment to finish his Zamorano Club keepsake that he had wanted to print for several years. His next challenge was finding just the right topic, something relating to the history of books and printing but also a facet of the subject that might be new to his colleagues in the club. He found the solution in another assignment at the Clark Company. In the winter of 1951, Jack wrote about dime novels set in the oil patch for the Baroid magazine. His contribution, "Rare Thrillers on Early Oil," was scheduled to appear in the March issue, and his design and production plans called for an accordion-fold pull-out reproducing seven of the covers prominent in this genre of popular reading. Most book collectors had not begun to pay attention to dime novels until the 1950 publication of *The House of Beadle and Adams and Its Dime and Nickel Novels: The Story of a Vanished Literature*, but Jack knew their story began in the 1860s and ran through the 1930s. Drawing once more upon a lesson learned from Lynn Ellis's approach to advertising, "to foresee all possible uses and applications of an idea and design it from the start to fit those uses,"[34] he printed an extra hundred copies of the accordion-fold pull-out and set them aside for his Zamorano keepsake.

For the new keepsake, his seventh Stagecoach Press publication, "a small bibliography on dime novels that related to the early days of the petroleum industry in America," Jack and Charlotte handset the type in Bembo. They printed the booklet on 9 × 12 inch sheets of a good paper often selected for special announcements. "When folded once and hand-sewn, they made a neat booklet."[35] The center section held the new accordion fold.

In the spring of 1951, Jack's Zamorano keepsake, *Dime Novels on Early Oil*, carried the imprint of his new venture, The Stagecoach Press, which he would operate for the next sixteen years. The booklet, 6 × 9 inches in paper wrappers with nine pages and the accordion fold of seven dime novel covers, was limited to one hundred copies. The first two lines of the titlepage were set in one of the nineteenth-century typefaces Jack had acquired in 1948, Mikita Shaded, designed by Julius Herriet and patented in 1867.[36] With vintage ornamental borders on the titlepage, Jack's keepsake demonstrated his good taste and restraint as an accomplished typographer and printer.

The friendly township of Sierra Madre was a good place for Jack to launch his Stagecoach Press and network with other printers. He submitted a brief notice for the local newspaper, the *Sierra Madre News*, announcing "Rittenhouse Has Press." It read, "Another name has been added to the growing list of 'private presses' in the West."

The notice identified him as the supervisor of printing design and production for the Clark Agency, who planned no commercial work on his Universal press at home but would concentrate on "experimental printing." By this time writing press releases was second nature for Jack who always scored column inches with newspaper editors recognizing a professional at work.

As soon as he learned that other private printers had worked earlier in Sierra Madre, a new collecting focus opened for him—books, pamphlets, and broadsides printed in the township prior to 1930. He began acquiring Sierra Madre imprints with plans to compile a bibliography.[37] From his own experience with the nascent Stagecoach Press, Jack knew that many small private press shops were beneath the radar in the large press industry. He believed they deserved more attention and pitched his concept to Roby Wentz, editor of the *Western Printer & Lithographer, The News Magazine of Western Graphic Arts*. Wentz liked Jack's idea, and they agreed on a series of articles for a new column, "The Private Press in the West," as well as a directory. In preparation for the series, Jack sent out questionnaires to as many private presses as he could identify in eleven western states. His estimate of more than a hundred such presses was probably accurate, but he never finished the directory.

Jack's six articles in *Western Printer & Lithographer* helped document and draw attention to developments within a sector of the small private press movement where proprietors were printing to please themselves rather than to earn a living. Over the course of six installments of "The Private Press in the West," Jack identified and discussed forty-four different private presses and their owners, their press marks, and twelve different makes of presses in use by private printers, from a table-top Kelsey to an Albion, a Chander & Price, a Reliance, and a huge Washington owned by William Everson. He discussed more than a dozen type faces and told how printers could acquire nineteenth-century type no longer available in any foundry.

In the spring of 1951, Jack presented his keepsake to members of the Zamorano Club at a dinner talk titled, "The Poor Man's Practical

Collector or Scholarly Misadventures Among the Highwaymen of Sixth Street." Having fun with his subject, his title referenced the locale where he regularly visited the shops of many of his Los Angeles book-dealer friends. He offered another approach to book collecting—to do so for the main purpose of using books, pamphlets, and ephemera in one's daily work and not being concerned about condition or the usual bibliographer's "points" noted in rare book catalogs.

> My library at home . . . confuses anyone seeing it for the first time. They have the feeling that they are in some peculiar sort of junk-shop. There are a thousand or so books, but much more space is devoted to dog-eared and spineless books, tattered pamphlets, peculiar catalogs, and similar ephemera. In this field there is an entirely different range of values and prices not found in Dawson's catalogs, for example. There is, for instance, a somewhat tattered catalog of horse-drawn fire engines, the rare old pumpers and hose carts. I got this catalog for a buck and a half from an upstate book scout, and now find it is worth $25.00 or more.[38]

In his talk Jack told how his work in advertising led him to explore and write about different topics of interest that shaped his unique approach to collecting. He spoke of his work being journalistic in nature, popular writing rather than scholarly, and how he found inexpensive items in print by always stopping in bookshops whenever passing one to ask about his topics of interest.

For examples Jack referenced how he used dime novels to write about a publication genre of interest to his clients in the oil industry. He spoke of vintage business catalogs becoming a "big new field of collecting" and how illustrations therein provided visual material that he could use in his work, thereby keeping down the cost for original art from other sources. He included the example of an article on Alaska he researched and wrote "from scratch" under a two-hour deadline, "with photos free" because he had collected a wide variety of printed material on the subject.

Jack closed his talk with tips on methods for his approach to collecting informed by his many hours conducting research in libraries. "Look for bibliographic leads in ads carried in back of books you buy, or in old trade magazines," or books that are mentioned by authors of books you own. "Know how to ask dealers if they have anything. If you are interested in square dancing the dealer may say he has nothing. He may not know his stock. See if he has anything on dancing, on amusements, on entertainment, etc." He suggested telling dealers about topics of interest and what one is willing to pay. He mentioned browsing Good Will stores, especially in smaller communities, and told about his discovery of records of historical significance in barrels of old papers that he found in an abandoned mining camp building in Bagdad Chase (Mojave Desert). "The farther you go, the more fun it is, and if you want to cash in the chips, you'll find a collection is worth more than the sum total of its pieces. . . . Certain it is that you will find yourself on a by-road of book collecting that is not beaten hard and stripped bare by previous travellers!"[39]

Early in 1951 the Clark Agency's second-largest client, the Baroid Division of the National Lead Company, faced major shifts in the oil industry when exploration and production in Texas moved ahead of California, developments that would lead to a major move for Jack. In addition to growing levels of production, the infrastructure in Texas was well established with huge multinational refineries near the Gulf Coast. The Port of Houston had become a key player as large quantities of gas and oil moved through Baytown, Texas City, and Houston. Baroid wanted to move its headquarters closer to the action without losing Jack's sure hand on the design and production of their award-winning magazine, the *Baroid News Bulletin*. As Baroid's discussions with the Clark Company evolved over the next few months, Clark saw the advantage of opening a branch in Houston with Baroid as a major client. Houston would offer promising opportunities to add other accounts in a thriving city where oil was king.

"Clark's problem was then one of choosing the head of the new office. . . . Eventually [he] asked me to head the Houston office. It was a problem for me, because I knew that if I turned him down, I would lose any future preference in promotions, perhaps start on that decline in fortunes that often happens to agency men."[40] The decision was difficult for Jack and Charlotte, happy in Sierra Madre and highly regarded in the Southern California book circles, enjoying their home in a close-knit, smaller community with new friends nearby. Even with his Huntington research privileges in one of the great rare book libraries in the United States and his strong ties to the book world of Southern California, he chose financial security for his family in a new city and in a new state.

In typical fashion, Jack always looked forward, wanting to learn more about the place where he was moving. He began forming a book and pamphlet collection on Texas. "I realized that I really knew little about Texas, so I set out to build a Texas collection á la Everett Miller. I ran around the Los Angeles area picking up anything I could find that did not cost more than a dollar; many pieces cost only ten to fifty cents. They were not rare books of course, but such things as local history pamphlets, rodeo programs, reports on oil wells, etc., as well as some novels, textbooks, and a few good clothbound books. Later in Texas, I was surprised to find that I had picked up some fairly good books; the collection as a whole was immediately worth five times what I had paid for it, chiefly because I had put together a <u>collection</u>. There were perhaps three hundred items, and altogether they had cost me no more than two hundred dollars. Of course, a book collector never counts the hours he spends in the hunt, any more than a fisherman measures his hours against the retail value of his catch."[41]

Moving books to Houston presented the next challenge. Jack pared down a little of his library by giving Ed Carpenter his collection of Sierra Madre imprints for the Huntington Library. In Texas there would be no opportunity to add to this collection. By the end of summer 1951, he had packed up his collection on petroleum and other topics of interest, along with his newly acquired Texas books. The moving firm quoted him a rate close to ten cents a pound; he checked with the US Post Office to discover their book rate was half that amount. At a corrugated box company in LA, he bought a hundred one-cubic-foot boxes, easy to handle and unpack. He marked each box with alphabetized subject headings so they could be quickly arranged before unpacking in Houston.

Jack and Charlotte packed their household goods for the move and listed their home in Sierra Madre for rent. Before the house at 223 San Gabriel Court, they had never owned a property as substantial or enjoyable. They would miss its location, spaciousness, neighbors, and community spirit. The Clark Company agreed to cover the cost of moving the household, growing library, and Jack's two presses and type. Jack was going to miss Los Angeles, the book collectors with whom he had bonded, the printers from whom he learned so much, the fine libraries with staffs who enjoyed helping experienced researchers, the writing projects on a large variety of subjects, and the bookshops, their rooms filled with books and friends. If he had to leave the stimulation of this community, he knew what he wanted to do next. He faced the move with an open mind and did not dwell on the community he was leaving. In Houston he would find space for his presses and type, perhaps add some more equipment to his printing shop, and print more Stagecoach Press books.

Chapter 6

The Houston Years

Some of the greatest benefits I found in Houston were the libraries.

—JACK D. RITTENHOUSE[1]

AS MOVING DAY DREW closer, Jack's book and printing friends around Los Angeles suggested he meet Carl Hertzog on his drive to Houston. El Paso would be one of several good points to break up the trip, and the legendary typographer and printer living there would give him a warm welcome. Hertzog could also introduce him to some notable writers and collectors. "The Printer at the Pass" responded to Jack's inquiry in good form. "If you stop by here on your way to Texas perhaps we can get you lined up for some book talk but all they do in Houston is count their money. If I can possibly get away you will not find me here because I want to do some cowboying before school starts. However, I have so much work to do you will probably find me at Texas Western College or you can call 5–1301 and my wife will think she knows where I am. . . . You probably didn't know that I am professor of advertising and job printer to the college. I can't eat off the books. Sincerely, Carl Hertzog."[2]

When Jack reached El Paso, he learned that Hertzog managed to catch a little vacation and was away. Although their initial meeting was postponed, their subsequent correspondence over many years reveals a warm friendship laced with discussions of books, presses, typefaces, and the general chat that draws printers together. Hertzog's accomplishments and welcoming cordiality reflected the vitality of the Texas book scene.

In one of his diaries, Jack documented the drive to Houston over ten days with stops in more than seven locations along the way.[3] Not exactly a direct route, it included many of the places in the American West he had not yet seen. He and his family reached Houston in early September where the heat was oppressive. "We lived first in a very unpleasant apartment, very hot, and where we became actually sick from the heat." Soon they found a duplex on Lanark Lane not far from Belaire, "a more attractive and bearable place."[4] Jack set up the Clark Agency office in a remodeled residence nearby. With no room at home for his petroleum collection, he shelved it prominently along an office wall. "Texans who saw it got the opinion that here was a man who was honoring their state by building such a collection, and who must already know much of its history. I did not disillusion them, but went on adding to the collection."[5]

Since Jack's new office would handle all of Baroid's publication advertising, he transferred printing for the Baroid News to a well-established Houston press shop. Still, operating Clark's first long-distance branch office created unanticipated complications. When Baroid's advertising manager chose not to relocate from Los Angeles, Clark helped Baroid find a new ad manager friendly to the agency, Donald T. Fowler, whom Jack knew from his years in the LA advertising community.

Quickly Jack identified other challenges. "Branch office operation did not work well because everything had to move back and forth" between Houston and LA. "We had no staff artist in Houston to do layouts, and the volume of Baroid business would not support a full Houston staff."[6] Jack tried to attract new accounts by networking with local agencies, but the Clark Company was regarded as a "foreigner" against whom others closed ranks. "So, in the late spring of 1952, Clark came over and said he was closing the Houston branch."

He offered Jack two options: return to the office with all moving expenses covered by the company or resign and set up his own company starting with the Baroid account as his sole client, no strings attached. For a professional man nearing forty in the ad business, neither option was attractive. Jack knew that if he returned to Clark's home office the failure of the Houston branch would follow him back to Los Angeles, but he also knew that a salaried employee without some type of agency partnership position was risky for any head of a household needing to provide security for his family.

He decided to go it alone and opened Jack D. Rittenhouse Industrial Publications Counsel on the first of July 1952, in a one-room office on West Gray. He arranged for another Houston agency to take on Baroid's advertising in trade publications while he kept the *Baroid News Bulletin* as his only account. Jack's fees and commissions assured him a steady monthly income of $5,700 in today's dollars. Hiring a student from the University of Houston as part-time help allowed him time to make outside calls and pick up jobs with local businesses needing manuals, catalogs, and handbooks. Before long Houston companies regarded the Rittenhouse agency as an accepted local business, not a branch of a "foreign" California company. Furthering his Houston identity, Jack joined the board of directors for the Houston Ad Club and became vice president of the Gulf Coast Industrial Editors Association.[7]

A former associate from his Ellis Plan work offered him an opportunity to boost his income with a month-long consulting job in Fort Worth developing billboard and radio campaigns for Foremost Dairies, milk purveyors to grocery stores throughout Texas. With this additional income he returned to Houston and secured other contracts for new business. "By now the situation was moving upward. . . . The office was becoming crowded, so I rented a four-room suite of small rooms in a converted apartment house at 1917 Westheimer Avenue. A couple of years later we also took over the adjoining suite. I added an artist, a bookkeeper, and a copywriter. Eventually we had ten or eleven people on the payroll." As his staff grew and Jack's managerial responsibilities increased, he decided to go after the entire Baroid account, including all its publication advertising. "They liked our work, and we got the whole account. We also added others, but Baroid was at least half of our total billing. Nearly all of our clients were in the oil field industry in some way."[8] Once again Jack's advertising work began winning awards. For three years in a row his campaign for Baroid placed him among Fifty Leaders in the country with the Direct Mail Advertising Association. His was the first Texas agency to win this honor, and it set Rittenhouse "among such giants as General Motors, Abbott Laboratories, and others." Readership studies measuring ad effectiveness ranked Rittenhouse publication ads near the top of the scale, with one ad in the *Oil and Gas Journal* recognized for being "most read" in that particular issue.

By the mid-1950s Jack and others who were experienced in analyzing the petroleum business market began to see "clouds on the future of oil field advertising. The great oil fields of Saudi Arabia and nearby countries were being developed and were pouring a . . . flood of cheap oil into American markets. It was said that a barrel of crude oil from Saudi Arabia could be unloaded at a Houston refinery for less than a barrel of American oil could be produced and piped from an oil field three hundred miles away. The result was a decline in the number of domestic oil wells being drilled."[9] As Houston began to experience the effects of the domestic drilling slowdown, so did its ad agencies. Yet Rittenhouse and Company was in a comfortable position for an agency of its size with annual fees and commissions totaling a half-million dollars. When Jack realized he could be facing a year or two without increased income, he doubled down on securing new work. His 1957 billing rose 49 percent over the previous year, and he predicted a 20 percent increase for the following year even as the petroleum industry was heading for a shakeout.

Since moving to Houston Jack had been approached once or twice each year regarding his interest in a merger. "In the beginning we resisted the idea. Then, as we observed the growing tendency to mergers among agencies, we realized that we should not overlook the possible benefits."[10] As he faced the uncertainties for projected growth in the summer of 1957, he received a letter of inquiry from Marsteller, Rickard, Gebhardt and Reed, a national agency with offices in Chicago, Pittsburgh, and New York. Marsteller, seeing market potential in all sectors of the Texas economy, was exploring the feasibility of opening an office in Houston. He wrote asking if Jack would consider the idea of some type of merger. Since the late 1930s when he had opened Mercury Advertising, his own one-man agency in Chicago, Jack had become acquainted with several other ad men now in the Marsteller firm. In the interim Marsteller had grown significantly through major accounts with Rockwell, the Ad Council (Keep America Beautiful campaign), Renault, and the Dannon Milk Company.

By the time Bill Marsteller reached out to Jack, his firm ranked among the largest industrial advertising agencies in the nation with annual billings of more than ten million dollars. Meanwhile, Jack had earned a reputation as an experienced agency executive with a thorough knowledge of production techniques for printed material and an ability to write engaging articles and deliver compelling lectures. Moreover, he had a good head for numbers. Knowing Jack's strengths, Marsteller invited him to Chicago to meet with key people in the head office. Following those meetings, Bill Marsteller's offer to Jack was especially attractive: a vice presidency, leadership of a new branch office in Houston, and a salary of $16,500, (equivalent to $177,400 in today's dollars), along with numerous other perks. Even with cheap Saudi oil at the Port of Houston changing the game, a corporate entity the size of Marsteller could withstand some economic tightening in one sector of the national economy and quite possibly attract new advertising accounts in and around Texas and the Gulf Coast.

The partnership with Marsteller, Rickard, Gebhardt and Reed placed Jack in the major league of American advertising. He and Marsteller set up offices near the Shamrock Hotel, a distinguished address in Houston.

In the shadow of the Shamrock, Marsteller's Houston branch

began to grow, and Jack's responsibilities expanded to include not only managerial work but also attracting new accounts in Houston, Dallas, and Tulsa. Now, riding the train to meetings, he remembered his early days riding the rails with hobos. "I often enjoyed an evening meal on one of the old Pennsylvania dining cars, with its efficient waiters, heavy silver table service, white napery, and [would] sit there eating a piece of deep-dish apple pie and drinking a cup of that full-bodied rich coffee, later lingering with a good cigar as the farms went past in the late evening glow. I had to admit that there was more than one kind of freedom. And as I sat there I knew that probably on the same train, or certainly on the freights that we passed, there were still hobos. I had no desire to trade places."[11]

He traveled extensively to professional conferences in San Francisco, Chicago, Cleveland, Pittsburgh, and New York where he often lectured. At times he framed a talk around something he learned as an accomplished printer. In his lecture, "Typography as an Art Form," Jack gave examples of how good typography and design helped readers engage with purposeful content. As his connections expanded beyond the ad business to include academics, executives, lawyers, and newspapermen, he began meeting individuals who also shared his interest in books, history, and collecting. Frequenting bookshops in Houston in his spare time, he also searched out booksellers wherever he traveled in Texas, from San Antonio to Austin and Dallas to El Paso. For his Baroid account he continued to amass clippings and cut sheets from magazines on interesting topics. For his library he acquired books on petroleum, Texas history, and a new category, New Mexico history. With his petroleum library prominently displayed in his new Houston office, word began to spread around town that Jack held the best petroleum book collection along the Gulf Coast. His library provided a certain cachet in the city where oil was king.

By the mid-1950s Jack's early experience working around newspapers led to his new friendship with one of Houston's eminent columnists at the *Houston Post*, George Fuermann, whose career spanned forty-nine years. Not long after they met, Jack told Fuermann about his research on early printing in Texas and his attempts to acquire vintage nineteenth-century type whenever he could visit small-town newspaper shops.[12] Fuermann, who knew a good story when he heard it, invited Jack to contribute a short piece about early Texas printing under a guest byline. He introduced Jack as "a friendly and inquisitive man, not to mention a staggering chain-smoker, who four years ago took to Texas as a duck takes to water. . . . Most of the following guest column was set by hand in Rittenhouse's private print shop, which is to say his garage, from his growing collection of old type faces.—G.F." Jack's text gave an abbreviated account of the first newspaper set (but not printed) in Texas (Gaceta de Texas, 1813), the first broadside printed in Galveston by Samuel Bangs in 1817, and the first newspaper and the first book printed by G. B. Cotton at San Felipe de Austin in 1829.[13]

The following year Fuermann invited Jack to contribute another short piece as guest columnist on the names of early Texas newspapers. In an introductory note Fuermann introduced Jack as "head of an advertising firm specializing in the oil trade. He smokes more cigarettes than any man I have ever known, he prefers to stand always, no matter the odds of how many are seated, and he is the only low-pressure adman I have known. He erupts in ideas—not fancy ones, but ideas that can be managed—and he is the only private printer in Texas. A private printer is a printer by hobby, and the type faces in this column are from his collection."[14]

Then Jack led off: "Nowhere is Texas' individuality shown more than in the astonishing names of its newspapers, whose editors at one time or another flaunted mast heads with the boisterous banners shown below. These are or were actual papers, and their names are recreated here in fancy, old-fashioned type." The list began with the *Grand Saline Salt Shaker*, the *Houston Musquito*, the *Vega Weekly Fizz*, the *Linden Longhandle Shovel*, and the *Galveston Rip-Saw*. For the "most aptly named small paper" he selected the *Kyle NUT-SHELL*, while the shortest was the *Waco DAY*. "Other pungent papers were bannered *Croaker*, *Sand Burr*, *Coyote*, *Kicker*, *Quirt*, *Crony*, *Gimlet*, *Rebel*, *Gusher*, and *Scorpion*."[15] Clearly, the two journalists were having a good time with the colorful history of Texas newspapers.

On the last day of 1955, Jack's first daughter, Anne, was born, an event he wanted to mark with a hand-printed birth announcement. Fuermann joined him that evening at the press, setting type and enjoying some champagne. As the two newspapermen celebrated Anne's arrival and the dawning of a new year, Jack had another opportunity to show his friend some newly acquired equipment at the Stagecoach Press now occupying its own room at his home on Fredonia Street. Featured in several newspaper articles over the next few years, his 1875 Washington Press, weighing 2,200 pounds. and standing more than six feet tall, must have impressed many readers.

Throughout the 1950s Jack found time to meet and visit booksellers around Houston. One of his first visits was with Joe Petty at his Book Mart in the 1100 block of Capitol Avenue near the main post office. Petty had bought the shop in the 1930s, established in 1916 by W. H. H. Miller, and turned it into "a rendezvous for book-lovers—both readers and writers—for so many years." When Jack first stopped by the Book Mart, he found a bookshop where he felt very much at home, "a hangout for the intelligentsia" and a "virtual landmark" where one could drop in and "meet stimulating people."[16] With shared interests and rapport, Petty invited Jack to join the Civil War Round Table, a respected group of historians and collectors in Houston. The group met regularly for formal talks by its members about aspects of the War between the States. When Petty moved his shop to Victoria, Texas, Jack stayed in touch and always visited Petty in subsequent years when scouting small towns in south Texas for books and vintage type.[17]

The senior antiquarian bookman in Houston, Herbert Fletcher also published books under the imprint of the Anson Jones Press. A University of Pennsylvania graduate, he had worked for Wanamaker's Department Store in Philadelphia as head of the rare books department. Jack was aware of Fletcher's standing in the community and probably knew of his reputation for an "acid wit" along with his determination to operate his book shop throughout the Great Depression. Fletcher had succeeded by opening a lending library in his shop so successful that he hired three women to take in and check out books. His fees were three cents a day for fiction, a little more for biographies, and a few cents more for history. Unfortunately, Jack did not get to know Fletcher very well after finding him "rather gruff and abrupt on my get-acquainted visit, and I never happened to go back, although I did not dislike him."[18]

The Houston bookseller whose company Jack enjoyed most was Ed Bartholomew, "a man of tremendous energy, enthusiasm, ability, and imagination." When Jack saw Bartholomew's ad for a self-published book on the history of Houston[19] he went to visit him at a large, corrugated metal building near what is now Hobby Airport where Ed dealt in surplus aviation parts and sold books. Bartholomew was always willing to share his knowledge of Texana and Western Americana. "One of the most interesting aspects of the rare book business is the manner in which the booksellers learn from each other. Except for those who have reached a high degree of success and become less approachable, they are always willing to talk about how they find books, how they establish prices, how they sell the books, and how they tell one rarity from another. . . . So I continued to learn from Ed and he from me."[20]

Bartholomew's deep and thorough grasp of the social and political history of the Borderlands matched his knowledge of the natural history and geography of the region. When John Steinbeck was writing *Travels with Charlie*, he learned about Ed and asked him to accompany him along the back roads of the Southwest to talk about what they were seeing.

As with many booksellers, Bartholomew enjoyed his book-scouting trips. In Washington, DC, he came upon a shop with a sign, "building coming down, everything must go." The sale had been going several days, but a "quick look through the store showed him that there were still many good Western items, so Ed asked about the price of the entire store. As I recall, it was in the medium four-figure range, so Ed planked down about half of the money and offered to take over the shop then and there and to pay the balance in two weeks. The deal was accepted. Ed locked the doors, checked every shelf and skimmed off the cream of the remaining stock, moving it to another room. He wired for his wife and daughter to come to help him, along with another Houston bookseller, Bill Morrison." After a massive sale, Ed shipped the remaining books to Houston. When Jack entered Ed's building at Hobby Airport, he saw "a monolithic pile of books, stacked solidly about ten feet wide, perhaps seven feet high, and more than forty feet long. 'Help yourself to a free book, any book,'" Bartholomew offered. "But as much as I love books I could not find one copy of real interest."[21]

With skill at ferreting out unusual collections, Bartholomew tracked down and bought all the Noah Hamilton Rose photographs after Rose died in San Antonio in 1952. The collection of more than two thousand images included many original prints and nitrate negatives of politicians, gunfighters, and outlaws as well as the towns in the west where they lived and died. After his teenage years in the 1880s, in Menardville, Texas, with a box camera and printing supplies bought by selling magazine subscriptions, he became an itinerant photographer and printer who drifted for thirty years from Menard to Sonora, Junction to Del Rio and then to San Antonio. From 1904 to 1919 he operated his own studio in Del Rio photographing news events, politicians, outlaws, and law men. He also began corresponding with Emmett Dalton and other personalities from whom he acquired original photographs.[22] Both Bartholomew and Jack must have had a grand time sorting his remarkable historic photographs and discussing the events they documented. Jack used many of these photographs to illustrate his ongoing *Baroid News* articles. For a feature on Pancho Villa he bought copy prints of seven Rose photographs, including burning bodies after Villa's attack on Columbus, New Mexico, in 1916, Mexican revolutionaries with a new machine gun, Mexican soldiers at Del Rio, and Villa wearing two crossed bandoliers and a large sombrero while seated on a white stallion.

In 1958 Bartholomew published a book based on the Rose collection, *Biographical Album of Western Gunfighters*, published by Frontier Press, Ed's imprint, and containing more than one thousand biographical entries with more than six hundred rare photographs of the most famous sheriffs, marshals, outlaws, and celebrated figures of the western frontier. Jack set type for the titlepage and cover. After fulfilling orders for copy prints over several years, Bartholomew sold Rose's images to the University of Oklahoma Library for its major photography collection.[23]

When Bartholomew and his wife eventually bought the old main lodge at Madera Springs Resort on 228 acres in the Davis Mountains of West Texas, they took along his books and airplane. Over the next ten years Jack and Charlotte visited them several times in this storied landscape when Madera Springs was on its way to becoming a ghost town.

The Civil War Round Table provided Jack a forum for lively discussions with a historical focus. While not "greatly interested in the Civil War," Jack found the membership "included some of the most interesting minds in the city. I knew such men as Frank Vandiver, Cooper Ragan, Palmer Bradley, and several historians, as well as bookseller Joe Petty."[24] Jack recalled they each "had fine homes with an entire room set aside as a library." He found the men at the Civil War Round Table much like his old friends at the Zamorano Club, well-educated, successful in business and academia, deeply interested in ideas and history, keen about books, and enjoyable to visit. Each member took turns reading a paper on one aspect or another in the Civil War. "The membership was about equally divided between home-boy Southerners and newcomer Yankees." Unlike similar clubs that would simply meet, listen to a talk, give polite applause, and then go home, at the Civil War Round Table "the debate that followed each talk was quite lively."

Carl Bond, a round table member, asked Jack's help to reproduce the talks for distribution to members. Bond arranged for copies to be mimeographed (most likely at the offices of Ragan or Bradley) and then went to Jack's home to help set type and print covers in the evening shortly after each dinner gathering. All members received copies at the next meeting, while extras were set aside for incoming new members.[25] When the University of Houston commemorated Civil War journalism in 1961, Jack printed the program invitation in antique type that read like a proclamation from 1861.[26]

Jack's circle of bookish friends grew as he reached out to Zamarano Club members in and around Texas including E. L. DeGolyer, known fondly as "Mr. De." Based on his use of seismology for discoveries of major oil fields around Tampico, Mexico, DeGolyer wrote technical articles that were soon required reading for geology students. He was already legendary in the petroleum world when Jack met him. His mentor and employer, Sir Weetman Pearson, had introduced him to London bookshops specializing in rare books. After the Mexican Revolution started, Pearson moved the company offices to New York where DeGolyer became a regular customer of the Eberstadts and other dealers in Western Americana, collecting rare books about early voyages and travels, the history of Mexico, the development of the Trans-Mississippi West, and other subjects. Unlike some collectors, DeGolyer was a voracious reader deeply familiar with the contents of the books on the library shelves of his Dallas mansion.

Jack had written to Mr. De before leaving Los Angeles, referencing their membership in the Zamarano Club. As their cordial exchange of letters began, he sent DeGolyer a copy of his dime-novel keepsake and his booklet on oil humor in 1865. DeGolyer replied by airmail, "I appreciate the 'Dime Novels on Early Oil' particularly because there are three 'Work and Win' numbers. The doings of Fred Fearnot used to be my favorite literature. My library at that time consisted of the space between the mattress and springs of my bed."[27]

On one of his first trips to Dallas, Jack arranged to meet Mr. De at his downtown offices of DeGolyer MacNaughton, a consulting firm that provided detailed analyses on oil reserves from China to Latin America and throughout the Middle East. DeGolyer explained that the books on the history of the oil industry, shelved throughout his office suite, exceeded the capacity of his spacious library at home, even after double-banking books on every shelf.[28] Jack recalled, "Perhaps I was equally impressed with the fact that he had a professional librarian to care for his office library. Imagine a collector able to hire a librarian!"[29]

On other occasions DeGolyer took Jack to lunch at the Dallas Petroleum Club in the Adolphus Hotel, "a sanctum that not many advertising men had a chance to enter" and to the DeGolyer mansion where they could talk about books in his Southwest collection "in a room with shelves so high that he needed a travelling ladder to get to the top shelves." He showed Jack his two variant copies of Cabeza de Vaca's *La Relacion y Comentarios* printed in Valladolid in 1555, "one with a title page in black and red and the other with a title page done only in black, and he expressed a curiosity about the printing. I was able to explain how some of the early printers did not lock up two separate forms for such color printing but simply blocked out certain lines with a frisket or mask and printed the same form in both black and red."[30]

> Once DeGolyer came up to visit me in my second floor office on West Gray to look at my books on Texas and on petroleum, by then housed on steel shelving along an entire wall. We talked of books and collecting for more than an hour, and at the end when he was ready to leave I asked him if I could call a cab. "No need to," he replied. "I have one waiting." I looked out of the window and there was a cab, its meter going. I felt honored by the gesture. In the years since, I continued an acquaintance with his son, E. L. DeGolyer, Jr., whom I saw each year at the Western History Conference.[31]

When Mr. De ended his own life in 1956, Jack wrote an eloquent tribute to his friend and included anecdotes and accolades.

> It is a tribute to [him] that when word flashed that DeGolyer had

> ended life, there were shocked men in petroleum social clubs, in the halls of learned societies, in the editorial offices of The Saturday Review of Literature, around the Zamorano table, and in the offices of dealers and librarians. In Houston, a private press printer, himself a Zamorano who had sat beside DeGolyer in that vast and unforgettable private library, was working late on a handset Christmas keepsake, musing how DeGolyer would like this one. And then came the word across the radio waves. The press was stilled . . . and then the antique flywheel began to spin again. DeGolyer would have liked it that way.[32]

The Christmas greeting on the press when Jack learned of DeGolyer's death was a poem by William Lawrence Chittenden, "The Cowboy's Christmas Ball," with original illustrations by Jose Cisneros, "of El Paso del Norte." It was handset and privately printed on Hamilton Victorian paper as Christmas Greetings from Charlotte and Jack Rittenhouse.[33]

Even though Jack and Carl Hertzog were unable to meet when Jack came through El Paso in September 1951, they soon made up for lost time. Within a few months Hertzog was in Houston and arranged to see Jack. When Jack opened the door, Hertzog's greeting was, "Let's talk printing." He gave Jack a copy of Ross Calvin's *River of the Sun* designed for the University of New Mexico Press in 1946. With colors of the earth and sun and a dust jacket echoing ancient Mimbres pottery designs from the Gila River area, the design for this book is still as fresh and engaging as it was more than seventy-five years ago. By the following summer Jack was writing Hertzog with gratitude for packets of material the Printer at the Pass had sent. Jack's response included much chat about printing. He told Hertzog about discovering the Houston Shopping News, a trade typesetter in town. Despite its name, the print shop had just acquired a "font of matrices for 10 pt. Waverley, with italic and small caps, for their machine." Hertzog understood well why Jack was pleased with this development. Shopping News could now set Jack's work in another preferred type face.[34]

In 1955 Jack drew once more from his collection of early type to create an elegant four-page, two-color keepsake titled "25 Lines on Old Type in Texas." He and Charlotte, reactivating Stagecoach Press after moving into their home at 1506 Freedonia Drive, produced this clever announcement for their printer friends in Houston, El Paso, and Los Angeles. They set the type by hand, with ten different ornaments and cuts.[35]

Herzog responded to Jack's appreciation for beautifully designed typefaces. On a visit in El Paso he gave his friend nine tied-up forms of Centaur 16 pt. type used in printing the Saddle Blanket edition of Tom Lea's *The King Ranch*. As Jack began distributing Hertzog's type into his cases at home, he kept meticulous statistics on use frequency of every piece his friend had given him, upper- and lower case, spaces and quads, caps, figures, and more so he could place an order with the Mackenzie and Harris foundry in San Francisco to balance out his assortment of Centaur and have everything needed for setting books. He must have thought fondly of his friend in El Paso whenever he opened his cases of Centaur to see type once used for a landmark book in Hertzog's career and the annals of fine printing.

Shortly after moving to Houston, Jack joined the Texas State Historical Association and regularly attended the TSHA annual meetings where he met Fritz and Emilie Toepperwein, printer-publishers from Boerne. Fritz, head of public relations for the Lone Star Brewery, planned and staged large events such as a homecoming pageant for Lyndon Johnson at the end of his presidency. The Toepperweins produced children's books with a Texas theme, the first of which they printed on a press at home. Later they designed their small format books to be printed at the Boerne Star newspaper plant and then bound by hand in their own press room. Whenever the Toepperweins, Carl Hertzog, and Jack met at TSHA gatherings they enjoyed "a feast of printing talk."[36]

Throughout Jack's life his range of interests constantly expanded. During his Houston years from 1951 to 1962, he began seeking more nineteenth-century type once common in small Texas-town newspaper shops. Using Houston library sources he compiled a comprehensive list of early Texas newspapers to carry with him. "In my travels around the state . . . in each new town I would seek out the local printer and try to buy type. Today there is a big demand for this material; back then there were few of us, and one of the best was a man named William Thorniley, from Seattle, who seemed always to precede me by a year or two, so that it was not often I could find a shop where he had left anything." Nevertheless, Jack did succeed in his quest and soon gathered about fifty fonts of original nineteenth-century type.[37]

Jack's search for vintage type led him to Giddings, Texas, where a colony of Wends settled in the 1840s on the road from Houston to Austin. When he learned of a printer, J. A. Proske (1857–1943) who established a shop among the immigrant settlers, he knew he needed to ask about early type possibly overlooked for a half century or more. In Giddings he met Albert Miertschin who learned how to print from Proske early in the twentieth century. Now the only printer in town, Miertschin was delighted to learn of Jack's interest in Wendish printing. Jack remembered "it was the custom . . . in central Texas to print a death notice when any local citizen passed on. In a region of weekly papers, this was the best way to spread the news and announce the funeral. The notices were printed on a black-edged card or folder, available from paper houses as a stock item. . . . These . . . were often seen in shop windows or under the glass counter top near the cash register. . . . No Wendish language printing had been done for many years in the shop, but [Miertschin] found an old type form still tied up, containing verse from the Wendish-language Bible and handset by the original printer in the shop." He told Jack the type had been "undisturbed over the years since it had been handset originally by drucker Proske. It was only a verse from an old Wendish hymn, set in type for use on a funeral announcement."[38] Jack paid Miertschin to lock up the form in his platen press and print 150 copies on a "small paneled card."[39]

On a return visit he met the widow of another printer who began working in Giddings in the late nineteenth century as the Wendish language was giving way to more German in Central Texas. She spoke only Wendish and German, but Jack broke the ice by saying, "Jah, ich bin eine drucker," telling her he was a printer. She gave him some old announcements and leaflets along with a copy of a Giddings newspaper printed in English, German, and Wendish, and a Wendish Bible brought from "the old country." From an antique shop about thirty miles away he bought the original sign that hung outside the Wendish printing shop in Giddings and an advertising blotter issued by the printer with his half-tone portrait printed on it. Later Jack sold these remaining pieces of Wendish printing to the University of Texas at Austin.

When Jack told Glen Dawson he was writing an essay about nineteenth- and early twentieth-century printing in Wendish, Dawson asked him if he might turn it into a small book. Jack did so and printed 128 copies with the Dawson bookshop imprint. Each copy of the book held one of the cards Jack had requested from the old printer in Giddings—most likely the last printing in Texas with nineteenth-century Wendish type cast in Europe.

Quickly Houston libraries became a familiar haunt for Jack. "Some of the greatest benefits I found in Houston were the libraries," he remembered. For a few dollars a year he joined the Friends of the Fondren Library at Rice Institute (later Rice University), took out a membership in the Friends of the Library at Houston Public Library, and conducted some of his many research projects at the University of Houston's M. D. Anderson Library. Ever since his early youth spending two evenings a week reading in a small public library, Jack was an inveterate library patron, the consummate researcher who had memorized the Dewey decimal system and was familiar with key books in every library reference room he visited. In those pre-Internet days large academic libraries and central public libraries maintained huge collections of reference books painstakingly compiled by scholars with a deep knowledge in specific fields of study. Reference librarians at home among the atlases, almanacs, bibliographies, biographical sources, catalogs, concordances, dictionaries, glossaries, handbooks, indexes, and style guides lining the shelves of library reference rooms helped patrons find the information they were seeking, literally opening doors to knowledge.

In Rice University's Fondren Library, Jack spent many evenings at the long, elbow-high tables in front of the card catalog searching for information. As he lost track of time, the librarians grew concerned for their patron who stood for hours. When asked if he might like to sit at a table, he politely declined. Information in the card files was so stimulating he did not have time to think about sitting or standing. At home he would often rise early in the morning to conduct more research on his projects before leaving for the office. Jack savored these periods of intense research, sometimes lasting for ten days, at the end of which he felt as if he was returning from a good vacation.

Everywhere he visited, librarians recognized him as a knowledgeable and seasoned writer with an infectious enthusiasm for whatever subject he was pursuing. They all enjoyed helping him. At the Houston Public Library Jack had two favorite departments, the Texas room with well-stocked shelves on history, and the photo-reproduction unit with "the best blueprint and map copying services in Houston. They could make a ten-cent copy by Xerox, a reduced microfiche, an enlarged full color print, and same-size black and white copies in any desired degree of quality. A reel of microfilm could be converted within minutes into a set of sheets for a book. All of this service was very fast, rarely more than a day." He felt this level of service outranked what he found at the National Archives or the Library of Congress.[40]

During vacations Jack and Charlotte traveled to New Mexico, remarkable for its variety of scenery from deserts and high plains to the Rocky Mountains and its rich history of the American West. First explored on numerous trips in the Bantam along Route 66, Jack and his family now vacationed in New Mexico in 1953 and 1954. The more they visited, the more they wanted to move there. Santa Fe had a special appeal. On their first visit Jack stopped by what had been Candelario's old store, recalling the Zamorano luncheon years earlier where a member told of his visit and speculated about treasures possibly squirreled away beyond the basement door. He took his time looking around, and "on a table near the back were about ten copies of the paperback edition of William H. Ryus's *The Second William Penn: Treating with Indians on the Santa Fe Trail*, published in Kansas City in 1913. They were priced at a dollar a copy. Now, when one finds an old copy or two of a book, this is no indication, but a pile of ten mint copies indicates a possible lode. I asked if they had more and was told they had a great many, so I bought one copy and took it back to the motel to read that evening."[41] Jack did not know the book or have any bibliographies from his reference collection with him, but he thought it could be the first printing of an early personal memoir by a traveler on the Santa Fe Trail.

"The next day I was back and dickered on a wholesale price, finally buying three hundred copies for a hundred dollars. When we went out to get the books from a back storage room, I noticed that there were shelves of this book, about 2,300 copies in all, still wrapped in brown paper in bundles of ten and sealed with the printed sealing tape of the Riley Company, printers. The books had been concealed by crates of pottery stored in front and only now were being revealed."[42]

Back in his reference collection in Houston, Jack learned the Ryus book had sold at auction for as much as fifteen dollars. Seeing an opportunity to cover his expenses, he offered Ed Bartholomew and Bill Morrison fifty copies each at a dollar a copy. In less than a week he recovered his hundred-dollar purchase and left it to his two bookman friends to reach the rare book market with a good margin on sales of what they bought from him. With his two hundred remaining books, Jack created newly bound copies by Stagecoach Press in red cloth over boards holding the 1913 booklet in its original wrappers. These he offered "for library use" at $3.75.[43]

Returning to Houston libraries, he began compiling a New Mexico bibliography of books and pamphlets published after 1800. His research started as a personal collecting guide, with the possibility of publication. "Over a weekend I made a list of about two hundred.

Within a fortnight it was up to five hundred; before the month was out it had passed 1,000 entries. . . . Within five years it had passed the three thousand entry mark and was still growing."[44] All of the entries were on the 4 × 6 inch cards he used to record his growing collection of books about New Mexico. Similar to his friend Mr. De, Jack read the books he collected, gathering historical facts and perspectives, adding to his knowledge about the Southwest. In years to follow he would draw upon this storehouse of information to shape his library and share information with friends.

In 1953 when he and Charlotte bought their ranch-style home in Spring Branch, a Houston suburb, he reassembled his printing press and also began forming "a better collection of Southwestern books, as well as bibliographies to guide me."[45] In 1954 he missed buying a key reference book as it went out of print, Wright Howes's US-IANA, probably the most important single volume on essential books relating to the United States. On his next business trip to Chicago, Jack visited Howes to examine his stock of Americana and to ask if he still had a copy of his recently published reference book. None were available, but Howes remembered "selling three copies to a bookseller named Rosengren, over in San Antonio. I'll bet he still has one." Back in Houston Jack learned that George Fuermann was soon going to San Antonio and would happily visit Rosengren Books.[46] Rosengren still had two copies. One Fuermann bought for Jack, the other for himself.

At about the same time, Jack acquired a copy of a book by his old friend at the Zamarano Club, Henry Raup Wagner. Among the most prolific historians of the Trans-Mississippi West, Wagner had written a landmark bibliography for the study of the West, *The Plains and the Rockies: A Bibliography of Original Narratives of Travel and Adventure, 1800–1865*. Jack observed, "without Howes and Wagner, no collector or dealer can work in Western books."[47]

Sometimes his small-town scouting trips yielded interesting books instead of type. Encountering Frank Lotto's *Fayette County: Her History and Her People* published in Schulenberg, Texas, in 1902, he knew where his next weekend scouting trip would take him. However, after driving to Schulenberg and asking at the local printing shops about the book and its author, he drew a lot of blank looks. When he remembered that the title page identified a steam press as the means of printing, the old-timers recalled there had been a steam press in LaGrange, twenty miles away. Soon he stood in the print shop in La Grange asking about the steam press that ran there about fifty years earlier. Yes, and it was named Sticker Steam Press.[48] "Did they publish Lotto's book early in this century? Yes. Did they still have copies? Yes. How much? Five dollars. Can a dealer get a reduction, say, three for ten dollars? Yes. I bought three."[49] Not yet a fulltime bookseller, he sold the books to Houston dealers, building good will among the bookshops in the region.

Evenings in the libraries, weekends in small towns searching for obscure, locally printed books and old type used in their production, along with vacations in New Mexico helped balance out Jack's stress from working in the highly competitive world of advertising. He could manage an office staff and crunch the numbers along with the best, meanwhile writing articles and lecturing at professional meetings. The single element in his professional work that most likely kept him in the ad world was his enjoyment of research and writing. At one point he realized he had written and published more than 250 articles. Those early writing exercises in college had paid off.

While Jack's agency was successful, he could do nothing to change the shifting business climate. He had already acknowledged that domestic oil production faced serious challenges from abroad. In the meantime he took advantage of his earning power with Marsteller. Over the next three years he acquired more printing equipment. In 1955 he bought a huge Washington-style handpress built by the Ostrander-Seymour Company. Sometime before the end of 1958 he also bought a cast-iron hand printing press made by R. Hoe and Company, New York and London, but with limited room to house it, he arranged for the San Jacinto Monument to store it temporarily as a historic object. No evidence suggests that he actually printed anything on the Hoe press before selling it.[50] He also bought and restored an extremely rare Adams Cottage Press (Civil War–era portable field press). Before long he would add a Linotype Model 5. In 1959 he also bought a new Vandercook Universal I Test Press known for producing superb results at the hand of experienced printers.

In addition to his presses, he also bought equipment for binding, gold stamping, and working with type, along with three favorite printing antiques, a two-foot mahogany composing stick, a two-handled ink roller, and a "shooting stick" for locking type in a chase.[51] His treasured cabinet of hundreds of stock electrotypes and engravings from 1870 to 1910 held cuts that enhanced his printed broadsides, announcements, and books for years to come.

While he had limited time for printing in the late 1950s, Jack did manage to produce one Stagecoach Press book, *The Man Who Owned Too Much*. It grew from his article by the same title about the Maxwell Land Grant for the *Baroid News Bulletin*. His subject for the historical article, Lucien Maxwell, (1818–1875), endlessly fascinating, secured a massive land grant from Mexico. The 1,714,765-acre grant was already known to historians, but Jack clarified part of the story for the first time with information from an obscure St. Louis newspaper clipping that he found in a scrapbook. It contained illuminating interviews with individuals who knew Maxwell. After Baroid published his article, he held the type, fleshed out the narrative, and printed *The Man Who Owned Too Much* two pages at a time on his Gally's Universal Press.

The Man Who Owned Too Much was Stagecoach Press's first hardcover book and was printed on ivory Strathmore. Normally, such high-quality paper might have exceeded Jack's budget, but he reduced production costs by buying a sizeable amount of discarded letterhead on Strathmore paper and using his guillotine paper cutter to remove the letterhead at the tops of the pages.[52] Issued in a slipcase, this elegant book included an account of the life of Maxwell along with rare photographs and the overlooked St. Louis newspaper article that Jack had discovered. The book sold out in a few years. Throughout its planning and production, Jack kept meticulous records on production time and costs as a "test run in book publishing [and] to set up procedures."[53] Clearly, he was already thinking about turning Stagecoach Press into a profitable business rather than a hobby. His chance came a few months later.

After three years of failing to attract sufficient business, Marsteller closed the Houston branch in June 1960. The firm had focused on large brand-name chemical companies, refineries, and related businesses, companies with headquarters in New York, Philadelphia, Chicago, and Los Angeles. These businesses made key decisions, including the allocation of resources for advertising, in their home offices thousands of miles from Houston. As agency growth stagnated, Marsteller tested the waters by asking Jack and his fellow VP, Douglas Craig, what they thought of moving to one of the company's major offices in the Midwest or Northeast. Neither man wanted to leave Houston. After his earlier experiences living in Chicago and New York, Jack was determined to remain in the Southwest.

Upon closing, Marsteller offered to give Jack and Craig all the accounts at no cost. Once more at a crossroad, Jack and his senior colleague "drove over to a nearby park and walked beneath the trees to discuss the matter," before going home to consult with their wives. "It was obvious that there would not be enough volume to support our staff at current salaries and expenses. After a couple of days, I told Craig that he could have my share of the accounts scot-free, if he could put together an agency of his own. He was eager to do this."[54] Craig soon formed an agency that lasted for over twenty years.

Briefly, Jack considered the possibility of opening his own ad agency in New Mexico, but he found little potential there. New Mexico had only three or four accounts in the entire state exceeding $100,000 in advertising per year. "I had been inside a couple of the 'larger' agencies and found them equal, at best, only to the staff and facilities of Rittenhouse & Co. I realized that New Mexico offered only limited opportunities for employment, and that the best way to get a job was to bring it with you."[55]

Moreover, Jack had become disillusioned with agency work. He must have felt a great sense of relief leaving the ad world behind. "The deep, inner truth was that I really didn't like the agency business," not so much from a "lack of faith in advertising as an instrument of society," but more around relationships with clients who did things "hypocritically to keep a job." Seeing the way some ad men worked reminded him of politicians making a show of churchgoing.

> I knew one young man who said that he intended to make a good career in advertising, and that as a preparation he had taken up golf and had joined the Republican party, because most clients preferred those. Jack also found some advertising managers quite unpredictable. They had the power to change agencies if they wished, and they let their agencies know this. Don Fowler, at Baroid, would sometimes say to another in his office, "Well, I guess I'll call ol' Jack and make him squirm." It was often necessary to cater to their vanity. I was told by one other large agency executive, "If you want to get that account, find out what the advertising manager's appetites are and gratify them. Get him what he wants. If it is girls or drugs, get them. But get the account.

Jack abhorred this approach to business relationships and managed to avoid it by working with top executives or owners of their firms. "They were businesslike and wanted a job done right, on schedule, and effectively." Still, he remembered "many late afternoons when I drove home from the office feeling miserable."[56]

At forty-eight Jack decided to move full-time into the world of books and printing, interests that had nourished his spirit for years. He had a shop full of presses and related printing equipment to guide Stagecoach Press on a steady and productive course.

"To go into business all I needed to buy was a push broom and a door sign. I was at work in less than a month after the Marsteller office closed."[57] Most important, he would be applying his decades of experience in editing and producing all manner of printed material, especially well-designed books of historical interest related to the Southwest.

Although he registered Stagecoach Press as a Houston business in 1956 at the Harris County courthouse, the never-ending demands of his advertising work had only allowed time to set type for Christmas cards, broadsides, and one book. Freed from the daily grind of the advertising business, Jack's Stagecoach Press sprang to life producing numerous broadsides and books. For one of his broadsides, "To All Employees," he proposed a radical innovation, the Work Break.

> We are asking that somewhere between starting and quitting time and without infringing too much on the time usually devoted to lunch period, coffee breaks, rest period, story-telling, ticket selling, vacation planning, and the re-hashing of yesterday's TV programs, that each employee endeavor to find some time that can be set aside and known as the WORK BREAK. To some this may seem a radical innovation, but we honestly believe the idea has great possibilities. It can conceivably be an aid to steady employment and it might also be a means of assuring regular pay checks. The Management.

With little time for breaks over the next six months, Jack printed more ephemeral and promotional materials and two books, *Santa Fe Trail: First Reports, 1825* and James C. McKee's *Narrative of the Surrender of a Command of U.S. Forces at Fort Fillmore, N.M., in July, A.D., 1861*. Both were reprints chosen wisely. He knew of their rarity and of historians' sustained interest in them. The Santa Fe Trail report by Augustus Storrs and Alphonso Wetmore originally appeared in documents issued by the US Government Publishing Office in 1825. With H. H. Bancroft and Henry R. Wagner emphasizing its significance, historians wanted the book in their reference collections. A reprint of Storrs and Wetmore issued by the Denver Public Library had long ago gone out of print, but the book was still in demand.[58] Text for Jack's promotional flyer opened boldly: "Here are the scarce government reports whose publication in 1825 helped to start the great surge westward over the Santa Fe Trail. Until 1824, no big commercial wagon train had travelled the Trail. In that year an expedition returned rich with Mexican silver. Excitement was high, and Congress asked for details." Jack set type by hand and printed the book on his supply of Strathmore paper.

Even though he enjoyed setting type by hand, it wasn't long before Jack realized he could not charge enough for books produced that way. "So I used type set by a man who had two Linotypes in a shop back of his house, where he set type for high school newspapers and such jobs."[59] Soon type was standing for the McKee book. When it was printed and published Lawrence Clark Powell promoted it in his widely read column, "Western Books and Writers," appearing monthly in *Westways*, circulation two hundred thousand. "Readers of this page know of my fondness for the un-ballyhooed labors of love in the field of Western Americana." He praised the "latest book from the Stagecoach Press of Houston, Texas, a handwrought product of the Press's master and sole employee, that too-long exiled southern Californian, Jack D. Rittenhouse" and suggested readers send a postcard to Stagecoach Press for a complete list "of this unusual publisher's works."[60] Before the end of the year the Southern Books Competition chose the McKee volume as one of the best designed books produced anywhere in the South during 1960. The book sold out in less than two years, and *Santa Fe Trail: First Reports, 1825* went out of print shortly thereafter.

Jack's next publication had a similar grounding with history, places, and friends. Associates in the Historical Society of New Mexico invited him to print a keepsake for distribution at its annual dinner where Lawrence Clark Powell would deliver the keynote address titled "Act of Enchantment." The *New Mexico Magazine* had recently published Powell's article, "50 Good Books about New Mexico," helping set the stage for the talk.[61] Jack remembered, "1961 was the hundredth anniversary of the opening of the Civil War, so I decided to compile and print a bibliography of books about the Texas Confederates' invasion of New Mexico."[62] For the keepsake he printed three hundred copies and made plans to attend the meeting in New Mexico where he would present a copy to Powell, one of his old Zamorano Club friends. All three hundred copies were distributed free at the meeting.

With type still standing from the paperback keepsake, Jack expanded its contents. Among the thirty-two different titles in the bibliography, one was a pamphlet with only two known copies in existence. He added text from the rare pamphlet to augment the bibliography for a 37-page cloth-bound hardback. Lawrence Clark Powell wrote in praise: "I want to salute the work of Jack Rittenhouse, who is devoting his skill as a bibliographer and printer to the recovery and preservation of New Mexican history."[63] In addition to positive reviews, *New Mexico Civil War Bibliography* won a Southern Books Competition in 1961, the second year in a row that Jack's work was honored for excellence in design.

After the Historical Society of New Mexico meeting, Powell wrote Calvin P. Horn, president of the Society, suggesting that they might be interested in publishing his talk. Horn liked the idea but said the Society did not have the money to do so in the manner it deserved. He offered a counterproposal: what if Stagecoach Press would "do a handsome printing job of the address?" Stagecoach Press could "give the Society enough copies to send to each member plus a few for some members of the legislature (we have a hard lobbying job coming up next month for the Society)." Jack could sell as many as he needed to break even, and Horn would guarantee him against any loss in the project.[64]

The plan worked, and a month later Jack sent Powell the galley proofs for *Act of Enchantment*. "Please return proofs and mss., even if you find no further changes. I will go to press immediately upon receipt of proofs. . . . Paper-bounds will be done within a week of your return of proofs; hard-bound will be out around Feb. 17, I hope."[65] Jack printed three hundred copies in paper wrappers for members of the Society and three hundred cloth-bound copies with dust jacket sold by Stagecoach Press.

When Jack wrote Powell about the proofs, he also mentioned

thirteen booksellers in California now handling Stagecoach Press books. All of them from the Dawsons and Jack Reynolds to Max Hunley, Warren Howell, and Peter Howard knew Lawrence Clark Powell and his reputation for writing about authors and books in a most engaging manner. Sales for Powell's new book were strong; it sold out in less than a year.

In October 1961, Jack was back in New Mexico at the organizational meeting for the Western History Association. With a national revival of interest in frontier and Western history, the time was ripe for a new professional organization devoted to the study of the Trans-Mississippi West. Early in the year Jack's friend W. D. Grisso alerted him to the autumn meeting being planned for Santa Fe. "There is on the planning board a new organization of historians, writers, collectors, etc., in the field of and about Southwestern Americana which will assemble in October. We will be there and hope you, too, are."[66] Jack was intrigued by the promise of a new organization that would encourage good scholarship on Western history. When he received the program for the meeting, he sent copies to friends such as the Bay Area historian and collector, Al Shumate, encouraging them to attend.[67] He then made reservations and drove from Houston to Santa Fe for the first annual meeting of the Western History Association (WHA). There, surrounded by such notable historians as Ray Allen Billington, Donald Cutter, John A. Carroll, Robert Utley, and many more, Jack found himself among like-minded people, serious about their pursuit of history and enjoying one another's company. They knew how to have fun while being good scholars, writers, collectors, and storytellers. One of the elements that drew Jack's devotion to WHA were the talks he attended at the inaugural meeting on Indian wars, mining, stock raising and agriculture, exploration and the fur trade, transportation and communication, and overland migration, subjects that resonated for a new citizen of the West who was already well grounded in its history. From its outset WHA welcomed "hundreds of historians teaching about the frontier and the West and thousands of collectors, buffs, journalists, and writers . . .

seeking ways to meet one another and to share their interests and findings."[68] In addition to the talks in Santa Fe, Jack began meeting members of the Westerners who helped organize the nascent WHA. The Westerners, an organization formed in 1944 to "encourage and promote interest and research in the history, literature, and culture of the North American West" were part of WHA from its start.[69] He returned home knowing he had found two organizations that he would enjoy immensely for their inclusiveness and comradery centered on history of the American West. Over the next twenty-eight years he missed only one meeting of the WHA, and in subsequent years he would help organize a Westerners "Corral" in Santa Fe.

The year 1961 looked promising for the Stagecoach Press with Jack's plans for four books to be produced for clients as well as four titles he would print for his own private press distribution. Since clients paid for contract work as soon as it was delivered and his Stagecoach Press books required capital in advance only to be recovered as the books sold, he needed both types of projects as a start-up business.

His contract work in 1961 included *Confederate Victories in the Southwest* (1,000 copies) and *Union Army Operations in the Southwest* (1,500 copies) printed for Horn and Walace in Albuquerque; *The Value of Business History in Oilfinding* (500 copies) done for the Texas Gulf Coast Historical Association; and *The Legend of Tok-Chock-Tow* (2,000 copies), a Christmas booklet for Maco Stewart. Among the four books that he chose as Stagecoach Press imprints, two were written by him, *New Mexico Civil War Bibliography* and *Carriage Hundred: A Bibliography on Horse-Drawn Transportation*.

For twenty-five years his interest in horse-drawn vehicles had never waned. Ever since publishing his second book, *American Horse-Drawn Vehicles* in 1948, he had kept detailed notecards on important and rare pamphlets and books issued between 1671 and 1954 on the subject. Since 1948 Jack had purchased and sold scarce titles about wagons and carriages. He carefully maintained lists of collectors interested in the subject. With his continuing interest in the subject, he produced a useful, forty-nine-page bibliography and promoted it among the most likely buyers around the country. *Carriage Hundred* was met with accolades, one of which was by Lawrence Clark Powell in his regular *Westways* book review article in June 1961. "This is one of the most unusual and interesting bibliographies I have ever read. It stems from Rittenhouse's earlier book, *American Horse-Drawn Vehicles*, and selects works to annotate from a time span of five centuries."

George Fuermann gave *Carriage Hundred* a boost in his *Houston Post* column. He called it "a beautiful small book by Jack D. Rittenhouse, the fourth book published by Stagecoach Press." He included an illustration of a "high gig of the 1890's, a sporting vehicle thought to be unsafe because of its height. The horse is wearing a fly net and fly-net cap, which Rittenhouse described as 'the equivalent of our gaudily-ornamented hotrods.'"[70]

Jack understood the importance of good publicity if he were going to make a living with Stagecoach Press. Journalists also enjoyed writing stories about Jack's printed replicas of outlaw posters. He placed ads for these in various book- and printing-related forums around the country and took orders to customize them with the recipient's name in bold, wood-block type. Appearing on the local TV station KHOU during the annual Printing Week, he talked about Benjamin Franklin and early printing. He also gave talks at the Houston Public Library, including one on publishers' methods and criteria for evaluating manuscripts for publication. For the Texas Daily Newspaper Association, he set title lines and stock heads for their newsletter, *TDNA Round-Up*, using typefaces dating back to some of Texas' earliest printing shops. The first page of the April 1961 issue of the *Round-Up* included a photograph of Jack at his large Washington press, smiling as he inked type with his favorite two-handled eighteen-inch roller.

As publicity about Jack and Stagecoach Press gathered momentum, George Fuermann wrote another "Post Card" in the *Houston Post* drawing upon Jack's collection of amusing typographic letterheads. The column opened with a reference to William Metzig (1893–1989), respected calligrapher and advertising artist from Germany who immigrated to the United States in 1939. His letterhead shows the

Pied Piper of Hamlin in the lead, piping a procession of dancing rats across a drawbridge and away from the castle. The text reads: "Pied Piper of Hamlin, Rodent Exterminator. Extermination Through Entertainment." Another example was for "Rip Van Winkle Mattresses—Guaranteed for 20 years of Restful Sleep."[71] Jack's penchant for collecting odd, overlooked examples of graphic design and cultural history caught Fuermann's attention once more with Jack's collection of wartime cigarette brands like Coffee-Tone Cigarettes, Salome, Puppies, O-Nic-O, Three Kings, Rameses, and Fleetwood. Soon Fuermann picked up on the Houston connection in Jack's newly published *Campaign from Santa Fe to the Mississippi* by Theo Noel, a history of Sibley's Brigade from 1861 to 1864.

While Jack's one-page press releases about his full-time work with Stagecoach Press were a model of well-written promotion, gaining him more attention and name recognition in newspapers, he also wrote personal letters to people whom he hoped would take notice. He invited Diana Hobby, book editor at the *Houston Post*, to visit his pressroom at Stagecoach Press. He also initiated *The Stagecoach Press Waybill*, a newsletter "issued at intervals to Booksellers, Librarians and Collectors." Sprinkling cuts throughout the text, he highlighted recently published books, others in production, demand from book dealers, and his approach to printing. He wrote about the press on which he could print four or eight pages at a time, turning out three hundred sheets an hour. "You can see why our house prints editions limited to 500–600 copies. Our experience shows that about one-third of a new edition is sold during the first month. We want to produce a *desirable* title, in an attractive format, to sell below $5.00 whenever possible." He noted some of the bookshops handling his books and mentioned "in Houston, the book department at *Foley's* now stocks constantly all titles we have in print."[72]

Whenever Stagecoach Press issued a new book or Christmas card, Fuermann mentioned it in his "Post Card" column. In December 1961, he reproduced Jack and Charlotte's Christmas card set and printed in the form of a rebus (using illustrated pictures with individual letters to depict words or a phrase) "Mr. R. printed the rebus in three colors. The puzzles within the rebus are what printers call 'type dingbats,' of which Rittenhouse has a collection of more than 600, some dating back 150 years."[73]

Shortly before the Rittenhouse family moved to Santa Fe, Jack published *Baca's Battle*, by V. B. Beckett. Fuermann took note of the book and Jack's introduction in which he wrote, "Another aspect of the forces at work in that time and place was the attitude of and toward the men from Texas. The continuing surface rivalry between some Texans and some New Mexicans is a condition to be deplored, but its roots are ancient."[74] The book told the story of Elfego Baca holed up in a shack in 1884 where he withstood a siege by eighty cowboys.[75]

With *Baca's Battle* off the press and back from the binders, the Rittenhouse family packed for their move to Santa Fe. The time had come to live in the place that had been calling them for years. Jack had transitioned smoothly from the advertising business into the world of editing, setting type, and printing books of interest. Stagecoach Press, well established and gaining an ever-widening reputation, published unusually attractive but affordable books and regularly won awards. Douglas was at home in the safe and caring environment of the Austin State School for Mentally Retarded, and their daughters would soon be approaching adolescence. His final years in the advertising world had boosted his financial stability and provided a comfortable living for his family in a ranch-style home in the suburbs with room for growing collections of books and printing equipment.

Even with reservations about Houston and Texas, Jack's years on the Gulf Coast had been fulfilling in many ways. His leadership in business organizations and participation in intellectual activities had brought respected members of the community together, and he expanded his network of friends and associates involved in history, books, and printing. He left advertising and entered another world for which he had been preparing over many decades—printing and publishing books that would contribute to knowledge about the West.

Leaving Texas would not be difficult. "My personal tastes did not align with the popular preferences in Houston. I did not care for football games, golf, prejudice against blacks and Mexicans, anti-intellectualism that couldn't handle polysyllabic words, a dearth of old book stores, provincial minds that proclaimed anything Texas as good and anything non-Texas as traitorous. These did not apply everywhere, but I often felt adrift, with few kindred souls."[76] To lighten his load he sold some of his collections and several of his presses. His books on petroleum history went to the University of Wyoming and his extensive Ellis Plan material, to the Medill School of Journalism at Northwestern University. As soon as the huge Washington press left his shop, Jack and his family moved to a new home in Santa Fe, New Mexico, fulfilling a ten-year dream.

(*top*) Figure 1. Jack Rittenhouse with homemade pedal car, Queen Creek, Arizona, 1918. © HBLT.
(*middle*) Figure 2. Jack Rittenhouse (right), Boy Scout Troop 35, Pine Tree Patrol. © HBLT.
(*bottom*) Figure 3. Jack Rittenhouse's model of Fulton's Steamboat Clermont, 1944. © HBLT.

(*top*) Figure 4. Jack Rittenhouse in his 1924 Model-T Ford. © HBLT.
(*bottom left*) Figure 5. Jack Rittenhouse, college junior, 1933. © HBLT.
(*bottom right*) Figure 6. Jack Rittenhouse at Long Lake, Indiana, summer 1935. New Mexico State University Library, Archives and Special Collections.

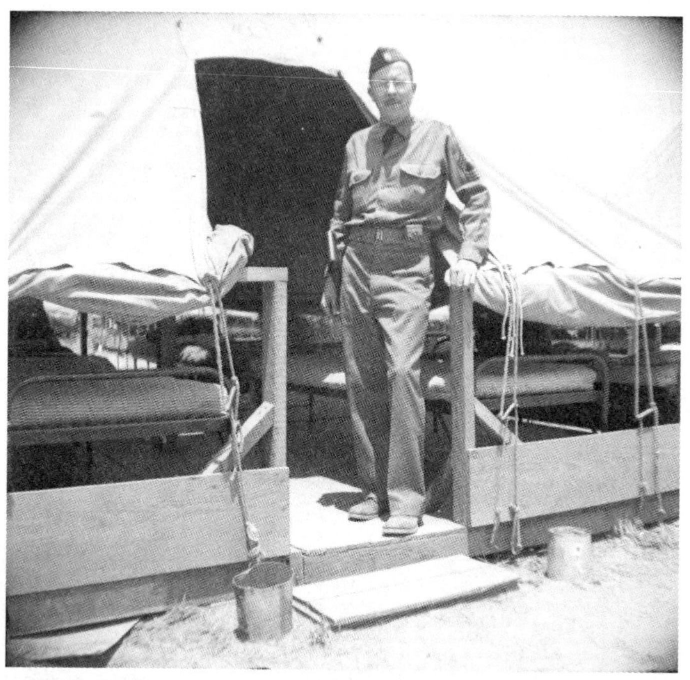

(*top*) Figure 7. Jack Rittenhouse, Mess Sergeant, California State Guard, 1942. New Mexico State University Library, Archives and Special Collections.

(*bottom left*) Figure 8. Charlotte at Union newspaper office, Chicago, 1944. J. Rittenhouse © HBLT.

(*bottom right*) Figure 9. Charlotte and Jack, wedding, St. Louis, September 17, 1944. © HBLT.

Figure 10. Charlotte at campsite, Last Chance Canyon, Mojave Desert. Photograph by Jack D. Rittenhouse. New Mexico State University Library, Archives and Special Collections.

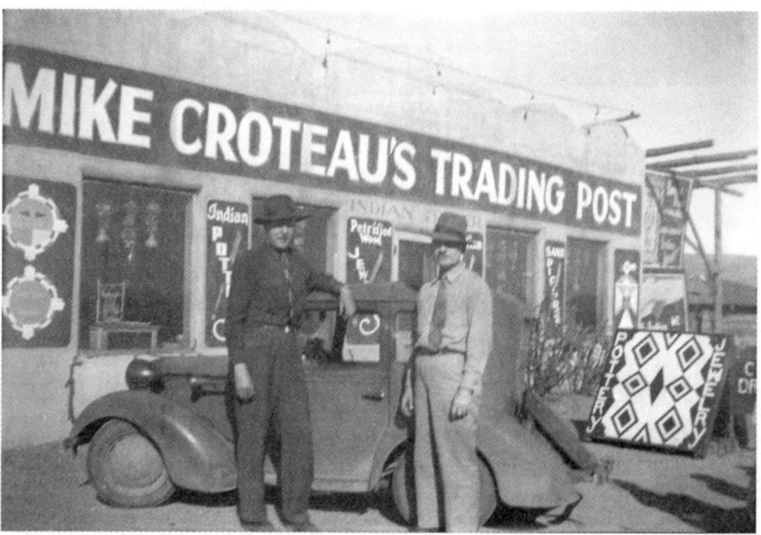

Figure 11. Jack Hillman and Jack Rittenhouse (right) beside Bantam coupe at Croteau's Trading Post, Route 66, Grants, New Mexico. New Mexico State University Library, Archives and Special Collections.

(*top*) Figure 12. Jack Rittenhouse at his Gally's Universal Press, Sierra Madre, California, 1950. New Mexico State University Library, Archives and Special Collections. (*bottom*) Figure 13. Printed inscription from Jack Rittenhouse to William Cheney accompanying first Stagecoach Press publication, A Showing of Type Faces. Courtesy John D. Randall.

DeaR BRO. CHENEY – MANY
tHANks for YOURT yPE booK
HopE I can geT UP neaR ITS QUaLIty In
Time BUT MUST clena MY
cASes 1st Jack

(*top*) Figure 14. Jack Rittenhouse setting wood type, Houston. New Mexico State University Library, Archives and Special Collections.
(*bottom*) Figure 15. Jack Rittenhouse with two-handle roller at his Washington handpress, Houston. New Mexico State University Library, Archives and Special Collections.

Figure 16. Jack Rittenhouse with his Adams Cottage field press, Houston. New Mexico State University Library, Archives and Special Collections.

The PHOTOGRAPHER
and the RIVER, 1889-90

FRANKLIN A. NIMS'
COLORADO CANYON DIARY

EDITED BY DWIGHT L. SMITH

DIARY OF
An Excursion
to the Ruins of
Abo, Quarra and
Gran Quivira
in New Mexico
in 1853

UNDER THE COMMAND OF
MAJOR JAMES HENRY CARLETON

OVER THE
SANTA FE TRAIL
1857

From the original 1905 edition by
William B. Napton. Introduction
by Donald C. Cutter Published by
the Stagecoach Press, Santa Fe, 1964

Figure 17. Stagecoach Press book covers.

Figure 18. Baroid Company publicity shot, Jack Rittenhouse, 1959. © HBLT.

Figure 19. Jack and Charlotte, street photo, San Francisco. © HBLT.

(*top*) Figure 20. Jack Rittenhouse on Route 66, Albuquerque, ca. 1988. New Mexico State University Library, Archives and Special Collections.
(*bottom*) Figure 21. Marc Simmons and Jack Rittenhouse, Santa Fe Plaza. © HBLT.

(*top*) Figure 22. Jack with granddaughter, Karen Briley, at Vandercook press on his seventy-fifth birthday, 1987. H. Briley © HBLT.
(*bottom*) Figure 23. Home Among Reference Books. Photo by R. J. Hart.

Figure 24. Jack Rittenhouse. Photo by Cynthia Farah, New Mexico State University Library, Archives and Special Collections.

Chapter 7

Santa Fe, at Last

> Real gems are the little local-history booklets cranked out by small town job printers and sold only in village gift shops. A four-bit pamphlet picked up this way, packs a small thrill when you later find it listed at $5.00 in a rare book catalog. Best of all, they are fun to read! Yes, Virginia, there are book shops in New Mexico!
>
> —JACK D. RITTENHOUSE[1]

JACK'S LIBRARY AND PRINTING equipment in Houston had expanded significantly to include a book collection insured for ten thousand dollars and a one-thousand-square-foot, fully equipped press shop. As sole proprietor of Stagecoach Press, now his principal business venture, he assumed full responsibility for the costs of leaving Houston and realized his budget would not cover moving tons of printing equipment and books to Santa Fe. To reduce moving expenses he offered to sell his New Mexico book collection to Larry Powell at UCLA, "the first move in making the sale that will ensure my move to Santa Fe," he wrote to his friend, W. D. Grisso. "Now I have to sweat out his acceptance."[2] Grisso told Arthur McAnally, library director at Oklahoma University (OU), about the New Mexico collection coming to the market, mentioning that although UCLA had right of first refusal, Jack was seriously looking for a buyer. When Powell bought only a small part of the collection, OU quickly stepped in with a major order.

Through connections made over the past decade in Texas, Jack also began selling some of his printing presses. A friend in Waco, Sam Lanham, wanted to start a private press and needed equipment to do so. He bought Jack's Adams Cottage Press, and with it started his own imprint, the Waco Village Press.[3] A short time later he also bought Jack's R. Hoe and Company platen press, once on loan to the San Jacinto Monument. In Houston, William Hudson, interested in launching his own private press, bought Jack's majestic one-ton Washington press.

Jack also bought a rebuilt 1912 Model 5 Linotype machine to save time and costs for his future typesetting.[4] He wrote Grisso,

> I really am not overjoyed at putting one in, but I have no choice if I am to get type at a price I can afford. The big shops who can handle my work charge extremely high prices. The small typesetters usually handle short jobs and they set large book jobs aside. My best supplier held a manuscript for six months without being able to "find time," and I finally had to pull it back. To give you some idea of the variation in costs, a small typesetter bid $350 to set one book; another wanted $500 and a third wanted $700. A year ago the $350 price would have been only about $275.[5]

Jack thought he might have to pay $1,195 for the Linotype, but he managed to close the deal with $850 cash. He told his friend, "It seems there is now a buyers' market in Linotypes because many smaller newspapers are switching over to offset printing."[6] Following these changes he wrote Grisso: "Tell Dr. McAnally that his purchases will move the Stagecoach Press to Santa Fe. Since my machinery and related equipment will be crated and shipped via freight, his purchases will pay their total shipping costs all the way."[7]

In Santa Fe Jack rented a small building at 115 Tesuque Drive, off Cerrillos Road, for his Stagecoach Press operation. At last, "a printshop where I could look out of the window and see a mountain, and print books about the old Southwest."[8] There he set up his Gally Universal and Vandercook presses, along with his Linotype and cabinets containing 150 fonts of type, "most of it old and unusual. Oldest font is a special casting made from matrices cut in the 18th century. Several fonts of fancy wooden type from 1880's, and many fonts of type secured from old newspapers in such Texas towns as Somerville, Meridian, Cold Spring, Georgetown, Austin, San Antonio and Houston. Special fonts have been imported from London, Paris and West Germany."[9]

He was especially fond of the type ornaments he had collected in Texas. "The best prize of all was a cabinet containing about 700 stock electrotypes and engravings of the vintage 1870–1910." The cabinet and cuts came from the Dealy-Adey Company in Houston, a major printer and stationer founded late in the nineteenth century. When the company closed in 1960, Jack bought a fifteen-drawer turquoise cabinet holding the dingbats and cuts he later enjoyed selecting for typographical elements in his books and other printing.[10] Near the presses he set a work stand acquired twenty-three years earlier in Sierra Madre to hold his small Kelsey press. Now the stand was just the right size and heft for a large Bavarian lithograph stone with its perfectly true surface on which he set type before locking it in the chase for printing.

He could anticipate settling back into the print shop routines he enjoyed immensely. "The move played hob with production schedules. One large book, Fallen Guidon, was in process at the time. Part of the presswork was done by a shop in Louisiana, and the book was sent to the bindery before we left Houston. Copies were delivered to Santa Fe, and it became our first book to bear a Santa Fe imprint."[11] Jack found sales for the new book refreshingly strong, but only after he navigated the bureaucracy of the Santa Fe Post Office.

> The P.O. men accomplish minor miracles every day, in spite of regulations from above that change every hour on the hour. The

> Santa Fe men are a tribe apart. Example: when you rent a P.O. Box you continue to receive all mail addressed to all previous holders of that box for years back. Example: when I went to the information desk to ask about a permit to use business reply envelopes, the clerk asked, "what's that?" When you wrote to 115 Tesuque, they said "no such street," but yesterday when my office light bill came they couldn't deny the existence of the place and the bill reached me all right. And so my business reply envelopes continued to stack up back inside the P.O. for two weeks and then someone must have wandered in somewhere and asked, "What do I do with these?" There were orders for about 150 copies of FALLEN GUIDON in that one batch, and I felt better.[12]

Over the following year, as Jack's routines smoothed out, Stagecoach Press issued four titles: *Mines of the Old Southwest* by Rex Arrowsmith; *From Where the Sun Now Stands* by W. D. Grisso; *Fort Union in Miniature* by Robert Utley; and *The Great Endurance Horse Race* by Jack Schaefer. When Arrowsmith's book sold out, Jack issued a second printing, but this success was offset by Utley's book on Fort Union. Designed as a miniature with pages less than an inch high, it was hard to market. "We hoped to tap the rich tourist trade—but we found that bookshops considered it a curio and the curio shops considered it a book—so both felt it was out of their field. Another rap on the wrist warning us to stick to our last! Only such specialist dealers as Glen Dawson did well with it." Jack scrapped plans for a series of four more miniature books. "The move to Santa Fe brought us to the heartland of the Southwest, midway between Houston and Los Angeles, and close to the old archives. At the same time, it posed difficulties in production: No trade typesetters equipped for trade book work, no paper houses stocking high-grade text papers, no trade binderies doing edition work."[13]

His Linotype became essential to the economics of Stagecoach Press. With a new font of matrices in ten pt. Caledonia "and every book we could find in print on how to operate or adjust a Linotype," he set to work. He had only a couple of hours' instruction on its operation, but over the next two years, he and Charlotte set type for six books. "Bit by bit, as the machine stopped, jammed, lurched, squirted and stuck I learned how to get it going again—a little better each time. There can be no greater tribute to the world of books than this experience, and my debt is immeasurable to Harding and Loomis' Linecasting Operator-Machinist and Ashworth's Operation and Mechanism of the Linotype and Intertype."[14]

Later, for his 1964 edition of *A Desperado in Arizona, 1858–1860*, he and Charlotte bound an entire print run of a book for the first time in their new shop, using an old Smythe curved needle book stitcher. "This was our most baffling experience, for no instruction books are available, and 96 per cent of our information had to be gained only through trial and error on the machine itself."[15]

A Desperado in Arizona offers a good case study on how he found interesting books that deserved to be reprinted. He did not know about the book until he opened an antiquarian bookseller's catalog that came in the mail and read the description of an unusual rarity from 1862. Checking two bibliographies on his reference shelves, he saw that the book had merit, so he wrote the Library of Congress, which had no copy but identified the two libraries that did. One of them sent Jack a microfilm negative from which he produced a set of prints to follow in typesetting.

Jack also kept his eye on the bottom line and knew precisely how to gauge costs and returns on each title. He kept meticulous notes on the time and money required for every step in making each book: documenting exact costs for editing, designing and planning layouts, setting type, securing paper and binding cloth, press time, binding time, publicity, and postage. He encouraged standing orders from libraries, booksellers, and collectors, while closely tracking the reviews each book generated. With Charlotte's help they kept clipping files of all the reviews for Stagecoach Press books, files reflecting widespread admiration for the contents and production standards of Stagecoach publications.

When speaking or writing about his private press experiences, Jack explained that small publishing ventures generated an uneven flow of income. One month would bring three hundred dollars in receipts; another brought three thousand dollars. At times he waited six months for payment from some of the large university libraries. To stabilize his cash flow, he quietly gave preferential status for Stagecoach Press books and antiquarian books to private collectors who sent checks with their orders. When ordering supplies he bought on a cash-with-order basis, earning a 2 percent discount. He projected that Stagecoach Press would eventually need fifty titles in print and in stock to become fiscally sound. "On some titles we would have a large first-year stock; on others we would have a small fifth-year stock. Each year we would bring out about ten new books, and about ten of the old ones would go out of print. Some of those going out of print would be recent books, but others would be older ones, as the rate of sale is uneven."[16]

When Jack happily informed his faithful Stagecoach Press customers in New Mexico about relocating the press to Santa Fe, they embraced his move. Among librarians with standing orders for every new Stagecoach book was William S. Wallace, librarian and archivist at New Mexico Highlands in Las Vegas. Soon Wallace invited Jack to the library to speak, and shortly thereafter printed part of the talk, "Hallmarks of Fine Printing," in the *Rogers Library Notes* through which Wallace cultivated friends of the library and kept them informed about library developments. He ran Jack's contribution as the lead article, followed by a note from Wallace heralding the move of Stagecoach Press from Houston to Santa Fe as "an important event in the long history of the printed word in New Mexico. . . . So far as I know it is the only private press in the state specializing in books of the finest design and workmanship. Rittenhouse books have been acclaimed by many leaders in the book trade and some of the leading university libraries have 'standing orders' for every title he publishes or designs. The librarians and book collectors of the state should feel honored to have Rittenhouse in our midst."[17]

In October 1962 Jack drove to Denver for the second annual meeting of the newly formed Western History Association. At the first meeting in Santa Fe a year earlier, he had decided he would only pay for a booth or a table in the book exhibit room every other year, so this was a year to work out of his briefcase.

> I sold about $300.00 worth of books and stuff; lined up one more good book dealer; spudded in on three more books to publish; added somewhat over 100 good names to my mailing lists; made the acquaintance of at least a dozen new customers who will become more or less "regulars;" made considerable progress on my New Mexico Bibliography; had good visits with three of my regular large-scale dealers; picked up some printing supplies not readily available closer than Denver, plus bringing back a load of paper with savings enough on freight to pay my gas one way; and checked out . . . all the bookbinderies in Denver in case I need one closer than San Antonio, Texas. In addition, I met Savoie Lottinville and got better acquainted; as well as meeting several other old friends.[18]

After listening to Bill Goetzmann's lecture on the Wheeler Survey, Jack visited Fred Rosenstock's antiquarian book shop on Colfax. There he read part of an 1879 book by William H. Rideing, a young newspaperman who traveled with the Wheeler party through southern Colorado, New Mexico, and part of Arkansas. Jack bought the book, and back at the conference persuaded Goetzmann to write an introduction should he select it for a new Stagecoach Press title.[19] Before the conference ended, he talked with representatives from Yale University Press who expressed interest in his bibliography of books about New Mexico (1808–1962). He also welcomed Archibald Hanna's offer to send copies of every card relating to New Mexico in the catalog files at Yale's Beinecke Library.[20] "This is quite an undertaking and will be a big help to me. Thus you can see that at these big 'camp meetings,' it is possible to get an idea and make immense headway on it all at one time with a minimum of beating around." With copies of the Beinecke Library cards on New Mexico, he could fill many gaps in his growing New Mexico bibliography. In another letter to Grisso he reflected on the WHA conference: "In my advertising days I 'worked' a lot of conventions, but this was the first time that I enjoyed every minute of the deal not only as business but as fun, because so many of the people are really friends."[21]

Soon after the WHA meeting in Denver, several Santa Fe participants organized the Corral de Santa Fe Westerners. James T. Forrest, director of the Museum of New Mexico, and Robert M. Utley, regional historian with the National Park Service, drew upon their experience in other corrals to help shape the organization. Most likely, Jack was part of the planning for the new El Corral, and without a doubt, he was central to its steady growth and outreach. As soon as the organization formed, members elected Jack as *El Alguacíl*, sheriff of the new Corral. He set type and printed a newsletter, *La Gaceta: El Boletin del Corral de Santa Fe Westerners*, for the next three years starting with volume 1, no. 1 in October 1963. "Space is too short—and routines not yet been set up—for book reviews in this issue, but with local Westerners Todd Webb and Jack Schaefer just out with new titles, we should not lack material for the next issue. One of these times we may devote an issue to the writers in our Corral, since we can field a better percentage than most Corrals in this regard."[22]

Jack also wrote in *La Gaceta* about the second annual meeting of WHA which he, James T. Forrest, Robert G. Ferris, and Bob Utley had just attended along with four hundred other WHA members. "Western publishers were out in force displaying an array of books almost overwhelming. The Stagecoach Press booth was observed to be transacting a healthy business. (Observed a Washingtonian: 'Rittenhouse is a low-pressure salesman. He told anecdotes for twenty minutes and I wound up buying every item on the table.')"[23]

Jack also printed the announcements for the Westerners' monthly dinner programs at La Posada. With the possible exception of one or two Corrals in California, El Corral de Santa Fe was probably the only chapter of Westerners throughout the country that produced handset letterpress notices for their meetings, attractively designed using original nineteenth century-display type. Some of the most notable were cards announcing talks by Jack Schaefer, Dr. Myra Ellen Jenkins, Curtis Schaafsma, Marc Simmons, Helen Greene Blumenschein, and John Gaw Meem.

The printing shop for Stagecoach Press was also a welcoming place for visitors to Santa Fe, drawn to good books and the smell of fresh ink on paper. For anyone spending time with printers or with press work, this aroma was the harbinger of interesting reading material. While Jack did not host gatherings at his press, visitors were always welcome even when unannounced. Carl Hertzog visited whenever he was in town to catch up on Jack's news and see what was just coming off the press. Marc Simmons, finishing his PhD in history at the University of New Mexico, stopped by one day because he heard about Stagecoach Press and wanted to meet its founder. He showed Jack a translation he had made of a 1773 document by Pedro Fermín de Mendinueta, the Spanish colonial governor of Santa Fe. It was a report on Indian and mission affairs, and Jack quickly offered to publish it. *Indian and Mission Affairs in New Mexico, 1773* was published in 1965 by Stagecoach Press in an edition of 250 copies. Thus began their long friendship working together on behalf of the Corral de Santa Fe Westerners, the Historical Society of New Mexico, the statewide historic preservation committee, and promotion and protection of the historic Santa Fe Trail.

Jack also began planning the launch of another newsletter, *New Mexico Book News* (*NMBN*) for 1964. He, alone, was responsible for this modest but influential monthly periodical, a statewide book and publication-related newsletter, and a first for New Mexico. Jack most likely drew ideas from a similar publication Lawrence Clark Powell had started seven years earlier at UCLA with *Books of the Southwest: A Critical Checklist of Current Southwestern Americana*. He was not seeking to match the scope of a monthly publication issued by UCLA with its team of bibliographers and reference librarians gathering information from thousands of new books published throughout the year. While Powell chose the entire Southwest for the coverage and distribution of his book news, Jack began bringing together a New Mexico community of authors, readers, librarians, booksellers, and publishers devoted to the printed word in his new home state. Even with the smaller geographical scope, *NMBN* was a large task for one man working with two assistants when all of them were also setting type and printing Stagecoach Press books.

Jack approached New Mexico as his backyard with a history worth telling and with readers all over the state ready to learn about books devoted to their history. Before moving to Santa Fe he had spent time in every town in the state with a population of five thousand or more. He had called on bookshops wherever he went, and he also photographed every town through which he drove, formulating plans for a photo-census of New Mexico townscapes. His approach to *New Mexico Book News* was similar to a small-town newspaper editor reaching out to their community with news of everyday happenings, writing in a relaxed, pithy style. In Jack's mind the interactions taking place all over the state among readers, writers, booksellers, publishers, and librarians contributed to an underappreciated New Mexico book community that was newsworthy and deserved more attention.

Jack printed *New Mexico Book News* on a single sheet folded twice to make a nine-inch by six-inch, six-page issue with annotated listings of all new books, pamphlets, periodicals, and bulletins relating to the state. He included news of authors and publishers in New Mexico, along with other book-related news. His press release announcing *NMBN* noted that New Mexico had more than thirty large and small publishers, "many of them not publicized in the usual book trade channels. Much of their output goes unnoticed. In addition, more than 60 national book publishers issue books of importance to New Mexicans."[24] The cost of a single issue was twenty cents, with an annual subscription for two dollars. Jack did all the research and writing while Charlotte helped maintain the growing subscription list, edited copy, and ran the linotype. A recent college graduate, Richard

Polese, helped with some of the printing and mailing. Jack's press release and gratis copies generated notes and stories in the *Santa Fe New Mexican*, the *Taos News*, the *El Paso Times*, the *Albuquerque Tribune*, *Books of the Southwest*, the State Historical Society of Colorado, and *Antiquarian Bookman* in New York. Mary Kate Tripp, books editor of *Amarillo Sunday News Globe*, devoted substantial space to the new publication within a month of its first appearance.

Jack followed his news release and launch of the first issue with a small broadside headed "A New Free Publicity Medium for You!," in which he described the scope of his coverage for books relating to New Mexico and also profiled the intended audience: all New Mexico libraries (school, college, and special), all New Mexico book dealers and collectors; and "all dealers, libraries, and collectors elsewhere who are interested in New Mexico." On a different card he printed the message: "Here is a sample copy of the first issue. Sorry you weren't represented, but we haven't heard from you since we wrote. Remember, we review EVERY new book or pamphlet we receive that has anything to do—in whole or in part—with New Mexico or is written by a New Mexico author. Keep us in mind. Just send a review copy to *New Mexico Book News*."[25] As the active subscription list for *NMBN* grew, he pitched it again with a free sample and a note card printed on his press: "Here is a sample issue of the *New Mexico Book News*, now in its second year. No other state has a bulletin like it! Each month it lists new books, pamphlets, maps, magazines about New Mexico—many not listed elsewhere. It tracks down elusive local-history printers, digs out hard-to-find items, covers major publishers, and makes your selection easier." He printed a subscription blank at the bottom of the card.[26]

NMBN documented the passing of writers and notable book collectors such as Oliver LaFarge and T. W. Streeter. It called attention to new publishers such as the Press of the Territorian in Santa Fe, noted articles of New Mexico interest in popular magazines such as *True West*, *Sports Illustrated*, *Atlantic Monthly*, and *Good Housekeeping*, and listed new administrative appointments to such organizations as the

New Mexico State Records Center and Archives and the NM Supreme Court Law Library, along with articles of interest to New Mexicans appearing in the historical journals of neighboring states.

The tone of the publication was noncritical except when poor writing got under Jack's skin. Commenting on an article from *New Mexico Business* for October 1965, he wrote, "The *Book News* departs here from its usual straight reporting to suggest that the authors read Rudolf Flesch's 'Art of Readable Writing.'"[27] Yet, Jack could just as quickly offer a mea culpa, as in his July 1965 note, "No More $100 Books."

> The article previously appearing here on rare N.M. books selling at $100 or more has brought mixed reactions. Some librarians said it had helped them decide which books should be placed in restricted collections. Other librarians said the list was a "handy guide for book thieves." Rare book dealers said the list was causing some book owners to demand full, sky-high prices for books offered to dealers. But other dealers said the list helped them justify higher retail sales prices. . . . Other collectors said the list was ending their success in bargain-hunting by causing dealers to hike price tags. Majority vote: negative. Hence no more such lists.[28]

Toward the end of the second year for *NMBN*, Jack added a new feature demonstrating his vision for a community of book people in New Mexico. He believed his readers should know where to find books wherever they traveled in the state. "YOUR SHOP LISTED IN OUR DIRECTORY—FREE. Look in this issue of the *New Mexico Book News*. Note that we are listing every bookdealer in the state, so buyers from out of town can visit or write for books. We want to list you. There is NO CHARGE, and you do not have to be a subscriber." He asked that anyone responding give the name and address for their book shop and to note whether books were a sideline in a gift, stationery, or drug store, or if their book business were conducted through an open shop, only by mail, or by appointment.

Jack's directory of book sources throughout the state was most likely inspired by a letter Spud Johnson ran in his regular column, "The Santa Fe Gadfly," published in the *Santa Fe New Mexican*. Spud wrote about an "unknown correspondent," Mrs. Pearson, and her complaint concerning the "dearth of bookshops in New Mexico." Jack responded: "If you'll give me until January 15th to double-check my facts, I can give you an interesting and non-quarrelsome reply to the lady who complained about 'no bookshops' . . . . I sat down today and listed 75 dealers in books in New Mexico, not including paperback racks in markets, junk bookshelves in second-hand stores or free-lance individuals who order books for a small clientele. This includes 31 communities. Not many are big-time shops, but I have found collectors' items, interesting local publications, etc., in places from Fort Union to Lordsburg and from Farmington to Hobbs. Mrs. Pearson drove right by some of her best bets." He went on to note that beyond the fifteen full-scale bookshops in New Mexico stocking five thousand or more hardcover titles, other sources included shops at the national monuments of Fort Union, Bandelier, Chaco Canyon, Gran Quivira, and Carlsbad Caverns. There, the Southwestern Monuments Association offered carefully selected books devoted to the Southwest. He mentioned book-and-gift shops in towns from Alamogordo and Artesia to Roswell and Ruidoso, along with stationery stores and book stalls at the Fred Harvey hotels.[29]

Jack's letter to Spud ended with suggestions from a "confirmed bookhunter." One "gambit," asking questions and telling a book dealer where you were headed next, might reveal such "off-the-path" experts as L. E. Gay in Lordsburg, Bob Kadlec and Stagecoach Press in Santa Fe, Claire Morrill in Taos, or Tom Davies in Albuquerque. "Another bookhunter's device is to look for a 'rare' book in a new book store," seeking books that were out of print but still in demand. "Real gems are the little local-history booklets cranked out by small town job printers and sold only in village gift shops. A four-bit pamphlet picked up this way, packs a small thrill when you later find it listed at $5.00 in a rare book catalog. Best of all, they are fun to read! Yes,

Virginia, there are bookshops in New Mexico!" Jack signed his letter with NEW MEXICO BOOK NEWS beneath his name. When Spud Johnson printed it in "The Gadfly" he said, "Mr. Rittenhouse might well have used the foregoing letter as the leading article in the next issue of his 'Book News,'" thereby giving another plug for the new publication devoted to books in New Mexico.[30]

At the end of the first year for *NMBN* Jack offered hundreds of review copies of books sent to him to the New Mexico State Library at 40 percent off the publisher's list price. The offer fulfilled a promise made earlier to the state librarian, an opportunity to acquire new, clean, unmarked books in perfect condition, all pertaining to New Mexico. He chose wisely the library of record for his adopted state.

With *New Mexico Book News* Jack helped lay the foundation for a vibrant statewide renaissance of the New Mexico book community starting to emerge in the 1970s and thriving for the next thirty years with emphasis on reading, writing, printing, publishing, bookselling, and collecting, the six legs of a very large table filled with many books. His sharing of information with all who were interested in books in as many forums and quarters as he could reach inspired others who followed him to organize and promote books in New Mexico widely and successfully. By 1994 the state was invited as the Guest of Honor Region at the Feria Internacional del Libro de Guadalajara. Hundreds of New Mexico books were featured at the largest book fair in the Spanish-speaking world and in the Americas, the second-largest book fair in the world. New Mexico authors reading and signing at the fair included Rudolfo Anaya, Demetria Martínez, John Brandi, Jim Sagel, Lucy Tapahonso, and Jimmy Santiago Baca, among others.

Jack's promotion of books for all led to lasting friendships, especially with some of his Stagecoach Press authors. He formed a warm relationship in the 1960s with W. D. Grisso of Oklahoma City whose book *From Where the Sun Now Stands* Stagecoach Press published in 1963. Grisso, president of the Van-Grisso Oil Company, reached out to Jack in the summer of 1960 trying to identify the authorship of an article in the *Baroid News Bulletin*. A friend, Col. John M. Virden, had brought the article to Grisso's attention. "This copy of the trade magazine Baroid, which came in yesterday's mail, has one of the most sprightly accounts of the Civil War in the West I have ever read. And I do wish the editor had taken the trouble [to] give the author of that piece a by-line. Whoever the author is he certainly does know his Civil War . . . and I pray that my piece in LIFE is even half so articulate."[31] After verifying Jack's authorship, Grisso introduced him to Virden, initiating a three-way correspondence centering in part on the Civil War.

As a history enthusiast, Grisso enjoyed reading in many subject areas, including the American West, the Civil War, and Oklahoma history. He observed in a letter to Jack that New Mexico under Spain, Mexico, and the United States "is a great, and barely scratched, literary mine, and I am not talking about more books about Bill Bonney." He was also among several people who informed Jack of a forthcoming meeting in Santa Fe. The gathering would include a variety of lectures on the history of the West and end by organizing a new society, the Western History Association. "We will be there and hope you, too, are."[32]

Jack's involvement with WHA over the next four decades would become key to his network among Western historians and writers as he anticipated his move to New Mexico, placing him in the heart of the Southwest. His cordial response to Grisso's letter set the tone for a more personal relationship going forward: "Dear Mr. Grisso, your letter of January 6 was a most pleasant start for the new year. Quite a coincidence that you met Calvin Horn and that my name came up during the conversation! Yes, we are planning to move to New Mexico, but it will probably not be for about fifteen months. We have a 13-year old son who is mentally retarded as a result of a brain injury at birth, and we can't move until we have completed all details of getting [him] placed in a proper school which has a long waiting list."[33] As their correspondence progressed, Grisso recalled an article about a log jam on the Red River for the *Baroid News Bulletin* and asked Jack if he had written it. After confirming he had written "The Biggest Log Jam in History," he sent Grisso his latest book, *New Mexico Civil War*

Bibliography, further strengthening their ties. Grisso enlarged Jack's circle, introducing him to the OU director of libraries, keen on acquiring a complete set of the Baroid publications for his library, already strong in petroleum-related materials. Jack contacted his former colleagues and bound volumes of the Baroid bulletin soon arrived in the mailroom at OU Library.

After a fishing trip on the Gulf of Mexico in late winter 1962, Grisso stopped by Jack's press in Houston before equipment was packed for the move to New Mexico. Jack's next letter reflects their shared interest in books and book talk. "Your visit was a real highlight, and I will be glad when we can get together for more such sessions. It's a lonely life down here in book-ways, except for the mails. There are so many personalities and ideas I wanted to talk about that were not germane to the purpose of our first visit: talk about bookshops in Oklahoma . . . the libraries at the universities . . . people such as Ramon Adams and Mrs. Zoe Tilghman and Jim Northe and the late Will Ransom and a host of others about whom my knowledge is vague . . . and more about New Mexico." Jack also shared his thoughts about what constituted a private press, making a distinction between printers like Hertzog who did not "seek all and any printing jobs" he could get, in contrast with

> printers such as Grabhorn, Ritchie, Dahlstrom, Kennedy, Marks and others (all in the Far West) who will print anything for anyone who will pay the price, but they do not issue such works as publication of their presses. . . . Such firms are generally known as "fine press" printers rather than "private press" printers, but there is no fixed definition. . . . Whether you talk about fine books, fine tailoring, fine sports cars, fine rifles, fine fishing tackle . . . the standards of the hand-crafted products have made the commercial producers raise their own standards. The "fine press" printer is therefore a useful burr under the saddle.[34]

Jack was helping Grisso understand some of the dynamics of

Stagecoach Press as publisher of *From Where the Sun Now Stands*, an anthology of memorable lectures by notable people in the West.

Regarding his book project, Grisso spent much of 1962 writing Jack mainly about content selections, an introduction, and a possible bibliography, all the while seeking advice from McAnally at the OU Library. Part of their exchange related to a bibliography at the end of the book, about which McAnally explained to Grisso the different types of bibliographies and what was needed. Grisso queried Jack about enlarging the scope of the book from thirty-four pages to sixty-four and then began having second thoughts about some of his selections. At one point, McAnally urged Grisso to finalize his decision of what to include so Jack could move forward with editing and production. Clearly Jack and McAnally realized their friend had little experience producing a book. Once the book was under way, Grisso asked Jack if "there would be any market for a book edited from Colonel Virden's letters?"[35]

Jack let the question of a book of Virden's letters rest for a day while he outlined how he would lay out their current book. "In my planning, I consider every page that goes through the press, including all the front and back matter. A 64-page book would lay out about as follows. . . ." A concise and clear description followed, item by item, page by page. "Now that I have my own Linotype machine, adding extra pages is not quite the chore it once was. My suggestion would be for you to work only roughly toward a limit of pages, and we can block out the approximate format when we meet in August."[36]

The following day Jack was at his diplomatic best with an answer to Grisso's question regarding a book of Virden's letters. "This is a tough one to answer, chiefly because I have seen only a few of his letters and can't fully visualize the scope or content of such a book. All I know is that he writes wonderful letters, intriguing to read and full of 'thoughty stuff.' Yet even with the highest merit, books that consist of a collection of letters or columns or articles by one person are in a class of book that is hardest to sell." He believed that Grisso's book of speeches "will do well because it is a western book, and I have the channels through which to sell a western book. Also, you have many already-famous names in the book." He gave Grisso names of several publishers with market channels through which to sell Civil War books should he and Virden want to contact them about a new book of letters. Jack closed with an insightful paragraph that again reveals why he was such a successful editor-publisher: "The only explanation I can offer for the difficulty of selling such a book is that the prospective purchaser has no clear idea of what the book is about. If you tell the . . . buyer that the book is a novel or a mystery story or a book of humor or a history, the buyer grasps the idea quickly and can understand what it will give him in the way of entertainment or knowledge."[37]

The next six months they exchanged letters about dropping or adding different speeches, who might write an introduction, whether an introduction was really needed, suggestions of where to sell the book in Oklahoma, Grisso's ideas for yet another book about saloons, and his query about a timeline for production even though final contents were still in flux. In measured tones Jack kept the focus on the book at hand and was able to begin setting type in November, with the first set of galley proofs going to Grisso by the end of the month. Amid this activity Grisso began organizing an Oklahoma Corral of Westerners and invited Jack to come speak in March.

Early in 1963 Jack revealed to Grisso some of the realities he faced as he began production of *Where the Sun Now Stands*.

> After months of small frustrations and delays, I am now running full blast, finally. 1962 was a confusing year for me. I knew at the start . . . that I would move to Santa Fe . . . somehow, and this became a part of every plan I made. Every project was gauged in accordance with this in mind, and it blocked many a good idea. Also, I had no idea of the tremendous amount of time required in preparing for the move and later getting set up again in Santa Fe . . . to say nothing of the expenses involved. Publishing-wise, January through August of 1962 were miserable. But September

through January, 1963, have been good, steady months that have [been] very promising.[38]

"Running full blast" meant Jack could also think more clearly about the Grisso book, now grown to seventy-three pages, too big to let Jack break even, let alone be profitable if he kept the price down to $4.95. He proposed an idea credited to Carl Hertzog—produce two editions to solve the problem of bulk and price. "One will be a regular edition, cloth bound and jacketed like all of my books, trimmed to the standard size of 8 1/4 by 5 1/2 inches (page size), in an edition of 650 copies, to retail at $4.95. The other will be a special edition, which I will call the 'Cimarron Edition' (named for the river that unites three great Southwestern states). This will be limited to 99 copies, printed on a deluxe deckle-edged paper, with the top edge stained, bound with more care and with special paper for end-leaves, and in a slipcase, with all copies signed by editor and printer, and with a larger trim size." This edition would sell at $15.00 a copy; Grisso would get five free copies of each edition; Jack would not offer the special edition to the general trade until he first sent a prospectus to his select customers.[39]

With Grisso's enthusiastic acceptance of the proposal, Jack printed the deluxe edition before the end of April and sent sheets to a craftsman binder at the University of New Mexico (UNM) Press. He followed this by printing the regular edition and sending sheets to a binder in San Antonio. Jack then wrote, "Now I can take a deep breath again and start printing the book jackets, ready for the bound books when they come back." He was confident the deluxe edition would be mailed first. Of the ninety-two copies, seventy-two were already sold. "As I told you I have about 30 old standby dealers who will raise the roof if they aren't given a chance to buy at least <u>one</u> copy, but already most of those 30 dealers are out of luck."[40]

In a chatty, single-spaced, three-page letter in November, Jack wrote Grisso in a more relaxed tone than previously. The summer had been "unusually slow," although reviews of *From Where the Sun Now Stands* were positive. His new author must have been inquiring regularly about sales, prompting Jack's explanation about lag time between release and uptick in sales for a new title, especially with the usual summer slowdown. In the meantime Jack received promising news. Stagecoach Press had been selected by the US Information Agency (USIA) in the State Department for four touring exhibits of work by small fine printers in America. Jack chose Grisso's book and printed ephemera for exhibits touring the Near East, the Far East, Latin America, and Europe. Jack also took Grisso's book to exhibit at the third annual meeting of the WHA in Salt Lake City. "None of us sell much over-the-counter at these meetings. Most of those attending are professors. They spend a lot of time looking at the books and scribbling notes; then, a month or so later you start to get orders from their librarians. So it's profitable, but only later on. To give you an example, the librarian at Princeton wrote me four months ago that he had started a purchase order through the mill. I met him in Salt Lake City and he said it was still 'in the mill' and would be along!"[41] Jack also explained how he generated interest in Stagecoach Press books through personal contacts among many people interested in Western history. "I have a way of making expenses, though. I take along a big aluminum suitcase full of rare books and peddle them to the rare books dealers who attend and the few collectors who show up."[42]

Correspondence between the two friends continued after Grisso's book was published, although not at the same pace as when it was in production. He continued to check with Jack, testing reactions to book ideas that were really not viable. After reading an article about different writing styles between academic and nonacademic historians, Grisso thought those styles could be the subject for a new book. With Alfred A. Knopf he shared a belief that the writing of some professional historians was rather dry. Jack did not encourage him to pursue such a book and carefully avoided expressing interest in it as a new project. "If I had my druthers, I'd druther have the dull facts, because a good creative writer can come along later and make it come alive, but no historian can put truth into fiction."[43] Although this was the second book concept from Grisso that Jack had diplomatically moved to the sidelines, their friendship remained close. They continued visiting whenever Grisso rented a home in Santa Fe where his wife could be more comfortable in summertime. When Grisso died at the end of July 1965, Jack wrote his widow, telling her that as long as he published books, he would send OU Library one of each edition in Dick's memory. "For a long, long time to come, whenever the shadow of a visitor blocks the doorway of my shop I will still look up to see if perhaps it isn't Dick come to sit again in the big walnut armchair and talk of books and the West and people, all of whom we both loved."[44]

As the economics of small-press publishing in the 1960s grew more challenging, Jack continued to draw inspiration from his circle of friends and associates in the book and printing world as well as from Charlotte. For twenty years she actively contributed to Stagecoach Press business. Beginning with *A Guide Book to Highway 66*, she organized notes, prepared mailings, kept records and clipping files of reviews, bound books, and later operated the Linotype machine. For the past ten years she had dreamed with Jack about moving to Santa Fe. After they realized their dream, she remembered fondly the printing shop where she sat at the Linotype with the sun streaming through the windows looking out on the Rocky Mountains, happily setting type for another Stagecoach Press book.

By the summer of 1966, even with Jack's knowledge of Western history, careful selection of manuscripts, cultivation of his market, and experience in printing, his press revenue began trending down. When he accidently cut off the tip of his left index finger while doing some repair work on the side of the platen, book production ground to a halt. "Deadlines slipped past, letters went unanswered, and I got into a tight financial bind."[45] Ever since his Depression years at college and in New York City, he had honed skills for pivoting when the economy turned against him. To economize he dismissed his assistant, remodeled a small adobe barn behind his house at 303 E. Berger Street for Stagecoach Press, moved his equipment, and ended the lease for printing space on Tesuque Street. These moves saved him four hundred dollars a month.

In his four years in Santa Fe, he had become friends with others in town interested in printing. Gustave Baumann and Willard Clark were among many in Jack's growing network of printing associates, as was Dale Bulloch at Rydal Press. Although no longer the fine printing shop where Walter Goodwin produced Writers' Editions and other beautiful presswork, Rydal remained a respected job shop printing letterhead, rodeo programs, menus, church bulletins, and other materials for numerous organizations in town. When Bulloch offered him a job, Jack accepted and applied for a journeyman's card, hoping the printer's union would consider his experience adequate. "I worked on the stone, the big imposing table where type is locked up in forms for letterpress printing."[46] He had no trouble doing the work and enjoyed learning more about routines in a small job shop in his adopted town. He told Carl Hertzog, "Still, there's no great fun in the jobs themselves: routine commercial work when there isn't a book on the stone."[47] He finished his work with Rydal before the union card arrived.

By the end of the summer, the Museum of New Mexico Press sought Jack's help with some part-time manuscript editing, obviously trying to fill a gap left when Robert G. Ferris resigned from the Museum to become executive assistant to the director of the Office of Manned Space Flight at NASA. Ferris, a good friend of Jack's, was an accomplished historian, editor, and publisher. As an active and noted member of the arts community, his departure from the Museum did not go unnoticed.[48] No surprise, it followed the vast reorganization of the Museum of New Mexico in 1963 with its deemphasis on education and publications.[49] Sadly, Ferris had come to Santa Fe only a year earlier as chief editor of museum publications. During his brief tenure he doubled the number of new titles and issued the first publication catalog in five years.

Two years after Ferris left for NASA, the Museum of New Mexico Press offered Jack a part-time job as director of the press, allowing him time to continue with Stagecoach Press projects. "The Museum of N.M. Press then was about as small as a publishing enterprise could be. The staff consisted of myself, plus sharing a secretary-typist with another museum worker, and when I was lucky I also had a student available to wrap packages for about ten hours a week. This was a pleasant interlude, but I was frustrated by the situation at the Museum, a condition quite typical of all museums: no funds, too much to be done, and a tangling web of bureaucratic practices imposed on the Museum by the state."[50]

In minimal office space at the Museum of Anthropology on Museum Hill, the press issued two types of publications, a series of modestly priced pamphlets sold primarily to visitors and tourists, and a series of extensive reports documenting archaeological digs conducted by the state archaeologist. With the federal government financing highways and dams, the state archaeologist was under contract to document sites that might be affected by new construction. Support for these federal-state projects included money for fieldwork as well as for printed reports on findings. No funds were allocated for the staff needed to edit and prepare copy for the press. Jack was responsible for all the editing, oversight of type setting (on an IBM Selectric typewriter), book design and preparation of pasteups, markup for illustrations, and delivery of camera-ready sheets to the printer.

"Each spring the state legislature assigned a small amount for printing museum publications, but it barely sufficed for the pamphlet series."[51] At the Laboratory of Anthropology Jack discovered a back run of reports so extensive he prepared a special mailer for selling them. He raised five thousand dollars and was planning to use the windfall for the publication program. The funds were immediately taken away for building repairs. After this happened a second time with the sale of back-run publications Jack found elsewhere in his building, he prepared and circulated a document titled "Methods of Financing a Publications Program" for the Museum of New Mexico Press. In it he outlined ten different methods by which publications could be financed, from an ordinary revolving fund to outside fund grants, grants for matching funds, cooperation with other institutions, and commercial cooperative agreements.[52] The museum regents ignored Jack's clearly stated, three-page document. In 1967 the administrative team at the Museum tried once more to promote its publication program when the museum director, Delmar M. Kolb, held a staff conference with Jack, Charles Proctor, and George Ewing to start planning a program "to make the Press the leading regional publisher in its fields." They produced a four-page document, "A Program for the Museum of New Mexico Press" for publications in anthropology, archaeology, history, fine arts, and folk arts. With sections devoted to administration, market possibilities, and "basic publications that every state needs," such as a catalog of all major historical maps, a central source for historic photos, and a guide to old newspaper files around the state, the document reflects many of Jack's long-time interests as a historian-publisher. Needless to say, the proposal was ignored up the line at the state level.

Years later in a discussion with a member of the Museum's board of regents, Jack learned he was "always opposed to any major publishing program at the Museum because he did not feel that a museum should become engaged in publishing. Perhaps that was why I met defeat every time I tried to urge the Museum to detach the Press and make it at least semi-independent, as the Library of Congress had done with its photocopying division, a move that transformed the division from an expense item to a highly profitable, self-supporting operation."[53] He was learning some of the differences between the business world where he had become a seasoned, experienced executive and the static universe of a state bureaucracy.

In October 1967, Jack took vacation time to drive to San Francisco for that year's WHA meeting. He carried Stagecoach Press books for display, along with Museum of New Mexico Press backstock, which he showed at no cost to the Museum. On the WHA exhibit floor he met and had a cordial visit with the new director of UNM Press, Dr. Roger W. Shugg. Shugg had only recently taken up his new post, and this was his first year at WHA. His credentials included a PhD in history from Princeton, four years as associate professor of history at Indiana University, and research for the Military Intelligence Service of the War Department's general staff. Earlier, while earning advanced degrees at Princeton, he served as an advisor on historical publications for Alfred

A. Knopf. He came to UNM after a distinguished, profit-making, thirteen-year term as director of the University of Chicago Press. Jack's visit with Shugg must have impressed the new director of UNM Press. By the late 1960s, Jack was a recognized public figure in New Mexico, knowledgeable about Western history, known for his Stagecoach Press books, consulted by newspaper writers seeking answers to historical questions, and highly experienced in editing. Such recognition no doubt strengthened his candidacy for a senior editorship at UNM Press.

Shugg made Jack an offer shortly after returning from the WHA meetings to come work with him three days a week while still devoting two days to the Museum of New Mexico Press. Jack started at UNM Press on the first of January 1968. In six months Shugg offered him a full-time position that he happily accepted. The new job at UNM Press carried a decent salary with benefits, while naming him the lead editor for selecting and editing manuscripts for new books on Western history. Jack's salary doubled immediately but was still only about half of what he earned in his advertising agency work in Houston. Nevertheless, he landed once more in his element, surrounded by books, writers, and the making of books.

UNM stipulated that employees could not engage in any outside business that might be considered a conflict of interest, so it was clear that he needed to shut down his private press, a bittersweet decision for Jack and Charlotte. For twenty years she had been at Jack's side at Stagecoach Press, a partner in life and in their publishing business.

The last Stagecoach book they produced was in 1967, David Weber's first book, *The Extranjeros: Selected Documents from the Mexican Side of the Santa Fe Trail, 1825–1828*. In September 1966, while still finishing his dissertation at UNM, Weber met Jack in Santa Fe at a Westerner's talk at the La Fonda Hotel. David knew about the Stagecoach Press series and Jack's relentless quest for lesser known but significant incidents in Western history, so he mentioned fur trade documents other historians had overlooked at the Archivo General in Mexico City, at the Huntington Library, and nearby at the New Mexico State Records Center.

These were *guías*, "letters of safe conduct proving that customs duty had been paid" that would be "of considerable interest to students of the fur trade, the Santa Fe trade and those interested in the Mexican period in general." Jack wanted to know more, so David outlined a book concept a week later; before the end of December he submitted a manuscript vetted by his dissertation advisor, Dr. Donald Cutter, and by Dr. Myra Ellen Jenkins, the first New Mexico State Historian and indefatigable authority on New Mexico history.[54] Jack began production immediately on a book that earned positive reviews. Subsequently, David's career included writing many more books, moving him into the top rank as a distinguished Borderlands historian. Before he died in 2010, he was honored by the scholarly world as well as by the king of Spain and the president of Mexico. Throughout his life he treasured the fact that Jack published his first book.

When *The Extrajeneros* was released in the spring of 1967, it ended a twenty-one-year run of Stagecoach Press books. Several of those books won design awards; all of them earned positive reviews. By the time it ceased publication, Stagecoach had a loyal following of librarians, historians, and collectors who placed standing orders for every new title. When new readers and librarians kept asking for earlier titles to fill out their holdings, Jack printed "The First Fifty, A Checklist of the Stagecoach Press." For him it was the fulfillment of a lifetime dream to produce well-edited books on Western history with sound typographic design and craftsmanship, all created in his own printing shop in the West. To this day many people remember Jack's legacy with Stagecoach Press while collecting and treasuring his publications. Perhaps no one explains Jack and his press more eloquently than Pam Smith, retired director of the Press of the Palace of the Governors, whose book, *Passions in Print: Private Press Artistry in New Mexico*, documents the rise of fine printing in the forty-seventh state: "With an unassuming manner, distinct authority, soft wit, and pipe in mouth or hand, Rittenhouse shared generously what he knew and often what he possessed. No appointment was necessary to drop in and chat with him about books, history, or printing."[55]

Chapter 8

The Albuquerque Years and the University of New Mexico Press

More than once I wished I could have been locked in the library stacks for weeks, with some kind attendant leaving a daily sack of hamburgers and a carton of buttermilk in my carrel.

—JACK D. RITTENHOUSE[1]

AS JACK BEGAN WORKING at UNM Press three days a week, Roger Shugg quickly discovered he had hired the quintessential editor's editor. Six months later he offered Jack a full-time position as editor of Western Books. Once more, the Rittenhouse family would be on the move, this time with two teenage daughters. As required by the Press, he placed on hold his own publication efforts but continued his volunteer pursuits, including a four-year term as president of the Historical Society of New Mexico and his work with the Old Santa Fe Association, where his friend and fellow Westerner Rex Arrowsmith was association chairman.

Jack adjusted quickly to his new academic setting. Already widely published, he moved with ease among faculty, press staff, and students of history. At the Press, he drew upon his deep familiarity with Western history, printing methods, and editing and publishing practices to evaluate book concepts and proposals, help present proposals for new books to the faculty press committee, edit manuscripts, work closely with authors to strengthen their manuscripts, and track projects through production. Along with regular attendance at academic conferences to promote UNM Press books, he participated in meetings of the Western History Association and state historical societies where he enjoyed discussions with others who shared an interest in the history and literature of the west.

He systematically proposed new book ideas to his colleagues in single-page memos. Lunchtime discussions or informal meetings with faculty, especially those in the History Department, often generated ideas for new books while previous experience in promotion helped him evaluate fresh book concepts in terms of marketability. However his proposals were received, he consistently created an atmosphere conducive to new ideas for book projects. On one occasion, after a meeting with Shugg and Donald Cutter, a widely respected and published professor of Western history, he briefly outlined a paperback book based on Cutter's syllabus for teaching Western history. As with all his book proposals, he concentrated on concept, content, and basic layout.

Manuscripts also came "over the transom" as unsolicited book proposals from writers unknown to the Press. When they were totally out of scope, the author received a short polite response, and occasionally, a suggestion of another press with a different editorial focus where there might be a better fit. When proposals had some merit but required the author to do considerably more work on the manuscript, Jack and his colleagues wrote and exchanged detailed internal documents to initiate discussions among themselves and the press director before writing their response to the author. For a book concept comprised mainly of articles on General John J. Pershing and his pursuit of Pancho Villa into Mexico, Jack offered his "ABSTRACT OF OPINION": "As it now stands, this manuscript does not merit publication by a university press whose program is limited. [The author's] material either supplements other books or is available in some form to scholars. . . . If more material is added, especially from Mexican sources, and if the work becomes more of a study in U.S.–Mexican attitudes, it would be sufficiently new and useful to merit publication. A market exists to support an edition of 2,000 copies."[2]

"This opinion runs counter to my personal enthusiasm. While I am no Villa buff, I have read at least four of the six books done on the Punitive Expedition and read many articles while doing research for a popular article on Villa published in 1956, one on Pershing done in 1962, and one on the Mexican rurales in 1967. . . . The weakness of this book, and indeed the weakness of all other books published in English about the Punitive Expedition, is that it draws almost exclusively from U.S. sources and presents the U.S. viewpoint. . . . It is here that [the editor] has an opportunity to make his book really a new and useful work by adding Mexican material." Jack then wrote two full paragraphs discussing books from the Mexican point of view and noting the bibliographies that took notice of them. "It is apparent that such a stereographic presentation would be an approach that might make the work useful in cultural studies such as are now being offered in Chicano courses."[3] The Press decided not to publish the book.

In spring 1969 he sketched out the concept for a book about attitudes toward the United States from the Mexican point of view without a particular author in mind. He recommended his memo be circulated to "some experts in this field, and if existing works are not adequate there might be both a scholarly need and a commercial market for such a book." Noting Mexico's dislike for Joel Roberts Poinsett, the first US envoy to serve in Mexico City, he also listed Mexico's suspicions that Sibley's 1825 survey of the Santa Fe Trail was a guise to lay out a military road. He included Mexico's opinion that the Texas Revolution in 1836 was a purely expansionist move against Mexico and identified how Mexico viewed with concern Shelby's failed attempt at the end of the Civil War to enlist en masse under Maximilian after refusing to surrender to Grant and then fleeing the United States. He also referenced many Mexicans' dislike of Porfirio Diaz's open arms policy welcoming American capital investments in their country. All these attitudes were ripe for discussion, and a new book by an accomplished scholar could fill the gap. While this particular book concept was probably ahead of its time and was not adopted, it voiced expectations for more diverse viewpoints in new books and acknowledged the recently emerging Chicano studies programs.

As Jack met and talked with people about favorite books and writers, he began thinking about books no longer available in print that deserved to be republished. With a new reprint series in mind, he built a list of worthwhile books UNM Press might consider. Marta Weigle, University Regents Professor of Anthropology at UNM, worked closely with Jack and her colleagues in literature, cultural studies, and anthropology to develop a list of books their students needed in an affordable format. They envisioned a series of paperbacks devoted to Western fiction and nonfiction. Each book would have a short introduction by a recognized scholar in attractive, yet inexpensive, format and would be marketed to the general trade as well as college bookstores. Through his research Jack confirmed the marketability of a series of books by Edward Abbey, Mary Austin, Harvey Fergusson, A. B. Guthrie Jr., Tom Lea, Larry McMurtry, N. Scott Momaday, Jack Schaefer, Frank Waters, and many more. With a list of forty writers and a five-category spreadsheet in hand, he pitched the idea for a new UNM Press series to his boss and colleagues. Everyone liked the concept; Jack suggested it become the Zia Books series, named for the ancient sun symbol of Zia Pueblo.

With strong approval from the Faculty Press Committee, he launched the new series in October 1974, with four new titles in the Press catalog: *The Conquest of Don Pedro* by Harvey Fergusson, *Tracey Cromwell* by Conrad Richter, *The Land of Little Rain* by Mary Austin, and *Far From Cibola* by Paul Horgan. In *Don Pedro*, Fergusson told the story of a small New Mexican town as the center of a clash of cultures. Richter, twice a Pulitzer Prize winner, set *Tracey Cromwell* in an Arizona mining town where others came seeking their fortunes. *Land of Little Rain*, Mary Austin's first book, was her masterpiece, while Horgan, also a Pulitzer Prize winner, described *Far From Cibola* as "a poem with as many subjects as it has characters."

At a brisk pace Jack kept the Zia Books list growing, announcing and publishing twenty-three books in only three years. Among the early titles in the series, John Houghton Allen's *Southwest*, first published by J. B. Lippencott in 1952 and out of print, was based loosely on experiences growing up on his family's sixty-thousand-acre ranch in south Texas between Laredo and Corpus Christi. Earlier at UNM Press, Roland Dickey had included one of Allen's poems in *Signature of the Sun*, an anthology published in 1950.[4] Jack admired *Southwest*, as did Lawrence Clark Powell, J. Frank Dobie, T. M. Pearce, and Mabel Major. In his *Guide to Life and Literature of the Southwest*, Dobie described it as "a chemical compound of highly impressionistic autobiographic nonfiction and highly romantic fiction and folk tales. The setting is a ranch of Mexican tradition in the lower border country of Texas, also saloons and bawdy houses of border towns. Vaqueros and their work in the brush are intensely vivid."[5]

While *Southwest* quickly gained approval of the faculty committee for inclusion in the Zia series, finding Allen to ask his permission was not so easy. Neither Jack nor his many contacts in the Southwest knew of a current mailing address for him. The last anyone heard of Allen, he was living in California, but Jack discovered he had moved again. "We have New York people trying to find old files in Philadelphia," Jack observed.[6] Patient correspondence finally solved the issue. The publication rights had reverted to Allen, and someone in the rights and permissions office at his publisher, Lippencott, helped Jack reach him in Tubac, Arizona. The author was curious but pleased with the proposal for a reprint by UNM. He wrote: "Have not been informed of this reprint or assigned Southwest to the University of New Mexico Press. No objection to its publication, but who gave permission, and do I get royalty? My copyright 1952. Lippincott and Bantam." In a postscript he wrote, "The University Press and I old friends. Even [was included] in *Signature of the Sun*. Later, Mr. Dickey of the Quarterly published poems and translations. . . . Where is Mr. Dickey by the way? JHA"[7] Allen's fond memories of working with UNM Press had begun more than twenty years earlier.

Jack responded as soon as he received Allen's letter, explaining that he had contacted the Lippencott rights and permissions editor in New York when he could not turn up a mailing address. He noted how Allen's book fit the newly emerging field of Western American literature in college studies and in general sales to bookstores. The press expected most sales to be chiefly to the public, although the college market was growing, and the sales in both sectors would benefit from their national distribution through bookstores.[8] Jack also sent a copy of William Eastlake's *The Bronc People* to Allen as an example of the Zia Series format. He closed with notes on recent developments at UNM Press and included updates on Roland Dickey. Soon, with permissions in place and an introduction by Orlan Sawey, chair of the English Department at Texas A&I University, *Southwest* took its well-deserved place on the growing shelf of Zia books from UNM Press.

As Jack continued developing the series, William Eastlake encouraged him to include one or two books by Ed Abbey. He chose *The Brave Cowboy* and *Fire on the Mountain*. Drawing upon an earlier meeting, he had the perfect opening for his letter seeking Abbey's permission: "Dear Mr. Abbey: It has been about eight years since you and Gus Blaisdell and I sat in the bar of the Pioneer Hotel in Denver, across from the Coliseum during the first Denver Book Fair. I saw Gus this noon and he told me I could reach you at Moab" [via General Delivery].[9] His reference to the Denver meeting with Blaisdell was indicative of the way Jack often reached out to others with a thread tied to personal recollections. Abbey had become a good friend of Blaisdell, a legendary writer, teacher, publisher, and editor in Albuquerque; the two writers may have met at Blaisdell's bookstore, the Living Batch, a magnet from 1969 to 1996 for creative people ranging from Evan Connell to Robert Creely, as well as a gathering place for regional poets and artists.[10]

Jack explained to Abbey his routine for trying to contact an author first about reprint rights as a courtesy in case those rights may have already reverted to him, or in case he might want to secure them before discussing a reprint. He related how the Zia Series had already grown with books by Eastlake, Fergusson, Horgan, and more. Abbey liked the concept and suggested Jack contact his agent, Don Congdon, at Harold Matson whom Jack already knew through his close friendship with Jack Schaefer. Congdon had been Schaefer's agent for years and had guided him through numerous contracts, including the book and film agreements for *Shane*. Jack began his letter to Congdon by referencing their last meeting, "when you were out here to visit with Jack Schaefer and both of you came to a party at Howard Bryan's in Old Town." He explained the focus of the Zia Series, with plans for an academic literary scholar to write a brief introduction that could "help classroom adoption." UNM Press wanted to release *The Brave Cowboy* in spring 1977. They would set new type for the introduction and produce the rest by facsimile from the first edition. He ended with a personal note: "I hope all continues to go well with you. As you know, we have lost Jack Schaefer to the Californios for the time being, but New Mexico always pulls people back. I hope it pulls you back for another visit; I enjoyed it."[11]

In the meantime, Jack's next challenge for his Abbey reprint was finding a first edition of *The Brave Cowboy*, necessary to make the offset printing plates for the new paperback. Published by Dodd, Mead in 1956, this was Abbey's second book and by far the scarcest. Twenty years after its first publication, Jack turned to some of his antiquarian book friends in California, asking them to call the book shops all around San Francisco and Los Angeles with offers to pay as much as fifty dollars a copy. In the pre-Internet years of the 1970s, a telephone call was usually the quickest way to locate a scarce book. Even in the two best book cities on the West Coast, the search was unsuccessful. He then tried another approach through channels known mainly to seasoned antiquarian booksellers, book scouts. Scouts with a reasonable knowledge of rare books make a living from estate sales, garage sales, and secondhand stores like Goodwill where they find books that ordinary buyers don't recognize as desirable. They neither maintain inventory, pay rent for shop space, nor advertise, but prefer to sell their finds to established antiquarian book dealers and head back out on a never-ending treasure hunt. As scouts, they play an important role in the food chain of the rare-book world wherein some of the most desirable books enter the market from some of the most unlikely places. Booksellers seldom acknowledge the role of scouts, especially in their catalogs. Jack contacted several savvy book scouts in the Southwest; again, he struck out. As a last resort, he ran an ad in the *Albuquerque Journal* and turned up only one copy the morning the item ran.[12] Finally, with a first edition of the book, signed permissions, and an introduction in hand, the press moved quickly into production. *Fire on the Mountain*, next in the queue, followed in time for an autumn release.

Jack relished his work at the Press and his proximity to an excellent research library. If he needed to verify a particular quotation or fact pertaining to a book he was editing for the Press, he would go to the Zimmerman Library whenever he needed to, but for his own research projects he only went on lunch breaks and on evenings and weekends. He also continued pursuing his volunteer interests with vigor, keeping up with his commitments as president of the Historical Society of New Mexico. Book people around New Mexico remembered how, as a Houston resident, Jack drew upon his own book collection to compile and print his *New Mexico Civil War Bibliography*. HSNM members had not forgotten how he drove from Houston for the annual meeting in Las Cruces and distributed his new book at the banquet where Lawrence Clark Powell saluted his work from the podium, and the president of the society, Calvin Horn, announced Jack would be moving his press to New Mexico in the near future.

In 1968 he had assumed full-time responsibility for Western books at UNM and also for running the statewide historical association dating back nearly a century. Yet nothing in his surviving correspondence indicates this period was any different from other times in his work-filled professional life. He was happiest when he could be working with books and the people who produced them, and he never lost his place or his pace because of a heavy workload. He could apparently focus on multiple projects simultaneously, solving problems, analyzing strengths and weaknesses, communicating next steps clearly and concisely, and doing so with a cordial, gentlemanly demeanor.

The Press supported his work in the Western History Association, filled with members writing, teaching, collecting, and promoting the history of the Trans-Mississippi West. Jack had attended the 1961 organizational meeting, followed by every annual meeting over the next twenty-eight years with one exception due to a health issue. Settling into his new job at UNM Press, he chaired the Arrangements Committee for the eleventh annual WHA conference planned for Santa Fe in autumn 1971. The logistics were formidable for a conference of more than six hundred people to be held in downtown Santa Fe long before the city built a convention center. Advance registration, registrant packets with programs, brochures, and badges, attendee check-in tables in the La Fonda Hotel lobby, guides for sightseeing buses, collecting meal tickets at the doors to dining halls, space assignments for program sessions and banquets, book exhibit space, and publishers' booth set-up all had to be carefully planned and manned. Jack estimated that he and his volunteer team spent at least one thousand man-hours on the pieces of the conference puzzle. His organizational skills made possible the production of a handout with the names of all participants, those featured as speakers and panelists, and where they were staying. This was the first "who is where" handout ever prepared for attendees at a WHA annual meeting. Jack believed it important in facilitating attendance at talks on topics of interest and promoting networking with seldom-seen friends and colleagues from different parts of the country.

Before the end of October 1971, only a few weeks after the conference, he submitted a full account of revenues and expenses for the meeting to Everett L. Cooley, secretary-treasurer of the WHA. Cooley wrote, "Once again, Jack, let me say that it was a pleasure working with you. I will never know how you survived not only the days of the

WHA but then the Western Publishers, too. You are a good man, and I appreciate all the work you have done."[13]

Previously, in 1967, Jack had been elected president of the Historical Society of New Mexico. There he had found a respected and important Western historical society hanging together with the help of dedicated volunteers but without the benefit of any modern organizational or business practices. He began a measured assessment of the situation, leaving aside the standard annual report and, instead, writing a "President's Report–1968" for circulation "chiefly to our officers, our Advisory Council, and those members who have shown a lasting and active concern over the Society." He briefly reviewed the administrative history of the society, starting with its finances. From the beginning of the *New Mexico Historical Review* in 1926 until the early 1960s, the society had received modest funding from the state, administered through the Museum of New Mexico and spent mainly on subsidizing the *Review*. Income from member subscriptions never covered costs. Re-incorporated in 1959, state funding ceased, leaving it to operate "for all practical purposes" apart from the museum. In 1963 the *Review* was transferred to UNM where the university paid for the editor and the costs of printing and mailing the journal, collecting dues, and sending out renewal notices.

Members paid six dollars per year; the university kept five dollars and remitted one dollar to the society. The ten to seventeen affiliated local societies around the state paid an annual charter fee of ten dollars. In 1968 the society had reported membership at 721, based on a count of journals mailed out. But journal mailings did not accurately reflect membership. "In reality, 259 of these [mailings] were college and public libraries outside New Mexico. 183 were private individuals living outside the state. 85 went to professors, libraries, and groups inside the state. Only 194 were individual members living in New Mexico. Thus, in reality we were a society with about two hundred really effective [paying] members. This number should be at least a thousand!"[14] His main recommendations to the society leaders were to increase membership, secure office space and hire a permanent staff member to handle correspondence, maintain membership, and keep subscription records. To grow membership, he called on his board to help coordinate society events such as public lectures and annual meetings and to maintain regular contact with members, perhaps through the newsletter.

Jack also referenced "one of the great, untangled matters of the society," the settlement of ownership questions regarding books and objects of material culture gifted in the nineteenth and early twentieth centuries when the society and the Museum of New Mexico were interwoven.[15] Some of these collections dated back to the Civil War–era as well as the 1880s and '90s when L. Bradford Prince was territorial governor. Prince held a deep interest in New Mexico history and in collecting documents and artifacts relating to it. In 1884 when New Mexico was only a territory and not a state, he arranged with the US secretary of the interior to grant space in the eastern end of the Palace of the Governors to the Society for holding its meetings, housing its growing collections, and eventually operating its museum.

In 1909 Edgar Lee Hewett gained permission to establish his School of American Archaeology (later the School for Advanced Research, SAR) in the same building. He soon opened his own museum at the opposite end from the society exhibits where he mounted exhibits of archaeological materials from his many excavations at major sites from Chaco Canyon to Mexico. Thus began the rivalry between two museums under one roof.[16] Over time major collections of the historical society fell into limbo as Hewett consolidated his control over the palace and later formed what became two separate state museums, the New Mexico History Museum and the Museum of Fine Arts, each with its own building.

Years later the Historical Society and the New Mexico History Museum established a plan for unraveling the tattered threads of ownership for tens of thousands of items collected for more than a century. Supported by patient diplomacy and careful documentation of provenance, the critical process began. In 1969 Jack and his board members at the society agreed to meet with Carlos Nagel, director of the Museum of New Mexico "to establish good faith in general ideas of cooperation and in obtaining an inventory of the Society collections."[17] Comprehensive listing of collections, along with the detailed review of old correspondence, required eight years to complete. Jack was no longer president, but the historical society remained committed and signed the documents transferring the massive collections as agreed. From the Historical Society of New Mexico, three hundred Spanish Colonial works of art went to the Museum of International Folk Art; more than five hundred items went to the Museum of Indian Arts and Culture; thousands of documents and photographs collected by the society went to the State Records Center and Archives; other manuscripts and photographs (ca. 60,000) were accessioned by the Photo Archives in the Fray Angelico Chavez Library at the Museum of New Mexico; and more than twelve hundred items stayed in the Palace of the Governors at the Museum of New Mexico .[18] By 1977 the Historical Society of New Mexico was no longer in the museum business.

While inventories of society collections were under way, Jack focused on generating a broader awareness of the organization and its mission. He reached out to other organizations in New Mexico offering to speak at their official meetings, beginning with the Highway Engineering Association. In 1968 he addressed the fourteenth Annual Highway Engineering Conference in Las Cruces with a theme of sharing information between agencies and organizations. Others on the program came from the Bureau of Reclamation, the Bureau of Land Management, the State Highway Department, the Bureau of Indian Affairs, the Forest Service, and the Department of Game and Fish.[19]

As the society announced its annual banquet for 1968, it took note of recent federal legislation to raise the profile of historical research on the local level. Two years earlier President Lyndon B. Johnson had signed into law the National Historic Preservation Act (NHPA), the most extensive preservation legislation ever enacted in the United States. It created the National Register of Historic Places (NRHP) to build "the official federal inventory of districts, sites, buildings, structures and objects significant on a national, State or local level in American history, architecture, archaeology, engineering and culture."[20] NRHP launched a nationwide program wherein local citizens and historical societies worked to identify and nominate sites for inclusion on the National Register. In New Mexico these efforts were coordinated through the State Planning Office and a statewide citizens council charged with evaluating site proposals for recommendation to the national level. With historic preservation very much in the news, the Historical Society of New Mexico arranged for a keynote speech by Arthur Ortiz, head of the State Planning Office to discuss the statewide historic sites program and its relationship to NHPA. In 1968 the governor of New Mexico appointed Jack to the Cultural Properties Review Committee where he served along with State Historian Dr. Myra Ellen Jenkins, archaeologist Albert Schroeder, State Archaeologist George Ewing, and historian Marc Simmons, among others. With help from thirty-one local advisory committees scattered throughout the state, New Mexico was among the first to submit a comprehensive plan for preservation of some 150 sites of unusual historic importance out of more than 600 nominated and reviewed.

Another of Jack's history-related projects during his HSNM presidency was a photo census of New Mexico to start in the 1970s and be repeated every ten years.[21] He envisioned a collection growing over decades to begin with "one good record photograph of the central street of each city, town, village, ghost town, or other settlement in the state." If the town had "historic structures or important buildings," he wanted to document them also. Jack's idea was "impelled by the fact that almost every year some significant structure disappears, from fire, decay, or new construction. This happened to the little hotel in Stanley, the stone lodge at Lybrook, and the old hotel in Cerrillos. Also, many significant structures may never have had a photograph taken that is readily available on short notice."[22]

To get the project started, he and Charlotte identified and listed 1,033 place names, drawing from key sources such as the official New Mexico tourist map, the latest postal zip code directory, large-scale historic maps, Sheldon H. Dike's list of places in territorial New Mexico that had a post office at any time, as well as a list of ghost towns and mining camps compiled by the New Mexico Institute of Mining and Technology. With their list complete, they gave a logical, unique number to each town, settlement, and post to aid in filing photographs.

In 1969 he included this project on the HSNM agenda, but apparently the board, with its increased responsibilities, did not share his enthusiasm. He promoted his concept to the president of the Camera Club in Albuquerque and in an open letter to Westerners and friends, headed "Save Those 'Old West' Photos," but he was unsuccessful.[23] Although he generated little interest among others, Jack continued to take his camera wherever he went, driving the small backroads leading to forgotten towns and taking photographs along the way for the rest of his life. On the wall of his office he kept a map marked with every road he had driven. Shortly before he died, he gave a collection of more than three hundred negatives and prints of New Mexico towns to the Rio Grande Historical Collections at New Mexico State University Library. NMSU mounted a traveling exhibit shown in several venues around the state and continues to house Jack's collection.

To engage citizens from smaller New Mexico towns in the Historical Society, Jack and his board planned program meetings outside of Santa Fe. Starting with Silver City as the site for the 1970 New Mexico History Day, he reached out to faculty and staff from Western New Mexico University to help with planning and to deliver talks. John Kessell and Jack also spoke, with Kessell lecturing on encounters with Apaches along the Gila River in 1756, and Jack talking about "Writing Local History for Publication."[24] At the close of the program, a guided tour of historic sites around Silver City helped draw attention to ongoing historic preservation efforts aided by federal funding throughout New Mexico. The following year in Albuquerque, site for Southwestern History Day, Jack lectured on the "Sesquicentennial of the Santa Fe Trail." Governor Bruce King proclaimed Santa Fe Trail Day, and a commemorative medal was issued for the occasion.[25]

Observance of the 1821 opening of the Santa Fe Trail continued into the following year with the Santa Fe Historical Society organizing a summer lecture series including talks by Myra Ellen Jenkins, Marc Simmons, and Jack, who spoke on the origins of the trail. These summertime history talks on Museum Hill drew large audiences from Santa Fe residents as well as from the many seasonal visitors attracted to New Mexico. Since 1953, when his deep interest in New Mexico began to grow, he had been working slowly on a major New Mexico book that was finally released in 1971 as the Sesquicentennial of the Santa Fe Trail celebrations continued for more than a year, generating substantial press attention. The history (and the mystique) of the trail and the town that gave it its name were key pieces in nineteenth-century expansion of the Trans-Mississippi West, and it held great interest for history buffs, historians, and book collectors.

Jack's idea for a book on the Santa Fe Trail had grown slowly, beginning with a 1953 vacation trip when his "interest in New Mexico began to simmer." He recalled later, "I foolishly decided to compile some sort of a checklist of New Mexico books, as a guide to my own collecting, and thought the list might go as high as five hundred titles. I began a card file, for those three-by-five cards have always been my own habitual solitaire. Over a weekend I had five hundred entries. By the end of a month I had a thousand. Within a couple of years the file had three thousand entries, and the end was not in sight. I could see that a bibliography of that scope could never be published if the entries were annotated, and I found such lists not really useful without annotations."[26]

Jack narrowed his research focus to the Santa Fe Trail and soon met William E. Brown, a historian with the National Park Service who had recently finished a long report on the trail and its historic sites along the way.[27] Impressed with the work, especially the bibliography at the end, he told Brown he thought "he had done a remarkably good selective bibliography." The NPS historian responded that his bibliography was more than selective; it included everything published on the trail. Jack invited Brown over to his home, showed him the thousands of his "own habitual solitaire" cards on books and pamphlets relating to the Trail, and offered to share his findings. With the 150th anniversary of Becknell's first trip from Arrow Rock, Missouri, to Santa Fe (1821–1822) coming up two years later, he began thinking it was time to finish his book.

When he pitched the idea of a Trail bibliography to his boss at UNM Press, Shugg responded unenthusiastically, saying that "university presses generally could not publish books written by its own staff members." At the next annual meeting of university presses, Jack told an editor he knew at Harvard University Press about his project, and he also ran the idea by Frank Wardlaw at the University of Texas Press. Both publishers were interested, but Wardlaw was the most enthusiastic, wanting to move forward with the project immediately. "When I reported this to Roger Shugg, he had a change of mind. 'Why should you be disloyal and go to another university with it? Let us try it.'" Shugg added that "my material would have to be approved by an outside specialist and be voted upon by the faculty Press committee, and that I could not be present during the voting. I replied that I would welcome any outside judgment, and I asked him to select two outside readers whom he thought would be strict in their opinions. He selected Ray Allen Billington, of the Huntington Library, and Professor Rodman Paul of Cal Tech."[28]

With vacation time approaching, Jack planned his next step, a train trip to Topeka to work in the library of the Kansas State Historical Society "to check on items from the Kansas end of the Trail. I also did some work at the Bancroft Library and at the Colorado State Historical Society, as well as at places in New Mexico." For the Topeka trip he took his typewriter, his entire card file, and his copy of Wright Howes *US-iana*, an important bibliography devoted to key books on American history. The library staff in Topeka were "remarkably cooperative. They brought out all the items I requested and also brought out things I did not request but which were adjacent on the closed shelves. In this way I found many more new items no one had mentioned."[29] About this time he switched from three-by-five to four-by-six cards to record more information and made a point of always carrying several dozen blank cards with him every day wherever he went. He stepped up his research routines and wanted to spend his first hour every morning on campus at the Zimmerman Library. Unfortunately, they did not open before 8:00 a.m. At least, on his way to the office, he could return books checked out the day before. On lunch breaks from 12:00 to 1:00, he was in the library standing at the card catalog making notes with a separate card for each book. On other noon hours he checked out books as systematically as he approached all his work. "The next noon I would arrange my cards by floor and gather six or seven books, starting on the top floor of the library and working my way down to the checkout counter with the least time spent on travel and with the least effort on carrying books. I seldom carried books up."[30] Many years earlier Jack had committed to memory the catalog classification system and knew where all parts of the collections were housed in the book stacks on the floors above.

Since childhood, libraries had been an important part of his life, places where he could find books he had never seen before, books holding answers to all manner of questions, telling good stories, and once read, possibly waiting for a return visit. For him, library systems that organized and located all these sources of knowledge were simply part of the way the world was supposed to work. It made perfect sense, just like his childhood phonics instruction on the relationships between the letters of written language and the sounds of the spoken word, all of which he easily understood and mastered for a lifetime of reading and writing about books.

"Later, as I began to run out of obvious books [for the bibliography], I would stand before the shelves in certain sections of the history books and pull out any book just to see if it had Santa Fe Trail material in it. I mined that vein until it pinched out." He then mined journals of historical societies for articles on the Trail, checking not just the articles for inclusion in his bibliography but also for footnotes with references to sources he may not have seen and documented. He searched for significant accounts of westward expansion in the nineteenth century, first printed in government documents holding full reports by those who led expeditions surveying lands west of the Mississippi River. "On government documents, I had previously done some massive spade work. I had bought my copy of Ben Perley Poore's checklist of government documents. It resembles the big unabridged dictionary or the Manhattan telephone directory. At home I built a reading stand to hold the big book, adjusted a proper light, and went through every entry on every page, copying . . . [those] related to New Mexico."[31] Jack remembered, "This was not unlike checking every name in the Manhattan telephone book to find all names whose third letter was an e. A card was made out for each Santa Fe Trail entry and then each suspected entry's number in the Serial Set was noted at the library. On long twilight evenings in a microform room, I checked the microprint edition of the Serial Set so each possibility could be either described or discarded."[32]

"There were several instances of pure and fortunate accident. Once, standing before the library shelves of material on California, I noticed a biography of John Sutter. I had never connected Sutter with the Santa Fe Trail, but I took down the book and glanced through it. Sutter had been on the Trail, active in trade, before he went to California." Another touch of serendipity came on a family vacation in southern California. "On the beach road south from Los Angeles I braked to a sudden stop outside a cottage whose sign said BOOKS. On one shelf was a previously unknown pamphlet, John Ashton's 1924 report on Missouri mules (they first came East over the Santa Fe Trail). It cost only a few cents but has seldom if ever been equaled on its precise subject."[33]

In recognizing others who helped him with the Trail bibliography, Jack paid tribute to fellow antiquarian booksellers. He had begun to think like a bookseller many years earlier when he was scratching out a living writing book reviews and selling review copies just to put the next meal on the table. In 1937 he wrote an unpublished overview and some perceptive observations on the book market in Fort Wayne when he was a twenty-five-year-old college dropout.[34] Twelve years, later after publishing his second book in 1949, *American Horse Drawn*

Vehicles, he issued "Advanced List No. 1 Comprising: BOOKS, MAGAZINES, PAMPHLETS And OLD CATALOGS Issued from 1837 to 1948 Relating to TRANSPORTATION (HORSE-DRAWN VEHICLES)," and was soon elected for membership in the Antiquarian Booksellers Association of America. Twenty-five years later he was on a first-name basis with all the notable dealers in Western Americana and wrote of them in his recollections about research for his bibliography. "The magnificent catalogs of such Americana dealers as Eberstadt, Decker, Dawson, Reynolds, Luther, and others were collected and read. They provided succinct summaries and critical comments, notes on values and variants, and new entries. On chance visits to New York, Chicago, and San Francisco, not to mention Nashville, Omaha, Helena, and San Diego, bookshops were visited personally, and from Argosy, from Acres of Books, and from Warren Howell more material was gained."[35]

Gathering information for *The Santa Fe Trail: A Historical Bibliography* was a giant treasure hunt, and Jack loved every part of the process. As with other collector-writers, he mused about actually living in a large library.

> More than once I wished I could have been locked in the library stacks for weeks, with some kind attendant leaving a daily sack of hamburgers and a carton of buttermilk in my carrel. No bibliography will ever produce an author's royalty that does more than recompense his costs of travel and photocopying. But there can be a side benefit: while this work was proceeding I naturally bought many items, not an expensive first of Kendall or Gregg[36] but those elusive bits of ephemera. They cost little when I acquired them, but after the bibliography appeared they rose in value. Ready to move on to another project, I sold the lot at enough profit to put a daughter through her first year at . . . college. But such is the nature of bibliomania that I have since acquired replacement copies of most, although these new children are not handled with the affection given the firstborn.[37]

Jack's manuscript returned from the outside readers with cogent suggestions for adjustments and strong recommendations to publish. Among other points, Ray Allen Billington thought a longer introduction of twenty-five to thirty pages should give a brief history of the trail for general readers who might not understand references to "the Snively expedition," or "the Santa Fe expedition." On his own initiative Jack had already sent his manuscript to Archie Hanna at Yale. Hanna, one of the most knowledgeable and highly respected curators of Western Americana, also made suggestions along with a strong recommendation to publish.

Shugg shared the two reports sent to him with Jack who responded with a single-page memorandum about making changes. "The scores of minor comments and suggestions on individual entries are all most helpful, easily corrected, and I consider myself fortunate to have had their guidance. Most books are expositions of the author's position or interpretation of a topic; a bibliography is a mere working tool, a piece of equipment. The bibliography must be of service to the user, who may be an undergraduate, a graduate student, a librarian, a collector, or a bookseller. Hence the bibliography should be market tested and the consumer's opinion respected. The critics have made an excellent contribution in this regard." As for changes that were needed, Jack told Shugg he would have it done in a month. "I foresaw that the ms. would need to be retyped completely with an eye to the particular style to be adopted, but this revision requires only a month of evenings. Once the ms. is adopted and the style fixed, this part is easy."[38] By mid-October 1970, Jack had retyped his manuscript and drawn up the "Final Typographic Standards," outlining precisely how each entry would handle font elements and spacing for the item number, author, subject, title entry, and physical description for each of the 718 titles in the bibliography, with the format and content of each entry consistent with all the others.

Jack made all the emendations needed and retyped his manuscript by mid-October. It then moved to his colleague, Bruce Gentry, book designer for the Press. When Gentry finished designing the book it went into production at the end of 1970, right on schedule for release in time for the Santa Fe Trail Sesquicentennial celebrations starting in 1971.

Jack received the first bound copy of his work on June 5, 1971. Dedicated to Charlotte, the book arrived on her birthday. Publication brought congratulatory letters from notable historians, librarians, booksellers, and collectors. In a few months strong reviews began appearing in newspapers and journals. Michael D. Heaston, curator of rare books at Wichita State University wrote, "I am quite impressed with your work and I can see why you have taken years to compile the bibliography. Your efforts to suggest a 'best' book list should be well received, as all are deserving books."[39] The list Heaston referred to came in the closing paragraph of Jack's introduction where he identified the thirty best writers on the trail, "For those who here make their first acquaintance with the full literature of the Santa Fe Trail." Dick Mohr of International Bookfinders in Beverly Hills wrote, "Altho most bibliographies are so pellucid as to be unreadable, I sat up late last night and read yours through. Then I went back and read the introduction, which I should have read in the first place, and the whole Santa Fe Trail picture is now much better in my mind." Mohr also commented, "I see from some of your evaluations that I undervalued some of the books on the Trail in the past, but I see also that I may have overestimated some that are just so so. . . . And how refreshing your Addenda, with the candid note that you did not examine them. I don't know another bibliographer who was that Honest!"[40] Ray Billington said, "How delightful to use a bibliography where the compiler has actually read the materials included—or at least scanned them intelligently—and who can produce such pithy and meaningful appraisals. This is a model treatment; the historian will benefit just as will the collector or librarian."[41] From the Beinecke Library at Yale University, Archie Hanna wrote of the book as "a foundation stone in the growing edifice of Western Americana" and was quoted in a blurb on the back of the dust jacket.

Reviews in scholarly journals, printed less frequently, took longer to appear in print. In the *New Mexico Historical Review*, David J. Weber led off with praise for the introduction, finding it unusual for a bibliography and identifying it as a "graceful and lucid overview of its subject . . . , a superb framework for the [work] that follows. . . . That the book will be useful to so many different groups—book collectors and dealers, librarians and scholars—is testimony to Rittenhouse's own wide-ranging interests as a bibliophile, printer, publisher, editor, historian, and bibliographer. We are all the richer for his having brought into print the results of years of assiduous searching and studying."[42] Other notable Western historians such as Max Moorehead and John Francis Bannon wrote of Jack's book as "indispensable" and "an admirable piece of careful, meticulous, judicious scholarship."[43] Reviews in daily newspapers and association newsletters tended to appear from towns and cities in close proximity to the Trail as well as from organizations with readerships interested in Western history. Nearly all of them were positive.

Late in 1971 the Border Regional Library Association announced that *The Santa Fe Trail: A Historical Bibliography* had won their award for the best Southwest Reference book published in the past year. Jack was honored at the awards dinner in Juarez, Mexico, in mid-November. A year later the American Association for State and Local History (AASLH) awarded two UNM Press books their Award of Merit, the association's highest honor given to only seventeen books that year. Along with Jack's new book, AASLH also chose Morris F. Taylor's *First Mail West: Stagecoach Lines on the Santa Fe Trail*. In his capacity as editor of Western books at the Press, Jack had chosen Taylor's manuscript and guided it through the UNM editorial board and production routines.[44] In the process of working together, Jack and Morris Taylor became good friends; Jack made a special trip to visit him in Trinidad, Colorado, where he taught.

While working at UNM Press, Jack enjoyed his proximity to highly esteemed academic figures on campus, especially the Western historians, such as France V. Scholes and Donald Cutter. Their discussions must have reminded him of the lunch table exchanges twenty years earlier at the Zamorano Club in Los Angeles, where he sat with a generation of notable historians and bookmen who would soon pass from the scene. At UNM, in the building where he officed, he also met the newly named chair of the Journalism Department, Tony Hillerman, whose first novel, *The Blessing Way*, would soon be published by Harper and Row. Sharing interests in Western history and literature, they began meeting for lunch across from the campus at University Rexall Drug Store on Central Avenue to talk about authors and their books, including what drew writers to New Mexico.[45] In a few years this topic would lead to a Hillerman book for UNM Press. Meanwhile, when Hillerman learned about Jack's advertising agency experience, he asked if Jack would fill a teaching gap left when a faculty member abruptly took a job elsewhere. Jack agreed to teach a single course in advertising at UNM in the fall semester 1968. Because the class, scheduled for an hour four days a week, started at 11:30 a.m., the university deemed the first half hour as "company time" away from the Press. For the remaining half hour from 12:00 to 12:30 p.m. the administration conveniently labeled him a volunteer taking time from his lunch break. Weaving and dodging to save pennies, they paid Jack no extra compensation for teaching the class. This course came on top of his full-time job at UNM Press in a year when he was still president of the Historical Society of New Mexico.

A few years later, the dean of the library asked what a course on the history of the book might cover. Jack's enthusiastic and thorough response was so well received that UNM asked him to teach the course and paid him for it. When the University listed Jack's History and Appreciation of the Book the first time in 1974, twenty-two students registered. For the next three years Jack taught this popular course, cross-listed at the Honors level by three departments—English, Art History, and Educational Foundations. The course outline for 1977 reveals Jack's widely knowledgeable approach to the subject. Starting with the origins of printing and papermaking, the design of typefaces and the aesthetics of typography, methods for illustrating books, methods of binding, book design, publishing practices, bookselling, book collecting, and book printers and publishers in the Southwest, it appealed to a wide variety of students. Whenever possible, he arranged for guests to speak to his class about their work with books. From his large circle of friends in the book world, his students heard and met such talented designers as Helen Gentry and Carl Hertzog. Gentry (1897–1988), a graduate of University of California, Berkeley, was a Santa Fe printer, book designer, and typographer who learned her craft in fine bookmaking and printing at the Grabhorn Press. Hertzog (1902–1984), the master book designer and printer from El Paso, had designed books for Texas Western Press at the University of Texas at El Paso as well as major publishing houses like Alfred A. Knopf.

In many ways, Jack had been preparing for decades to teach a thorough and engaging course on the history of the book. When he was twenty-three and living in New York during the Depression and working in the mailroom at Alfred A. Knopf, he had kept notes on all the points about book publication revealed in the incoming correspondence from noted Knopf authors from H. L. Mencken and Willa Cather to John Galsworthy and Langston Hughes. At Knopf he observed Sidney Jacobs, head of advertising and promotion. Jack's notes included listing, organizing, and charting the workflow for all of Jacobs's responsibilities. Working for Hillman-Curl the following year, he learned more about book promotion and also studied advertising, copywriting, typography, and printing. By the time he bought his first press some years later, he had already assembled a collection of vintage type and learned about the history of type design. With years around presses, publishers, book people, and book production work, he had the knowledge and experience to outline his course. He gained permission from Roger Shugg to hold office hours for students during his day job at UNM Press. With his class scheduled one evening a week for a semester, Jack was soon teaching his second university course.

In the same year that UNM released Jack's bibliography, Marc Simmons, leading authority on the Santa Fe Trail and close friend of

Jack, began writing about the Trail. Having published a small pamphlet, *Opening the Santa Fe Trail: One Hundred and Fifty Years, 1821–1971*, Marc followed with six highly readable books about the Trail, generating nationwide interest through his writing, lectures, and leadership in organizing the Santa Fe Trail Association. Soon the National Geographic Society invited him to write about the Santa Fe Trail in their book, *Trails West*. After that, when anyone, especially at the *New York Times*, had a question about the Santa Fe Trail, they called Marc at his small, remote ranch in the Galisteo Basin south of Santa Fe. Little did they know he was answering on an old dial phone mounted on the porch outside the adobe library he had built entirely by hand. Thanks to his lobbying efforts, the National Park Service added the Santa Fe Trail to the National Trails System in 1987.

In 1986 when Jack published his own second printing in paperback of *The Santa Fe Trail: A Historical Bibliography*, Marc approached him, seeking permission to reprint the introduction to meet growing interest at the Santa Fe Trail Council (renamed The Santa Fe Trail Association). Marc wanted a short history of the Trail, noting, "No such publication has been available since Stanley Vestal's little pamphlet, Wagons Southwest, went out of print thirty years ago."[46] Jack, owning all the rights to his book, gave permission to the Council to reprint the introduction without a fee and with freedom to "distribute it free or sell it at any price. . . . This permission from me would extend through December 31, 1997, renewable then by agreement of both parties, or extended in perpetuity if I am dead."[47]

Gratefully, the Council distributed Jack's introduction to his Trail bibliography as a booklet titled *Trail of Commerce and Conquest: A Brief History of the Road to Santa Fe* at the 1987 Trail Symposium in Hutchinson, Kansas. The council also bestowed on Jack their Award of Merit in recognition of his book published on the 150th anniversary of the opening of the Trail.[48]

As Jack approached retirement in 1978, he realized the Press did not have an organized record of its development. To gather and preserve it, he offered to write a short history of UNM Press "to provide staff members and members of the UNM administration and the University Press Committee with a record of events at the Press that will portray the experiences, traditions, and policies upon which the Press was founded and has operated. Such knowledge of tradition affects our current morale and method at any time, but it also provides a method by which we can consider past mistakes and triumphs when we consider new proposals." He also felt such a document would be helpful for new people joining the staff.[49] His notes grew into an abbreviated fifty-five-page document titled "A Condensed History of the University of New Mexico Press," a succinct but insightful overview. He set the context by noting the Territorial Legislature passed an act in 1889 establishing the University of New Mexico. He referenced earlier establishment of university press publishing in the United States, beginning with Cornell in 1869. West of the Mississippi River the University of California led with their Press in 1893. In New Mexico in 1915 the School of Mines began printing its own publications, but the Regents did not establish a university press until 1929. Jack also clarified different connotations of the term "university press," a designation that did not necessarily indicate a full-scale publishing office with staff and well-defined editorial and production routines.

The UNM Board of Regents assigned multiple responsibilities to its first Press director, Paul A. F. Walter Jr., including assistant director for the Museum of New Mexico and the School of American Research (SAR) in Santa Fe. In 1929 the boards of the Museum of New Mexico and SAR moved printing equipment used in Santa Fe for *El Palacio* to the UNM campus in Albuquerque and expanded production responsibilities to include *El Palacio*, the *New Mexico Quarterly*, and the *New Mexico Historical Review*.[50]

For the next eight years until 1937, UNM Press operated more as a printing facility than a traditional university press, producing the official course catalog for each semester, a "Bulletin" series for publishing the results of faculty research deemed worthy of print, books under a joint imprint with the Laboratory of Anthropology, and journals and bulletins of academic interest for organizations managed by boards and committees outside the university. Definition of responsibilities at the Press evolved slowly after the university established a Committee on Publications in the spring of 1937. As the Press began documenting its activities, it still had no policy requiring payment to outside readers who helped evaluate manuscripts. It later corrected this practice by requiring and paying outside experts from other universities to review manuscripts before acceptance for publication.

After a thorough search of old committee minutes, internal memos, and directors' annual reports, Jack located no evidence of a handbook or manual for the operation of the press similar to the "Faculty Handbook." He observed that the early lack of oversight was not surprising. Few administrators had even minimal training in business management methods. He also observed that when policies were not codified as standard practices documented in a handbook, they were likely passed down only piecemeal from the oldest employees to newcomers. By 1976 the duties and responsibilities of the University Press Committee were clearly explained in the UNM "Faculty Handbook," but leading up to that time implementation of professional standards was, at best, challenging. With tireless searching Jack was still unable to locate all the Press records he hoped to see. Ultimately, he pulled together a unified set of the files and records kept by various people in their offices under a variety of file names and categories over many years.

Jack also documented how the university presses at Oklahoma and New Mexico began to establish their reputations.

> Oklahoma had an ambitious and effective program for its editorial operation, and during the 1930s moved quickly into a strong position. In those early days of university press publishing everywhere, presses could draw manuscripts from professors who had spent many years of specialized work. Many of these great scholars had manuscripts that represented a life's work, and they

> wished to see their material published, more as their contribution to knowledge. Most of them already had tenure and a reputation. Across the country, many were willing to forego royalties, often paid for final typing of manuscripts, and in other ways aided publication without recompense. The result was a series of landmark books that probably will never be seen again in such a general scope and quality.

OU Press quickly developed a series of books on Native Americans and on frontier exploration and marketed them to the public as well as to scholars.[51]

At about the same time OU Press was charting its course, UNM Press participated in two multivolume joint-book projects that strengthened its reputation in academic publishing. The first, Coronado Cuarto Centennial Publications, was planned by a statewide commission organized to mark the four hundredth anniversary of Coronado's expedition entering what is now New Mexico. Pulling together federal and state moneys, the planning committee arranged for UNM Press to produce the books in two series: the Coronado Historical Series and an Anthropological Series. The authors included some of the most distinguished figures in Borderlands history at the time—Herbert E. Bolton, George P. Hammond, France V. Scholes, Agapito Rey, and Frederick Webb Hodge, among others.

The Press also participated in an early series of books associated with the Quivira Society, planned by George P. Hammond in the History Department before moving to UC Berkeley. Along with some of his associates, he formed the Quivira Society described by Jack as "a book club whose members received books as issued." Their ambitious publications program resulted in a highly regarded series on the early history of the Southwestern part of the United States and the Northern part of Mexico, all based mainly on English translations of original Spanish documents. Dr. Hammond raised funding for the series, selected the texts, and edited them for publication. At the beginning of the series, the Society paid UNM Press to handle the printing production and deliver finished books to the society. Because of this arrangement, inquiries in the ensuing years assumed the Quivira Society books were a UNM Press project. They were not, but the series brought prestige to the Press for its scope, focus, scholarship, and production standards. Later titles were produced in California.

In time the Press benefitted from membership in the Association of American University Presses (AAUP), formed at the end of World War II. As with many professional organizations, the AAUP promoted standardized publication practices. However, the economic impact of wartime recovery did not trickle down to the Press. A few years later, for lack of funds, UNM Press could not even attend the AAUP annual meeting.

Until 1965, the Press ended each year with a large backlog of manuscripts awaiting publication and remained unprofitable. When the UNM Press Committee recommended an operational assessment by an outside university press director, the president selected one of the best, Frank Wardlaw. His leadership at the University of Texas Press had placed it in the top tier of academic presses in the country. He identified two areas in need of strengthening: production time (sometimes as slow as five or six years between contract and release of a finished book), and inadequate sales efforts. His recommendations described a clear roadmap for strengthening workflow through delegation of both responsibility and authority to editorial and production staff. He recommended working steadily on each manuscript until everything was finished, then turning it over as a complete package to the production department to move without interruption through manufacturing. He recommended time schedules for all phases of the work. Not all of Wardlaw's recommendations were implemented, but when Shugg came on board, he and his team brought the professional backgrounds and experience needed to set UNM Press on a steady course to success.[52] In Shugg's first full year at UNM, the Press published sixteen new books compared to nineteen in the previous three years. Sales income increased 58 percent and the operation deficit decreased from $65,000 to $61,200, a distinct improvement over the predicted deficit of $70,000 for the year.[53]

Throughout his tenure at UNM Press, Shugg and his staff closely monitored book sales and balance sheets. Early in January 1972, Jack announced that UNM Press books would be sold nationwide through an arrangement with Columbia University Press. He reported that the Columbia sales team calling on bookstores in 225 major US cities would add UNM to their list of academic presses that included Cornell, Penn State, and the University of Texas.[54] In May Shugg noticed an ad in *Quill & Quire*, the principal Canadian book trade magazine, and asked Jack, "What should we do to increase our Canadian sales? Please investigate and recommend." This was precisely the type of marketing question that Jack enjoyed tackling. The next day he gave his boss a four-page, single-spaced report titled, "The Canadian Market for Books of the University of New Mexico Press–A Report." It opened with a summary: "This is a preliminary study, drawn from limited data and subject to revision as we secure more data. It indicates that we should be able to increase sales in Canada as do other university presses. The average university press sells to Canada about 2% of its net annual billing; we have been doing about 1/2 of 1%, or about $1,500 to $2,000 annually. The major move we should take is to secure representation there through a Canadian publisher." He then backed up his conclusions with the details needed to make an informed decision, starting with brief summaries on the nature and size of the Canadian book market, the number of booksellers and publishers, and the trade areas from Montreal and Quebec to British Columbia, the book trade centers, literary publications, Canadian readership, exports to Canada, and key Canadian representatives. He devoted the last part of his report to the level of UNM Press business in Canada, gleaned from files of invoices. He found the Press did not "keep ledger accounts by customer or by area. During the past two years we have dealt with 78 Canadian booksellers. Two-thirds of them have sent us only one order in a two-year period." Jack then cautioned that collections from Canada were slower and more difficult than with US booksellers and libraries because cross-border transactions were always delayed. He ended with an eight-point set of actions by which the Press could increase its sales in Canada, including the idea of engaging a Canadian co-publisher, securing more market data, building a better mailing list, sending mailings into Canada, building a minimum review list, writing to wholesalers, considering conference book exhibits in Canada, and examining special export discounts and remainder sales. Jack's report gave Shugg everything he needed to promote increased sales for UNM Press books in a country that read as much if not more than the United States.[55]

When Roger Shugg's retirement date approached, UNM opened a search for a new Press director. Jack's name was on the list of possible candidates for a replacement. He submitted a resume and cover letter highlighting his range of experience in book publishing over thirty-eight years. He included two statements focusing on the job: "Role of the Director in Any University Press" and "Role of the Director of UNM Press in Particular." In the first, he specified the need for a good knowledge of the book industry, the ability to manage business affairs, skill in acquiring manuscripts and dealing with authors, and demonstrated ability to hire and direct good people. Regarding UNM Press, he wrote of a smaller press with both regional and state constituencies. At UNM in the 1970s, he likened the press director to being one of the instrumentalists in a string quartet, someone who in an emergency could "handle any post on the staff: edit a manuscript, design a book, write advertising copy, make a sales call, or prepare an invoice." He stated clearly that he had experience in all these categories.[56] For his references, Jack listed Ray Billington at the Huntington Library, Archibald Hanna at Yale, and Lawrence Clark Powell, retired from UCLA but by 1972 in semi-retirement in Tucson as special advisor to the president of the University of Arizona.

After considering Jack's application, the search committee decided to seek someone who could head the Press for at least ten years. When they saw Jack was sixty and only five years from mandatory retirement, they told him he did not qualify. By then his relationship with his boss had become strained. He never forgot when Shugg pressured everyone in 1971 to "work all possible days in December . . . and my usual winter trip to Texas was called off." Ever since moving to New Mexico, Jack and Charlotte saved some earned vacation days each year so they could spend Christmas with their son at the Austin State School for developmental disabilities. They had not missed spending the holiday with Douglas since his admission to the school, and Jack would long remember being pressured not to see his disabled son. For this and possibly other reasons he "became deeply unhappy with Shugg," and his retirement "made my life [at the Press] much brighter."[57]

In mid-1973 UNM hired Hugh W. Treadwell from Random House as the new director of the Press. Combined with his earlier experience at Holt, Rinehart and Winston, he brought sound credentials. Shortly after taking up his new post, Treadwell asked Jack to assume responsibility as business manager at the Press in addition to his role as editor of Western books. For his expanded responsibilities, the Press offered him a 10 percent raise in salary. None of these additional duties slowed him down. Before long he and Richard N. Ellis in the UNM History Department were discussing the need for a guide to New Mexico documents of historical significance. They had already worked together on an earlier book by Ellis, *New Mexico Past and Present: A Historical Reader* (UNM Press, 1971), adopted by the New Mexico Public Education Department for use in schools around the state. This textbook adoption was a first for the Press. Soon Jack and Ellis collaborated on a new project for bi-lingual publication of key documents relating to New Mexico history. Jack had already identified the idea for such a book in his first weeks at the Press when he drew up a three-page document, "Books Needed in Every State–A Checklist." It is a remarkably complete set of subjects with 105 book ideas ranging from place names and plant life to a Who's Who of famous writers and a school history of the state.[58] Published in 1975, *New Mexico Historic Documents* drew favorable reviews, including one by Alice Bulloch in the *Santa Fe New Mexican* writing about her realization that many New Mexicans may have heard about the Kearny Code, Gadsen Treaty, and separation of New Mexico and Arizona but never read them.[59]

Bulloch noted how good it was to have the material in one compact volume. "It's such a good idea, one wonders why it was not done long ago, and we are glad that Ellis has done it now."[60]

Out of their lunchtime discussions about writers, books, and publishing, Jack and Tony Hillerman decided how to answer their question of what drew authors to New Mexico. They decided on key writers revealing the reasons through their own work and began gathering their top choices for a new book titled *The Spell of New Mexico*. It included contributions by D. H. Lawrence, Ernie Pyle, Oliver LaFarge, Mary Austin, Lawrence Clark Powell, and Conrad Richter, among others. When UNM Press published the book in late 1976, it drew numerous positive reviews, including one by Jack Janowski in the *Albuquerque Journal*. "What a handful of gems!," he wrote. Hillerman and Rittenhouse "have assembled a sparkling collection of introspective looks by 11 authors about 'The Land of Enchantment.'" The book remains in print today at UNM Press, a testament to its enduring popularity.[61]

In the summer of 1978, with the university adhering to a state requirement for mandatory retirement at sixty-five, Jack prepared to step down at the end of June. Counting a few months of part-time work at the beginning of his tenure at UNM, he spent more than a decade at the Press, shaping its list of new books on the Trans-Mississippi West, creating and building a successful series of paperback reprints, Zia Books, and serving as business manager with responsibility for tracking, analyzing, and reporting all the numbers that measured the financial well-being of an organization with many moving parts. Jack recalled his early time on the job:

> My first task was to handle incoming manuscripts on books dealing with the American West and to handle the advertising. We had no sales manager; [we] had one person typing all invoices. Shugg brought in Bruce Gentry, an extremely well qualified book designer and production manager. Bruce was ready to retire from H. Wolff & Co., the big eastern firm, and welcomed a chance to

come to New Mexico, where he had once worked at the original Rydal Press in its golden period.[62] Bruce lived in Santa Fe and he and I shared the driving for the first several months. Another new member was John Scoon, who had been experienced in New York publishing circles. The four of us: Shugg, Scoon, Gentry and Rittenhouse together comprised almost a century and a quarter of combined experience. We all knew that within four to ten years each of us would be replaced by new, younger people.

And we made it work. We tripled the number of books the Press produced each year; within the first year we increased sales by fifty percent and for the next four years usually increased it around 25% each year. Sales were below $100,000 when Shugg came in mid-1967; by the end of his sixth and last year the volume was up to $387,000 and a flywheel effect carried it in the next year up to almost $500,000. Under Gentry, we raised production to a point where we were averaging either a new book or a reprint [from our] backlist every week, or about five times its old rate.

My experience enabled me to fill in at times on various jobs, at least well enough to keep the wheels turning. During the summer before Gentry arrived, I handled the production manager's job after the previous production man left. When the invoice typist was absent I typed invoices. I had no secretary but typed my own letters. I did the annual catalog section for Bowker, produced mailing pieces, ran an exhibit program, and dealt with authors on some incoming manuscripts. Most other staff members were doing the same.[63]

At Jack's retirement party, his colleagues at the Press surprised him with a book of seventy-two letters from people he had known in the world of books. "These people included authors, historians, professors, printers, artists, booksellers, a newspaper editor, a judge, book designers, librarians, bookbinders, university administrators, heads of university presses, and co-workers and other friends."[64] Frank Wardlaw wrote from Texas A&M University Press where he was the director, "I hear it rumored that you are going to retire June 30. You will beat me by exactly two months." After some amusing remarks, he closed by saying, "Seriously, Jack, few men who have engaged in the dangerous sport of publishing in the Southwest have had such broad knowledge of the history of the region and of its books. This knowledge, plus your own prowess as a maker of beautiful books, has enabled you to make a rich contribution to our knowledge of this land which claims our allegiance."[65] In their letter from the Taos Book Shop, Claire Morrill and Jenevieve Janssen recalled buying copies of the Stagecoach Press book, *The Man Who Owned Too Much*, two decades earlier and over the intervening years watching "these little books come out, distinguished in content and an illustrious example of the bookmaker's art."[66] Carl Hertzog included a note about a collection of books about books and about book people that he established in the library at Texas Western University, where a "sizeable Rittenhouse assortment [stands] alongside Grabhorn, Nash, Bruce Rogers," and more. "Your craftsmanship shows care and knowledge resulting in that elusive element—Taste. And I know that you worked extra hours to maintain quality when underfinanced and underequipped. Congratulations on a job well done and best wishes for you and Charlotte in the years ahead."[67]

Bruce Gentry remembered the dynamics of Press meetings with Jack. "There were those weekly staff meetings, where I usually sat thinking about how much design or production I could be doing instead. You always contributed to the meetings well, even if sometimes unexpectedly. I'm recalling the discussion of a possible publishing project and our each being asked our opinion of it, such as, 'How do you feel about this?' And your reply was 'Compared to what?' That kept the stuffiness at an acceptable distance!" Gentry closed by remembering the collegiality among the staff. "We were capable, confident persons. We knew we could do our jobs. We worked together well, even though we found plenty to gripe about. And if our self-confidence ever weakened we knew we could rely on you, for when all else seemed to fail, there you were, always ready with 'Plan B!' (What the hell was Plan B anyway?)"[68] Gentry signed his letter "Sincerely and admiringly."

Tony Hillerman began his letter by saying he was aware that Jack had been looking forward with pleasure to his retirement.

> That attitude certainly is not shared by those of us who have come to depend upon you for information, wit, wisdom, good advice, good spirits, and—rarity among rarities—engrossing conversation. We're going to miss you, old friend. And don't try to tell us that no one is irreplaceable. Who else can we ask when we want to know if the Rio Grande is really 30 miles shorter than it used to be; if the "muerto" of Jornada del Muerto was really a Dutchman and, if so, how he got so far from Amsterdam; and if Zane Grey, sent by his publisher to inspect the West, really hated it so avidly that he locked himself in his hotel room at El Paso and wouldn't emerge until he could get passage back to New York?
>
> Most people are replaceable. But there's only one Jack Rittenhouse and those of us you are leaving behind will feel your absence. With respect, gratitude, and affection, Tony Hillerman.[69]

Chapter 9

Dean of New Mexico Bookdom

> The farther you go, the more fun it is, and if you want to cash in the chips, you'll find a collection is worth more than the sum total of its pieces. Certain it is that you will find yourself on a by-road of book collecting that is not beaten hard and stripped bare by previous travelers!
>
> —JACK D. RITTENHOUSE[1]

EARLY IN 1978, JACK wrote Carl Hertzog, "I am really straining at the leash to get out into bookselling and to start doing some Stagecoach Press things. The NM Press has begun the formal search for my replacement, and I leave June 30. Twenty-two weeks, four and a half days to go."[2] The morning after his retirement party at UNM Press, Jack took little time basking in the accolades from the event. After breakfast he walked down the hall and into his office filled with books, starting his first day as a full-time antiquarian bookseller, a career he had dreamed of and planned since the 1940s. Shelves he designed and built on the first floor and in the basement of his home at 600 Solano Street in Albuquerque held nearly ten thousand volumes, all desirable Western Americana. Drawers of 3 × 5 file cards documented his full inventory. Closest to his desk stood an extensive reference collection, the envy of every bookseller and savvy collector who visited his home. Throughout his career he had started every new project in a library reference room with source materials pointing him in new directions. Now he was going to work each day in his own personal reference room at home.

His card files held basic, vital information for catalog descriptions. In addition, his cards included annotations from major bibliographies on the subject, the number of copies handled, sources for his copies, costs, and prices realized. In a nearby cabinet he maintained up-to-date, annotated mailing lists with more than one thousand names, addresses, and notes on specific collecting interests of each customer. Completely at home in this world of books, he had created a system so carefully that it had become second nature to him as he conducted his business efficiently, following routines to maximize profitability.

Jack's approach to bookselling had begun in 1946 with his publication of *A Guide Book to Highway 66* and his mailings tailored for different audiences. The first, a mimeographed letter to 200 advertisers and 800 agencies, brought notices in many publications such as *Westways*, *Motor Court Age*, *Trailer Travel*, and more.[3] The second mailing went to 652 prospective dealers (motor courts, hotels, cafes, and stores) along Route 66. To track results he assembled a card file on those who bought books and others who required follow-up mailings.

Two years later, after publication of his wagon book, *American Horse Drawn Vehicles*, collectors began inquiring about sources for books cited in his new book. He quickly realized that his research material could become the needed inventory to start a small bookselling business focused on a subject no other bookseller was pursuing.

From the outset he tracked annual expenses and revenue. His year-end notes from 1949 document receipts of $1,215.70 and expenses of $1,043.34, with a profit of $172.36.[4] In the postwar economy this sum, equivalent of $2,200 in today's dollars, became a modest fund for buying additional obscure and overlooked books about wagons sought by collectors who were buying his wagon book. He also bought an ad highlighting his specialization in the new journal, *Antiquarian Bookman* (*AB*), soon to become the leading trade publication in the antiquarian book world.

Over the next decade, he broadened the scope of his inventory, acquiring books and pamphlets about the West while growing his client base and mailing list to match his new offerings. As with all booksellers, he carefully maintained and closely guarded his mailing list. On rare occasions he would exchange samplings of names on his mailing list with trusted fellow-booksellers, usually ones working in another part of the country. On one occasion he exchanged sixty-six names with Robert Greenwood at the Talisman Press in San Jose, California, making sure all were collectors he regarded as good paying customers who had bought Southwestern Americana in the past six months.[5] Periodically he would purchase a mailing list from another dealer with several hundred targeted names and addresses to add to his master file.

Forty years later when Jack decided to sell his complete run of the *AB Yearbook*, he described the yearbook as a landmark reference work. "Each issue had articles by leading book people, which appeared only in the annual issue. There were ads of new-book publishers, lists of specialists and of books wanted. These copies were well used and often have marks. Reading them is equal to a full course on the trade."[6] These were among the books Jack studied as he practiced the art and substance of antiquarian bookselling, starting on a small scale and growing his business to the point where he became "Dean of New Mexico Bookdom" by the end of his life.

The title for his new catalog in 1978 revealed one of the ways he had amassed an inventory sufficient to launch his full-time business so soon after retiring. The cover reads: *Old, New & Rare Books on the American West . . . Featuring Scarce Works from the Library of Mr. J. L. Perry, Jr.* Some years earlier he had begun taking entire libraries on consignment. Through his earlier catalogs on Western Americana, some issued when he lived in Houston and others in Santa Fe, he had developed lasting relationships among collectors, some of whom were later interested in consigning their libraries to a dealer whom they trusted and admired. As long-time customers they had found him ethical and fair in his dealings and always willing to share information about Western books. In many cases what began as a business relationship became a longstanding friendship. As these collectors retired and stopped buying books, they turned to Jack for help selling their libraries. By the summer of 1978, about 20 percent of his inventory was on consignment under arrangements that did not require an outlay of cash, just an annual accounting for the books sold and a check for the collector's share on a 50/50 split.

With a substantial inventory of books in the summer of 1978, he launched his new full-time occupation. Announcing his move to Bob Hesler, a friend at the University of Arizona Press, he wrote, "Well, I retired from UNM Press on June 30, having reached the age limit. As I had promised, I have gone into the bookselling-by-mail business and am doing so well I wonder why I didn't do it long ago. I sent Marshall a copy of my Catalog #44 and hope he showed it to you. I simply picked up the catalog sequence where I had stopped it long ago."[7]

Immediately successful, he wrote Marshall Townsend, director of the University of Arizona Press, "I have been on my own for a year now and as happy as a toad in a puddle of buttermilk. Had one month that came to nearly $30,000, which isn't bad for a mom 'n pop business done out of a home. Will probably see you at the WHA in San Diego in October, although I won't run my own table but will lure a few collectors up to my room."[8] He wrote Jerry Keenan, another publisher friend that his business continued to astonish him. "The income matches what I would have been making at UNM Press, perhaps better, and I am enjoying life. Before long I will reach the physical limit of what a man and wife can do in the way of searching, accessioning, cataloging, billing, and shipping, together with the accompanying correspondence. But at age 68 I don't want to add the overhead of store rental and employees, but prefer to relax, work out of my home, and just do what I can handle."[9]

Between his consignment books and his own inventory, his first two years as a full-time antiquarian bookseller were astonishing, even to him. By 1980 he had sold first editions of Zebulon Pike; Pat Garrett's *Authentic Life of Billy the Kid*; one of the earliest books printed in New Mexico by Padre Martinez; Pedro Bautista Pino's 1810 report from Cadiz on New Mexico; Ugarte's *Instrucción Formada* of 1786; and a copy of Hakluyt's *Voyages* of 1599–1600. Tracking down the Hakluyt and finding the best home for it was one of Jack's favorite bookselling stories. In November 1979, the Friends of the Library at UNM asked the Special Collections Department to propose a possible millionth volume for purchase. Jack remembered, "I decided to join the competition. Every dealer has a few great titles in mind, shining like a pole star, dream books whose acquisition would be like Hillary's triumph in topping Everest." He ruled out certain books as too expensive for the Friends' budget and turned to two books for ideas: Henry Raup Wagner's *The Spanish Southwest, 1542–1794*. . . and *Printing and the Mind of Man*, edited by John Carter and Percy Muir. "Wagner could point to early books, Carter and Muir could confirm the importance of their impact on western civilization. Where the two lines of thought crossed, there might be the book I should seek."[10] He chose Richard Hakluyt's *Principal Navigations, Voyages, Traffiques and Discoveries of the English Nation*, published in three volumes in London, 1598–1600, and containing some of the earliest printed accounts of New Mexico and the American Southwest.

Jack began calling and sending letters of inquiry to book dealers scattered around the country. "When I telephoned my old friend Jake Zeitlin, he chuckled and asked, 'What are you trying to do, become the top Western Americana dealer?' I told Jake that I had no such ambitions at my age but wanted this particular book." Then Jack thought, "But what if I invested in this expensive work but it was not selected by the committee as a final choice? I sent letters to every major university in four surrounding states and learned that only one, in Texas, had a copy of this early edition. Perhaps if UNM did not select the Hakluyt I could find a buyer elsewhere."[11]

With no success from his barrage of inquiries, he attended the LA antiquarian book fair where he met Alan Mitchell with Frances Edwards, Ltd., in London. Fortunately, the firm was negotiating with an estate for a library that included the Hakluyt, subsequently offered to Jack. When the books arrived, he found an "added fillip to the volumes" as he looked at their old bookplates from Ashby Castle. Remembering his high school days, Sir Walter Scott's *Ivanhoe*, and the tournaments at Ashby de la Zouch, he reached for his *Britannica*. "Yes, there had been an Ashby Castle there when the Hakluyt was published. Mary Queen of Scots had been detained there in 1569, Charles I had visited in 1645, and it had been dismantled by order of Parliament after the civil war in England ended. Apparently its library survived."[12]

Several months passed before the selection committee notified Jack that the Hakluyt had been selected, along with two manuscripts offered by Ray Walton and a small album of sketches by Frank Cushing offered by Bart Durham. The official observance and presentation of books on May 2, 1981, included remarks by the governor of New Mexico, a message from the university president, and an eloquent talk by Rudolfo Anaya. Jack wrote an account of his happy book adventure a few weeks before the dedication event, ending with, "Home was the hunter."[13]

While he ably found high-spot books for special client requests, Jack also shaped his catalogs to include a variety of books and prices focused on history and related subjects in the westernmost seventeen adjoining states. When occasionally someone asked him for books about Texas and California, he explained, "I can't help you much on Texas books. The dealers down there are so experienced, so close to sources, and with such good customer lists that it is folly for me to compete. The same would apply to Californiana. On all other Western states, I can do well. I only pick up Texana when it comes as part of a collection I am buying."[14]

As his business increased so did his consignments from friends and former clients. His consignment agreement with Jess Perry, a wealthy book collector in Nashville, lasted twelve years until he had sold all of Perry's books. Through their letters they developed a warm friendship with inquiries about each other's health, updates on Jack's flourishing business, Perry's move to a new top-floor condo in Naples,

Florida, and mutual recollections of booksellers they both admired over the years, such as Bill Kelleher in New Jersey. Moving to his condo, Perry consigned one thousand volumes of Western Americana to Jack, gave three hundred volumes to the Nashville Public Library, and still had ample books in his new residence. "So now all I have left is about 64 shelf feet in Nashville and about a hundred in Naples." Jack responded, "I hope this finds you in good fettle, Jess. Out here it is a typical New Mexico summer, with spasms of heat broken by a few days' cycle of daily thundershowers. There are noticeably fewer cars on the roads, although we have no lines at gas stations in Albuquerque . . . yet."[15]

On another occasion Jack wrote to Perry about his success selling to university libraries. "Fortunately the years I spent at the University of New Mexico made me acquainted with the librarians' attitudes and interests. Most antiquarian dealers have troubles with librarians. . . . I know the ins and outs of the paperwork and red tape involved in libraries' buying and can be tolerant." He shared news of the WHA meeting in San Antonio, including a move for him and Charlotte to the Menger Hotel when the St. Anthony Hotel air conditioning failed. He came home "with only three or four fine books, plus a carton of standard stuff. Fewer and fewer of the Old Guard are present at these meetings. I didn't see LeRoy Hafen, Art Woodward, George Hammond, etc., and I know that many have gone to the Roundup. But the younger men are still enthusiastic. As long as you can be enthusiastic, life is at its best."[16]

The following year Jack wrote Perry about the growing Santa Fe book scene and its effect on his business. "There are now five antiquarian booksellers in Santa Fe, where they once had only one. None are large, but all are doing fairly well. This leads to some competitive pricing on the run-of-the-mill books about New Mexico, but I saw this trend coming and began to upgrade my stock. When I sell four books at $25 each, I do not replace them but use the money to buy one book that I can sell at $100. By this means I keep my shelves from expanding and carry the books the others do not have. However, I keep one copy in stock always of the old standby books, as this brings in trade who then can see the higher items. So my business remains good."[17]

In spring 1989, Jack thanked Perry warmly for allowing him to sell his library. "Jess, I owe you a great gratitude for letting me handle the original collection. When I became 65 and had to retire from the University under rules then in force this helped me get back into my original occupation. I should have been back in it twenty years earlier, but it was what I learned in those years that made it possible.

"It is actually now only a retirement occupation, but I make each year about as much as a young history professor earns around here, and I don't work as much as he does. I work at my own pace and greet each day with joy. Another university here, New Mexico State, gave me an award as 'the most knowledgeable bookman in New Mexico.' If you have any other books for sale, send me a list. At my age, I no longer sell on consignment. I now buy for cash, and I prefer the better books. I will be away on a book-hunting trip April 18–May 4."[18]

For twelve years Jack sold books from Perry's library, and Perry also helped him secure another notable consignment in 1978. He wrote,

> Dear Jess, thanks to your fine help, I have secured the book collection of A. B. Guthrie, Jr. up in Choteau, Montana. He told me you had written and said that if he had any more letters of recommendation such as that he would have to nominate me for Pope.
>
> The collection consists of about six hundred books. It is not as valuable as yours or as well chosen, for it is a working research library and not a collector's collection. Naturally it is heavy on the fur trade, with some rare items in that line, and there are many books on the cattle trade and on the northwestern states.[19]

Jack had the perfect reason for another road trip through western landscapes he loved and drove to Choteau, Montana, to pack up Guthrie's books. Before leaving he had gained a new friend with plans for a visit the following year. Back home he made an inventory for Guthrie and assembled a sequence of catalogs offering his books for sale. A good example is Catalog 48, *Old, New & Rare Books on the American West . . . Featuring More Books from the Library of A. B. Guthrie, Jr.*, with Jack's note in the front: "Where abbreviation phrase 'sgd ABG' appears in the description of any book, this indicates that it is from the working library of A. B. Guthrie, Jr. the Pulitzer Prize–winning author, and the copy is signed by him." What Jack did not mention in the catalog headnote was that Guthrie had also written the screenplay for *Shane*, nominated for an Academy Award. Of the 198 books in Catalog 48, more than 75 percent were from Guthrie's library. He wrote Jack, "What a lot of books I had and how carefully you have listed them! In the beginning I had wondered whether I had number enough to justify your trip. Now it appears I did, and I am glad about that. I will mail out to likely prospects the copies of your catalogue, which haven't reached me yet. But good Lord, man, you needn't have sent me stamps. Your consideration humbles me."[20]

Perhaps Jack's earliest consignment of desirable Western Americana came from William S. Wallace three years before Jack retired from UNM. Jack had initiated correspondence with Wallace seventeen years earlier when he learned that Wallace was compiling a bibliography of New Mexico, a project similar to one Jack was working on at the same time. In a five-page, single-spaced letter Jack was at his cordial best, explaining how he had come to work on such a massive project, his approach to its scope and organization, and what he had done earlier with the Route 66 book and his wagon book.[21] As their correspondence continued they each decided independently that the scope of a New Mexico bibliography would be prohibitively expensive to publish, but they moved on to other subjects, discovering their mutual interest in books and collecting. Jack commended Wallace on his book-collecting article in *New Mexico Magazine* and shared some of his own book-scouting experiences. He told Wallace about his second trip to Santa Fe in 1954 when he found and bought three hundred copies for one hundred dollars of William H. Ryus's book, *The Second William Penn Treating with Indians on the Santa Fe Trail, 1860–66*, at Candelario's Old Curio Store. He had only twenty-five copies left when he wrote Wallace.

Jack wrote,

> These examples of "literary detective" work fascinate me. Ramon Adams found the remainders of *Memoirs of Ike Fridge* at Electra, Texas, I understand, and made out handsomely. Glen Dawson dug out the balance of Crichton's book on Elfego Baca in Santa Fe about four years ago. Ed Bartholomew for years sought the remainder of *Life of John Wesley Hardin* which was bringing $15.00 a copy, and finally found 300 copies in an attic. There just might be some similar loot still lying around in Clayton, Raton, Las Cruces, etc. I have never found anything else of a sizable nature, although I located the printer who did Latta's *History of Fayette County, Texas* (1905), selling at $20.00 through dealers, but by the time I got there he had only three copies left at the original price of $3.00 each.[22]

While still living in Houston and becoming more active with his Stagecoach Press, Jack printed two books for Wallace under contract with the Horn and Wallace imprint in Albuquerque.[23] Their friendship grew, and when Jack moved to Santa Fe, Wallace wrote enthusiastically about Stagecoach Press. "This Fall Jack D. Rittenhouse moved his Stagecoach Press from Houston to Santa Fe. So far as I know it is the only private press in the state specializing in books of the finest design and workmanship. . . . The librarians and book collectors of the state should feel honored to have Rittenhouse in our midst." Walace invited Jack to write the lead article in *Rogers Library Notes*, "Hallmarks of Fine Printing," and also to speak at the library at New Mexico Highlands University in Las Vegas.[24] Years later, in failing health, Wallace consigned his library to Jack with a 50/50 split on the sales price for his books to be listed in Rittenhouse catalogs. In 1985, with all the books sold, Jack wrote the trustee of the Wallace estate, enclosing the final check and remembering Bill as "a longtime friend of mine. In 1975 he knew that he had to move to a lower altitude and did not feel up to moving all of his books, so I agreed to sell them on consignment. We worked out a written agreement and signed it. At first he wanted nothing in writing. I asked him how much he thought he might eventually get as his share, and he said about $8,500. With this enclosed check, he and Almina actually got $14,642.91. The day he brought the last of the books, he went home and had his final heart attack. I will always remember those two, fine people."[25]

Maintaining an inventory of nearly ten thousand books, Jack compiled and published four catalogs a year. If a book did not sell, he would wait a year before relisting it. In contrast, he would relist key books in high demand whenever he could find them. His concise summaries of their contributions to the history of westward expansion in the nineteenth century helped find buyers for works such as Susan Shelby Magoffin's *Down the Santa Fe Trail and Into Mexico* (1926), George W. Kendall's *Narrative of the Texan Santa Fe Expedition* (1844), and Josiah Gregg's *Commerce of the Prairies, or the Journal of a Santa Fe Trader* (1845), among many others.

With Catalog 49 he began including a topical index to the contents of his 220 and 250 books for sale.[26] By mid-1982, Catalog 54 noted that clients approved his A–Z author listings and new index. Sales for the first half of the year remained stable, with 48 percent of his dollar volume generated from individual collectors, 42 percent from libraries, and 10 percent from other dealers. Laying out Catalog 50, Jack noticed the index with two columns per page often left blank space before the section ended. He decided to use the space for a unique feature in the annals of booksellers' catalogs—more personal notes about bookselling, collecting, and occasionally, the passing of old friends. Carefully framed with a relaxed and sometimes avuncular tone, these short pieces were written to generate a reader's interest in collecting books and gain an appreciation for the comradery of the book trade.

In Catalog 74 Jack wrote about the importance of foreign editions of Western Americana included in his offerings. In another catalog he posed the question, where do we find books? "For Charlotte and me it is the most exhilarating form of hunting. Some weeks ago we made a circuit of the Navajo Nation. Went to tribal museums, missions, schools, and trading posts. We came back with some interesting items. We went down into Canyon De Chelly, of course, where we had been before but still ride the trail with awe. At home, we bought 700 books from a retired professor, heavy on Spanish Borderlands items. We got 125 fur trade books from a Minnesota woman now in New Mexico. She is now collecting bird books and needed the shelf space. There was a small haul from an estate, and so it goes. Long distance calls, from Vancouver to Florida, brought other choice items."[27] Ordering by phone was the subject of his notes in Catalog 76, as he tried to prevent clients from becoming discouraged when they missed buying a book they wanted because someone else got there first. Jack noted that that happened to him, also.

With a great love for road trips by car, knowing they could lead past a book shop they had not yet explored, Jack and Charlotte were always up for another journey, just the way they started their honeymoon. In Catalog 82 Jack wrote about the thrill of discovering good books while on the road again. "One of the collector's joys is to find in some unexpected place a pocket of what an old prospector called high grade ore. Once we found some Texana letters in Toledo, Ohio. In Big Spring, Texas, we found two full shelves of New Mexico books in a junk shop, all nearly mint. More than once we have found books we had long sought in places usually not considered bookish towns."[28]

Jack also enjoyed examples of other book collectors on the road and on the phone. "A little . . . trade [from visitors to New Mexico] comes our way, too. A discerning Chicago woman found we had a scarce Fremont book for which she had abandoned hope. Last week a New York photographer telephoned and got a Laura Gilpin volume that she couldn't find in the east. A Connecticut collector of books by and about women came in and said we had more such books than she had found in any shop this side of Dorothy Sloan's."[29]

In another catalog Jack mused about the joys of printing and Stagecoach Press. "In Catalog 58 we offered to give away our old Linotype, and it is now with a young printer up in the town of Santa Fe. One of these future days we will start selling off some of our old type, but we will always keep the [Vandercook] press and a basic assortment of type. The soft click of a piece of type going into the composing stick is a pleasure that only printers can know." In the same column he pitched his few remaining Stagecoach Press books and then reminisced about his first bookshop job:

> Like homing pigeons, some of our Stagecoach Press books come back to us as we buy collections or see them in other shops. We have found them as far away as Vancouver in British Columbia and in London. If you have a Stagecoach Press collection and need certain items, let us know.
>
> Fifty years ago this coming May, I landed my first paying job in the book business, as the only assistant in Harry Smolin's shop at 89 Park Row, in New York City. He dealt mostly in back number magazines but had some books. I worked a ten-hour day, seven days a week, for $5 a week and the right to bed down in a back room. I was 21 1/2 at the time. Talk about your halcyon days![30]

He devoted his notes in Catalog 78 to the memory of Helen Gentry with whom he had worked at UNM Press: "Seldom have we been so saddened as by the death of our friend, Helen Gentry late in 1988, in Santa Fe. Helen was one of the nation's top book designers, but she entered that craft by accident, as a result of wandering into a display of fine books. Determined to make this her career, she apprenticed to the Grabhorn Press to learn typography. After two years she moved to a commercial plant where she learned presswork. . . . She knew 'the art that preserves all arts' from hands-on experience. In New Mexico she never received full honors. We list two Helen Gentry items in this catalog and as a small tribute to her we will henceforth always have an index section on Women: Books by and About. We will miss her visits to our house for book talk. Ave atque vale, Helen!"[31]

In between some of his more personal reflections, Jack interspersed notes on the nuts and bolts of bookselling. In one of these notes he told about the twenty-two thousand cards on file, begun in the 1940s, and listing every antiquarian book he had handled: "We enjoy cataloging more than any other aspect of bookselling, except for the thrill of finding a good collection for sale. Time records show that we generally spend an average of one hour per book. A catalog of 200 books requires 200 work hours. This includes everything, from advance 'thinking' to final mailing. . . . Some books take ten minutes; some take three hours. But along the way, the cataloguer gets to know the book once and for all. J.D.R."[32]

Another of his catalog notes reveals how much he was devoted to the Western History Association, with each annual meeting a chance for another road trip! "This catalog goes to press as we leave for the Western History Conference in San Antonio. We have attended every one including the preliminary meeting at Santa Fe in 1961, except the 1973 session when I was laid up with a broken arm. At that first meeting I called home in excitement to say, 'The great ones are all here! Hafen! Billington! Hammond! Woodward! Scholes! Winther! Morgan! Ewers! They aren't legends, they are here!' The ranks are thinned now, but their books live. And the young scholars are now deans."

"In late September we made a book-hunting trip to Arizona. At a motel in a small town we found the owner to be a Ph.D. who had studied under J. Frank Dobie, and a woman dropped in whose father is an 84-year-old ghost town hermit, laid up with bruises from a fall off his motorbike. We sat around and talked about Elfego Baca's gunfight, vanished towns, and such, while a tourist hung around with his jaw slack."[33]

. Each of these notes was most likely written as Jack prepared final catalog copy for the printer. With the extended routine all done for selecting books and writing entries, he could relax, reach back through a long book career, and reflect on what he wanted to say. In his catalogs he included Western Americana of interest and significance to a variety of potential buyers, from the neophyte collector to the most seasoned rare-book librarians seeking to fill gaps in their collections. By offering books in the $10, $20, $40, and $50 range, with $100, $200, $300, and $400 books sprinkled throughout, he appealed to a wide range of budgets. In order to keep the lower-end books interesting and attractive, he included important newly published titles to complement the rare books for sale. He carefully selected new books with an eye to selling multiple copies. He also tried to surprise his collectors. "In each catalogue I like to spice the mix with a few strange, unusual books, not necessarily at high prices, but to pique the reader's interest. 'Hey, look, Rittenhouse has a book on dowsing!' The prospective customer may not buy that book but is encouraged to keep on reading, in search of other unusual items."[34]

As he had done throughout his life, Jack enjoyed sharing what he had learned with collectors, graduate students looking for a thesis topic, other booksellers, and writers who frequently talked with him about books on the American West. They often came away from a conversation with Jack having learned something new and useful to their own interests.

In the last decades of his life, Jack wrote numerous articles for the book-trade magazine, *AB Bookman's Weekly*. His 1986 article titled, "Putting Out a Bookseller Catalogue," could serve as an outline for a course on antiquarian bookselling.[35] After the article appeared, a bookseller on Long Island wrote a "good, long letter" about it, asking where he could learn more about the antiquarian book trade, and how one sets a price on a book published in the past decade. Jack responded with a two-page, single-spaced letter recommending the Colorado Antiquarian Book Seminar offered in Denver each summer. "In time and expense it costs money, but sooner or later you play every card in the deck, so the choice is whether to get the knowledge all at once at a price or in bits and pieces over many years at a higher price." For pricing newer books he recommended other booksellers' catalogs, *AB*, and Bowker's *Books in Print*. If he found a book had gone o.p. (out of print), he would raise the price 25 to 50 percent if it had intrinsic merit and was like new. "But most of all, I do not buy any recent books unless I know from experience or intuition that the book has real, unrecognized merit and will rise in steady demand. You just have to learn that." He compared the cost benefit of getting a new computer or the less expensive Brother WP-500 word processor. Opting for the latter, he figured it would save him at least $300 in time on each of the next catalogs. "As the machine cost only $600 complete, it will pay for itself in the next two catalogs." He closed with the recommendation that one needed to know as much as possible about "(a) business, any business, and (b) the book business."[36]

Another bookseller in Victoria, BC, followed Jack's approach to writing catalogs and sent him a copy of his first one. He responded,

> Dear Colleague, your catalog #1 arrived today and was read thoroughly within the hour. This is a good catalog, and I am flattered that you followed my own suggestions. I enclose a copy of my own latest catalog. When I wrote that article, I hoped that others would write in to add their own ideas, but little has been forthcoming. I don't say that my catalog is the best, but it works and works and works for me. On a scale of 1 to 10, I would rate mine as a 5 or 6. Whose is a 10? Maggs or Kraus or Quaritch or Bill Reese or Dorothy Sloan or Mike Heaston. If I had their books and their mailing list, I would do as they do. But I am quite happy as things are.[37]

Jack also easily shared his enthusiasm for trade books that made new contributions to knowledge about the West. This was not only evident in his catalogs but also when visiting bookshops. In 1984 the University of Nebraska Press published *Carl Bodmer's America* by William H. Goetzmann, David C. Hunt, Marsha V. Gallagher, and William J. Orr to wide acclaim. Jack read it as soon as it was released and wrote Darla Beckman at Nebraska that when he was typing his new catalog copy, a customer stopped by and bought the book on Bodmer that he was describing, so he was ordering more copies. He also said, "I was out at Plaza Books, a new-book store here in Albuquerque, and I praised the Bodmer so much that Wayne Hammond, the owner there, is sending you an order."[38]

To graduate students making inquiries, he wrote letters filled with information and encouragement. After talking with Lynn Bevill who was searching for a thesis topic, Jack commended him for starting a bibliography on the history of the southwestern New Mexico counties of Luna, Grant, and Hidalgo. He sent a copy of his article on writing a Western bibliography and cited recent work in the field. He also planted a seed for including the earliest European travelers to the region, including Don Jose de Zuniga who came up through the Mogollons from Tucson in 1795 and wrote his account in Spanish, published in 1835. He gave names of others to contact for information, booksellers such as L. E. Gay in Alpine, Arizona, and collectors Lucile Gray in Silver City and George A. Caldwell in Deming. "The late Carl Hays of Deming was reputed to have had a fabulous collection, but his widow has stored them somewhere and they are inaccessible, I hear. The Lundwalls in Silver City also are great collectors." Jack ended by observing that the southwestern part of the state was not covered by any major published annotated bibliography and wished Bevill good luck.[39]

Jack's business correspondence was not as relaxed or affable as with students of history or aspiring booksellers. He never asked for favors or price breaks on new books (or on rare books), yet he applied a laser-like focus on discounts when writing publishers. From the beginning of his press with his first two books on Route 66 and wagons, he always paid cash or sent a check with orders for business supplies. When buying rare books, he continued this routine, especially with dealers who paid postage on orders accompanied by a check. He was constantly contending with the wide variety of discount policies at publishing houses. In a letter to his friend Marshall Townsend, director of the University of Arizona press he wrote,

> Ordering is still the greatest maze in this business, for everyone is a little different. For instance, some publishers grant a discount on the quantity ordered, others allow the discount only on the quantity shipped, so that when I think I have placed an order for enough to get 40%, I find that they have cut me back to 33 1/3% because one title went o.p. Most houses allow discounts on quantity ordered if based on the latest published PTLA [Publishers Trade List Annual] list, and if one title has gone o.p. they notify me that they will honor the order this time but cannot allow it if I try to run in a repeat. What is your policy on this? This is only one of several gopher holes I must ride around when ordering.[40]

The gopher holes got deeper when ordering from Brigham Young University Press. In 1978 Jack asked a friend in marketing for an invoice in addition to a packing slip enclosed in each shipment. "A packing slip does come with the parcel, but it does not show any list or net prices or postage. I cannot put the books on sale until they have been entered on inventory, and they cannot be entered until I know their cost including incoming postage. . . . [With publishers] I frequently find that the postpaid policy has been abandoned and/or that list prices have been raised without notice, and this turns up only on the invoice."[41]

From his experience as business manager at UNM Press, Jack knew how ledgers should be structured and maintained, so he could suggest a possible cause of the fulfillment problems at Brigham Young University (BYU). "I can guess how this happens: few bookstores pay cash with [an] order but operate on your money. Most cash-with-orders are from individuals, who do not need an invoice. So you run such an order through a 'cash sales' procedure and it has no invoice. However, you would have no ledger sheet to show debits or credits outstanding or to show how much you do with a customer. And as time goes by I may be one of your very best accounts in New Mexico, although your salesman will never know I exist."[42]

Another gopher popped up at the Western History Conference in

Kansas City in 1980 when Jack placed an order at the BYU booth and "wrote a check on the spot at trade discount as usual." When the shipment arrived, he found the representative at the booth had taken orders for books no longer in stock. The partial shipment came with a refund, but also with a paperback substitution for a book he ordered in cloth. One of the books missing from the order came later, postpaid, with another following even later at full price and no discount. Jack was furious and wrote the director of the press.

> I operate on an unconventional principle: I always send full cash with my orders, and I never return books unless there is a mistake or a defective book. Don't you wish all your retailers did this? But from now on, I will attach a note to all orders to BYU: If you cannot fill this order completely, now, return the order and the check and let me know what you can send now and the proper full amount therefore, so I may reorder; never backorder an item to Rittenhouse; never make substitutions (such as paper for cloth). Your computer is a great benefit to you, I am sure, but it benefits only one side of the transaction. Handled as this Gowans item was handled, it only makes a bookseller hesitant to order any BYU books except in case of necessity. This time-consuming letter is written only because I like BYU books and want to handle them regularly and in the hope that somewhere human thought and concern can enter into the printout.[43]

In another case, Jack simply stopped ordering books published by the University of Illinois Press and wrote the director saying so. Apparently, the press at Illinois had signed a contract to move all their order fulfillment off campus to Harper and Row. The problems that followed required so much of his time away from more productive work that he told them goodbye. After ten years on a team at UNM Press that put in place a smooth-running distribution system, he had no patience for anything less.[44]

While Jack was a stickler for a rational ordering process, he also never asked other booksellers for a courtesy discount. Writing to collector Fred Rochlin, he said, "If they offer one, I take it; but I don't bring it up. I do this for two reasons: unlike some dealers, my prices are not structured to include discounts. . . . I do 'exchange' discounts with booksellers who send me catalogs and from which I buy, or who operate shops that give me a discount when I walk in and buy. So, even though it has cost me some customers and has cut my volume sold to dealers to ten per cent of my total sales, I still follow this policy."[45]

In addition to selling books through his catalogs, Jack offered collections or key books directly to individual collectors or libraries whenever he thought they would be interested. He had been selling books this way for years before starting Jack D. Rittenhouse, Bookseller. In 1977 he offered James P. Dyke, director of the library at New Mexico State University, the first chance to buy "the best collection on the New Mexico poet Haniel Long that has ever been offered at one time." When Dyke bought the collection, Jack wrote, "You acquired more than the contents of that carton, however. I will keep on looking for Haniel Long material and will forward everything as a donation, so we can keep building the collection. Only if some super-deluxe work comes along at an inconvenient price will I query you. Please spare your staff the trouble of acknowledging these as gifts."[46]

Closer to home, the head of Special Collections at the Zimmerman Library, Dr. Donald Farren, turned to Jack in 1979 with a special request for books the library did not have. In March, Farren learned that funds were available for purchasing rare and out-of-print books, but they had to be found, selected if in good condition, delivered, and invoiced before the end of nine weeks for payments to clear by the end of the fiscal year. Farren kept the focus for this crash effort tight: UNM wanted certain titles in Wagner-Camp's *Plains and the Rockies*, with preference for Southwest items in Colton Storm's bibliography of the Graff Collection. He also wanted to fill gaps in the UNM holdings from Jack's Santa Fe Trail bibliography. After five days at the card catalog, Jack created an itemized want list of 437 titles that library staff members double-checked, finding many books in the open stacks and subsequently moving them to Special Collections. At home he checked recent catalogs from John Jenkins, Fred White, Tal Luther, Dawson, Mike Ginsberg, Jack Reynolds, and others. With state restrictions requiring a month's advance travel requisition, Farren could not make a buying trip, so Jack conducted his own trips with his personal bank financing to pay "spot cash for all purchases or leave a deposit check on books taken on approval." Over the next weekend in Scottsdale, he and Charlotte visited Van Allen Bradley, and on Sunday Aaron Cohen opened his Guidon Book Shop just for them. Jack then flew to Austin where he visited the Jenkins Company. "I worked late each evening and slept in the living quarters at the shop.[47] I made the circuit of the famous 'Eberstadt Vault' at least three times, checking every title on the shelves, and then checked other rooms.[48] I spent a few hours at the shop of Ray Walton." He returned home with many items on the want list and started preparing an ad for *AB Bookman's Weekly*. The next morning he caught an early flight to Los Angeles and the shops of Dawson, Heritage, Zeitlin, and others. As he scouted for books, this trip must have felt like "old home week" in LA bookshops that he knew well from years earlier. In the Bay Area he visited Randall House, Howell, Argonaut, Brick Row, Ross Valley, and others. Each night of the trip he called Charlotte with the titles he found so she could remove them from the ad they were preparing for *AB*. Once home he checked with Bob Kadlec, Bart Durham, Tal Luther, and Fred White Jr. in New Mexico. Along the way Jack was buying for his own inventory as well as for UNM. He examined books in English, Spanish, French, German, Italian, and Danish. One of his happy discoveries was the German first edition of Friedrich Wislizenus's report of his 1846 trip through New Mexico and down the Chihuahua Trail. It was not in the Graff or Streeter collections and wasn't on the list, but Jack took a chance that the Zimmerman Library did not have it. He was right. His final step was the preparation of 3 × 5 cards, one for each book, with proper bibliographical entries and notes on their applicability to the UNM collection. Jack filed the original cards in his growing documentation on the books he handled and would list in future catalogs whenever he could find them again; a Xerox copy of each card went in the book destined for UNM.

Jack recalled his quest as "an exciting and challenging operation with 164 of the 437 items sought put on the UNM library shelves." It enhanced his reputation as a major dealer, gave him much pleasure and pleasant travel, and allowed him to handle books in a price range he had not previously enjoyed. Always a quick study when working with books, he remembered all the details learned on this adventure. In later years he would draw upon this new knowledge as he upgraded his stock with books of greater rarity. There was also another takeaway from his whirlwind book adventure: even with a good want list and money to buy, "rare books and scarce items are simply not readily available. Building a good collection requires much time and vigilance."[49]

A few years later, the library at UNM responded favorably to his offer of a collection he formed as the Albuquerque Balloon Festival grew in popularity. By 1983 he had amassed 119 important books on landmarks in the history of ballooning. He included in the collection Faujas de Saint-Fond's *Description des Experienes de la Machine Aerostatique de Mm. Montgolfier*, Paris, 1783, containing descriptions of the first tethered balloon flight, sending several people aloft and deemed safe only after an earlier successful flight with a sheep, a duck, and a rooster as the only passengers. The UNM Friends of the Library funded the acquisition of the balloon collection.

On other occasions he sent lists to numerous libraries at the same time, alerting them to individual items that were for sale to the first letter or telephoned reservation. This was the case with a collection of novels set in New Mexico, some of which Saul Cohen had identified in his bibliography published in *Book Talk* in 1984. As customary, Jack went the extra mile to find additional titles unknown to Cohen, bringing the collection up to 268.

With an exclusive offer to Taos bookseller Tal Luther, he sold his complete run of the *New Mexico Historical Review* from 1926 to 1977. Closing his letter to Luther with a little inside joke, he wrote, "If you resell this to a collector, there is an association item that 'this set once belonged to a past president of the Society,' for I served 1967–71. I have not heretofore sold a full run to anyone, so it is no repetition of the way Bat Masterson sold his gun, over and over."[50]

At the same time that Jack was buying important books, compiling catalogs and steadily selling Western Americana, he was also continually writing and lecturing. For decades he had worked evenings and weekends on research and writing projects. When Dwight and Carol Meyers launched the New Mexico Book League in 1972 and began publishing *Book Talk*, Jack became one of their regular contributors with book and history essays. He wrote about private presses, printers, rare-book values, early New Mexico newspapers, the first press in the state, and historical essays about various publishing ventures. For his two-part essay on the Writers' Editions, he arranged to meet the notable printer who had put Writers' Editions on the map of fine printing in New Mexico.

> During the past summer I drove north of Santa Fe to spend a memorable morning and luncheon with Walter L. Goodwin, Jr., at his horse ranch just east of Pojoaque on the winding road that goes on to the pueblo of Nambé. He described his role in the project and showed me many of the books. Later, other details were furnished in letters from Bruce Gentry and Dale Bullock. . . . Writers' Editions, Inc., was a Southwestern phenomenon, a gathering of writers, poets, artists, designers, bookbinders, and printing craftsmen who produced many of the most beautiful books done in the Southwest during the first half of the twentieth century.[51]

He also consulted with Peggy Pond Church for recollections about working with the Writers' Editions on several of her books.

In another contribution to *Book Talk*, "The Bookseller, the Library, and the Collector," Jack suggested ways bookshops and libraries could help collectors enhance their enjoyment of books and develop more collecting skills. "Collectors are good for the book trade and for libraries, but neither of the latter are doing as much as they should to encourage new collectors in New Mexico." He suggested bookshops devise small signs about collecting in certain sections of the shop and set out mimeographed leaflets offering a search service for books that readers couldn't find. As readers asked for help, the shop could begin building a mailing list and working it. He encouraged libraries to invite collector-patrons to help with special displays and to participate in special programs, something Jack had done for decades.[52]

In addition to twenty-three articles over nineteen years that he contributed to *Book Talk*, Jack enjoyed writing for *AB Bookman's Weekly*. By the 1980s he had met Jacob L. Chernofsky, editor of *AB*, and both enjoyed their visits several times a year at professional meetings where books were exhibited, especially at the Western History Association. Jake produced a Western Americana Issue of *AB* each year to help promote the WHA meeting with a complete lineup of conference papers to be delivered, articles by well-known figures in the Western book and art trade. He also published numerous ads, especially by every antiquarian dealer who offered Western Americana for sale, as well as trade reviews of new books relating to Western history, many written by scholars attending the meeting.

In October 1983, Jack contributed a lively essay titled, "The West is Wider Than You Think" about some of his book-hunting adventures in places and on topics not often associated with the American West. In his UNM days when Pearce Grove asked Jack for suggestions on unusual collections that might add distinction to his academic library in Macomb, Illinois, he asked Grove how far Macomb was from Nauvoo. Grove guessed it was forty or fifty miles. "Then I told him about how [Étienne] Cabet . . . tried in 1848 to settle in Texas and in 1849 moved north to take over the Old Mormon buildings at Navoo, after the Mormons had migrated westward." Jack pointed out that there was no major collection of material in America about Cabet, though there were many books and booklets published in France about the Icarian experiment led by the French socialist. Grove asked Jack to help form a collection while he went back to his university library and enlisted colleagues and friends to help start a Center for Icarian Studies. This project for Western Illinois University Library lasted for three years, during which Jack's Paris contacts made on a vacation with Charlotte helped him assemble the best Icarian collection in America.

In the same article Jack also included the account of another project showing how books can be related to the American West without being written about the West. Alan Clark, director of the Albuquerque Library, had told Jack he wanted books that children could handle demonstrating worldwide interest in *Don Quixote* by Miguel Cervantes de Saavedra. "Elementary school teachers had been telling Hispanic children that Shakespeare was the world's greatest writer. This was about like telling Indian children that Columbus discovered America. The Hispanic boys and girls needed to be aware of their heritage." Rather than a rare book exhibit, Clark wanted books in as many different languages as possible, preferably paperback reprints. He wanted children to handle the books so they could see how a legendary literary landmark had spread around the world because people on other continents wanted to read it in other languages, even though it was originally written in Spanish. When Jack's letters to specialists selling foreign language editions brought an underwhelming response, Charlotte wrote to the cultural attachés and consulates of various countries seeking addresses for bookshops handling editions in their native tongues. She also contacted ethnic organizations in the United States, such as the Sons of Norway where they helped her find a copy of *Don Quixote* in Norwegian. An Irish source provided a copy in Gaelic. After talking with editors from Hong Kong and Tokyo at a conference, Jack secured editions in Chinese and Japanese. Friends who were traveling abroad found French, German, and Greek translations. "Spanish editions were easy, through the many American firms dealing in that literature; I even found a good facsimile of the first edition, the most expensive item in the collection. One edition was difficult to find, a copy in Arabic." At that point Jack remembered a new book fair that had recently opened in Cairo with the Spanish ambassador attending. The ambassador was a book collector, and Jack wrote him as one collector to another, asking for help. Not long afterward, a handsome two-volume Arabic edition arrived by diplomatic pouch from Egypt. "Finally, I had about 26 examples, not representing all languages but still dramatic and satisfactory, and it came in under the budget. Western Americana? Yes, in a way, because it traced the early Southwest to its roots [in Spain]."[53]

In addition to writing essays for book-related periodicals, Jack lectured throughout his bookseller years as frequently as he had done in the ad business. With confidence gained as a prize-winning member of his college debate team, he never lost his enjoyment of public speaking. When Jerry Wise, the executive director of the Friends of the Library at UNM, pitched the idea for Jack to deliver the opening lecture for a series on the book arts in New Mexico, he was on board. The other speakers, all known to him, included Richard Hicks, a master woodworker and craftsman who built wooden printing presses; Linnea Gentry, the book designer; Courtney Sheehan, master bookbinder widely respected for his restoration work on rare books; and Dwight Myers who, with his wife Carol, launched the New Mexico Book League in 1971 and published *Book Talk* for thirty years. Jack titled his talk, "The Enchanted Printers–Book Arts in New Mexico," and once more assumed his role as a goodwill ambassador of books. "A series much as you propose has special significance and importance here in New Mexico. Among the young people of this state there are many who might develop a deep interest and high capability in the world of book arts, but someone has to open the door to that world. On the east and west coasts there are many lectures, exhibits, workshops, and group meetings where people can be introduced to this field. . . . Your series is the best way to start, and your Library now has rich holdings to support further study."

He outlined the introduction of printing in Mexico, the first press in New Mexico, and its use by Padre Martinez to print schoolbooks. Then he turned to the region and its intellectual climate, how it attracted fine-press printers, and how the landscape influenced their designs. Topics and names for discussion included Gustave Baumann, Rydall Press, various "Fifty Books" prize winners, Bruce and Helen Gentry, Merle Armitage, and the move of the Tamarind Institute lithographic laboratory and master printmaking program from Los Angeles to Albuquerque. Wise agreed to Jack's outline and launched the series in October 1980.[54]

On another occasion Jack teamed up with Edgar Award–winning novelists Tony Hillerman and Richard Martin Stern, bookseller Nicholas Potter, attorney-collector Saul Cohen, and binder Courtney Sheehan for a program sponsored by the Library Associates at St. John's College. In a round-table discussion the panel covered points relating to book collecting as well as the steps required to move a manuscript through production to its final form as a printed, bound book.[55] Programs such as this were typical of the book-related activities one could find in Santa Fe in the late 1970s and early 1980s. In the autumn of 1979, at Jan Nelson's shop, The Santa Fe Bookseller, near Canyon Road, book lovers attended a two-day exhibition and sale, The Book as Art. The exhibit included examples of calligraphy by Mary Lou Cook, fine bindings by Virginia Gannon and Courtney Sheehan, artist's books by Paula Hocks, and marbled paper by Pamela Smith, along with publications from the Palace Print Shop, the Limited Editions Club, and artist's books by Robert Rauschenberg, James Michener, Jack Levine, Pablo Picasso, and more.[56]

The next year Pam Smith at the Palace Press launched a series of annual book-arts festivals with demonstrations of ink making, calligraphy, lithography, typesetting, bookbinding, papermaking, letterpress printing, type making, and paper marbling. The patio behind the Palace of the Governors provided a graceful setting for this activity and close proximity to the Palace Press where Jack had helped the History Museum start assembling a remarkable collection of historic presses, type, and print-related material. School children came throughout the year for printing demonstrations grounded in New Mexico history, while Pam Smith and Priscilla Spitler designed, printed, and bound notable books eagerly awaited by serious collectors. The first annual Book Arts Festival in 1980 drew nearly four thousand people, and the event continued to grow over the next few years.

Jack's reputation as an engaging public speaker on behalf of books and libraries took him to Farmington late in 1981 as a guest of the Friends of the Library. The *Farmington Daily Times* described him as "Mr. New Mexico Bookman" as they wrote about his lecture titled, "Why the West is Western: How the Land Shapes the Books and the Books Shape the People." His talk included something for everyone, from a discussion of books relating to the Four Corners area to ways for learning if an old book might be valuable.[57] Once more, in 1988, the Friends of UNM Libraries invited Jack to speak. In "Cities of Gold–Books of Silver" Jack described Hubert Howe Bancroft (1832–1918), his history of Arizona and New Mexico, and his book collection of sixteen thousand volumes amassed in his late twenties and early thirties.

Amid Jack's bookselling, writing, and lecturing, he was invited back to New Mexico State University late in 1982 to receive the Rio Grande Historical Collections' *Pasó Por Aquí* Award. Dwight Myers made the presentation, speaking of Jack's "outstanding contributions toward the preservation of the historical and cultural heritage of New Mexico. This inscription on El Morro recognizes one who not only passed by but who cherished the lore of the land and gathered it with love and pride for the enlightenment of later travelers in time."[58] Jack treasured the award more than any other honor bestowed in his lifetime. It came from an organization deeply committed to preserving New Mexico history while referencing one of the most historic sites in the state, the El Morro rock cliff where Juan de Oñate carved the earliest dated Spanish inscription in 1605, fifteen years before Plymouth Rock. The plaque still hangs proudly in the home of his only remaining son-in-law, Harry Briley, husband of Jack's late daughter Anne.

"Mr. New Mexico Bookman" recognized Jack's aspirations and contributions to his favorite state. He was so quietly old school while appreciating the accolades. His deep interests were in people, history, books, and sound business practices. Between 1980 and 1990 he averaged more than four hundred invoices per year for annual gross receipts of just over $56,700. His two daughters had finished college and were happily married, and he could concentrate on what he loved best: selling antiquarian books, traveling to lecture and scout for more books, and visiting with old and new friends along the way. In the meantime he still attended the Western History Association annual meetings, writing articles about books and bookselling, and always sharing his knowledge of books with collectors and colleagues in the book trade. Yet, aware of his mortality as his seventy-fifth birthday approached, he wrote a memo to his files marked "CONFIDENTIAL." It contained a short list of names and addresses for antiquarian booksellers he judged best prospects in case Charlotte needed to sell his inventory and close out the business. Bill Reese in New Haven, Michael Heaston in Austin, Kenneth Nebenzahl in Chicago, and Jan Nelson in Santa Fe were at the top of the list. Others included John Jenkins and Dorothy Sloan in Austin. Regarding Sloan, he cautioned, "She will bid very low; drive a hard bargain."[59] The memo revealed no premonitions of failing health, but as always, Jack was acting prudently in business matters.

In 1988 when UNM Press proposed publishing a facsimile edition of *A Guide Book to Highway 66*, Jack agreed. He wrote a short preface recapping the salient points of his now legendary project, remembering how at the end of World War II he foresaw a major migration from the East Coast to California where many young men and women had received their training before being shipped overseas. They would be driving the Mother Road, Route 66, and a guidebook could prove useful. He recounted how in 1946 he had driven the entire route one more time in his midget Bantam automobile from LA to Chicago and back, checking the mileage, making his final notes on yellow pads because there were no portable tape recorders at the time, and typing his first draft late into the night in small, dimly lit motels along the route. Reviewers ignored the little book, but Duncan Hines, best known for his restaurant guides, wrote Jack a letter praising his guidebook because it would help travelers slow down and enjoy the countryside. He ended his preface by saying, "Now, as with the old US 66 signs, that first edition has soared in price as a collector's prize. So keep this book as your own souvenir, or use it as you try to retrace the old road. Happy traveling!"[60] UNM Press published the facsimile in 1989. It remains in print today and has sold more than fifty thousand copies.

At the close of the 1980s, Jack D. Rittenhouse, Bookseller, saw its best annual gross receipts to date in excess of $81,000. His catalogs included more highly priced books than ever before. In addition to nineteen titles priced between $200 and $500, Catalog 77 (January 1989), included a two-volume set of the Paris 1812 edition of Zebulon Pike's account of travels up the Arkansas into present-day Colorado where he was captured by the Spaniards and taken to Mexico. Jack offered it at $2,250. Another item, unusual for many booksellers but not for Jack, was an original mold from England used in making paper by hand. The watermark wires woven into the mold read "J. Whatman Hand Made 1921." Jack had bought it on his trip to England in 1977 for £50 to use in the course he was teaching at UNM in the history of the book. For the two subsequent catalogs of 1989, Jack offered fourteen landmark volumes of Western Americana priced between $900 and $2,875, including the first edition of the great Wheeler survey in eight volumes, a first edition of Garrard's *Wah-To-Yah and the Taos Trail*, a complete set of the *Works of Hubert Howe Bancroft*, and the first and only edition of Clarence King's *Report of the Geological Exploration of the Fortieth Parallel* in seven volumes. Jack was reaching deep into his choicest inventory. The decision to do so was most likely motivated by a diagnosis of cancer in August, even though it was surgically removed without any serious problems. Jack's doctor leveled with him, saying it would probably come back, sometime, somewhere, and the success of any treatment would then depend on location, severity, and rate of growth. "I did not mentally climb the wall. Usually, I always had a certain amount of self-restraint and tended to accept major events philosophically, as inevitable. That November, I [turned] seventy-seven. Most newspaper stories in 1989 on life expectancy said that an average white male would live to seventy-six, so I should have already been dead a year."[61] What he did do was begin thinking differently about his business, how he would simplify it to reduce any burden on Charlotte if the cancer returned, and keenly focus on a handful of projects he wanted very much to finish. Whatever time was left, he would make the most of it, and he would be extremely well organized in doing so.

Chapter 10

Closing Down

> I seem to have left half-erected structures strewn across the landscape of my past. But my pleasures have always outweighed my misgivings. Central to everything was a passionate interest in the literature of the West. I wanted to write it, read it, print it, sell it, collect it, evangelize upon it, talk about it, teach about it, study about it, and travel to all the places mentioned in it.
>
> —JACK D. RITTENHOUSE[1]

CATALOG 80 IN JANUARY 1990 reflects changes Jack decided to make while continuing with bookselling. His diagnosis of cancer that could reappear was a clear call to start planning so it would be easier for Charlotte to settle his estate should his condition worsen, and his doctors could not treat it successfully. Assets such as a nine-thousand-book inventory and the Stagecoach Press shop could prolong the probate of a will. He listed more of his higher priced books in Catalog 80 while adding several pages at the end for lower-priced books. He signaled additional books for sale with the following notice: "SPECIAL SUPPLEMENT—LOWER PRICED BOOKS. Note: These good, standard books are offered at low prices that will not support long catalog descriptions. All books have been selected for cloth bindings, in dust wrappers, in good or better condition." Among the fifty offerings was the WPA American Guide volume on Death Valley, Vine Deloria Jr.'s

We Talk, You Listen: New Tribes, New Turf, and Ross Parmenter's *Week in Yanhuitlan,* desirable books but not often found in other booksellers' catalogs. Priced below $30, they provided a good counterpoint to other books ranging from $750 to $1,750.

Catalog 80 also included small, choice collections such as one with books by his friend, Tony Hillerman. He introduced Hillerman's mysteries with a headnote: "The following books . . . represent a collection seldom offered. All are 1st editions, all in dust wrappers where so issued, in very fine condition with no price clipped, tears or other defects unless specifically mentioned. All are signed or inscribed and in cloth."[2] With copies inscribed to him by Tony or duplicates in fine condition he had saved for a rainy day, this was a choice offering. Although he had not publicly revealed his cancer diagnosis, his later catalogs contain small but uncharacteristic errors, perhaps an indication of increasing fatigue. His pace slowed for issuing new catalogs from five a year in 1987 to three in 1990.[3] Even when slowing down his business to preserve his strength, his spirits were boosted by an invitation to deliver the 1990 keynote address at the Denver Seminar-Workshop on the Out of Print and Antiquarian Book Market. Keenly aware of the distinguished individuals in the book world who had spoken or taught in previous years, he began crafting his talk, writing three drafts in the process. Since its founding in 1977 by Dean Margaret Goggin at the University of Denver and Jacob L. Chernofsky, editor and publisher of *AB Bookman's Weekly*, the Denver seminars gained prominence with speakers from the Library of Congress, the American Antiquarian Society, and luminaries in the book trade.

Jack considered his keynote speech "the summit of our book career" and worked diligently to polish his talk. While writing his lecture he took a bad fall. "In June yr. bookseller stumbled over three stupid little steps into the garage, fell, and broke his right hip. Now I have a full metal artificial hip. Recovery of the hip is going well, but it drained away so much energy that I have not yet caught up, and things still run behind. Sorry!"[4]

Along with Catalog 83 in November 1990, Jack included a special note to select customers that his recovery had been "hampered by a pulmonary embolism and a few other matters" but would not stop his book business. "We will have some help in packing, and we never deposit a check until the book is on its way."[5] Despite his physical challenges, Jack delivered his keynote address on August 5, 1990, barely two months after his fall and hip replacement. In Denver, wearing his favorite seersucker suit and tie and standing with the aid of a walker, he delivered a beautifully crafted speech. He opened with an appropriate quotation, framing his talk, "Foundations for Castles in the Air'": "'So you have built castles in the air,' asked Henry David Thoreau. 'That is fine. That is where they should be. Now build foundations under them.'" Jack continued, "And you have come to the right place to do just that. This fever-heat, fact-crammed, week-long seminar will be remembered in your years ahead as one of the great landmark ridges dividing two eras in your life in the book world."

Jack described bookselling as one of the very few businesses left in the world where the merchant could be as individualistic as he or she might choose. In the process of finding one's niche at whatever level each aspired, they could also find happiness and satisfaction right where they settled.

> Down in Texas we used to say that such people are as happy as a toad in a puddle of buttermilk. It is not that they have lost all ambition; instead, they have realized all ambition. One of the best booksellers I ever knew was Franklin Gilliam, who ran the Brick Row Bookshop in Austin and later in San Francisco. Once I wandered into his place and asked for any novel by Mary Hallock Foote. She is one of the better but less-recognized women writers of the Rocky Mountain West at the turn of the century. Foote has yet to be given her pedestal, despite a fine biography by Rodman Paul and a stunning appearance as the central figure in Wallace Stegner's Angle of Repose, the prize-winning novel.
>
> Gilliam's eyes lit up in recognition; he darted to a shelf and

> brought me a volume. The price was fair, and the sale made. Then Franklin said nine words I shall always remember: "Gee, I like to handle that kind of book!" In those nine words, Franklin Gilliam told me more about his personal tastes and preferences than I could have learned in several business luncheons. And he told me more about the possible breadth and quality of Brick Row stock than I would have gained from a dozen advertisements. For here was a man who knew not only the main roads but the bypaths of his book specialty. And he kept in stock books he felt deserved to be sold on their own merit, not placed on or off the shelf according to some printout.[6]

As Jack spoke about the hallmarks of shop inventory, standards, ethics, and manners of those in the "ancient guild of book people," he included other elements important in the trade with examples from booksellers such as Madeleine Stern and Leona Rostenberg in New York, Sir Basil Blackwell in Oxford, Glen Dawson in Los Angeles, and Nico Israel in Amsterdam. In emphasizing the importance of a comprehensive reference collection, he gave a heartwarming example of a student who became a customer and later a friend who wanted to compile a bibliography on the California-Oregon Trail. Lannon Mintz could not spend evenings in the library, so Jack loaned him his best reference works one volume at a time, for night study.

> In time, his bibliography, entitled *The Trail*, was published and was well received. Mintz died soon afterward, of cancer, but he left a fine legacy. I recall the snowy evenings when Lannon came to the house, to talk books. I recall also that old French poet, François Villon, who asked, "Where are the snows of yesteryear?" They are here, François, in this book. They are here. And to me the greatest surprise of all was Lannon Mintz's dedication, to me. A bibliography dedicated to a bookseller! Over on the campus, one measure of a scholar is the number of books dedicated to him by his graduate students. Score one for the bookseller![7]

Near the end of Jack's talk he referred to a subject close to his heart—the sharing with others of what one learns in the book trade. He practiced sharing knowledge throughout his life and urged others to do so. "If you go back through the files of *AB Bookman's Weekly* over the years, you will note that with few exceptions all of the prominent book people have written unpaid articles on the craft of bookselling. And talks have been given at book fairs, public events, and library meetings. Pull your end of this crosscut saw."[8] The record does not reveal if Jack received a standing ovation at the end of his talk, but such recognition would not have been surprising.

Barely three months after lecturing in Denver, Jack consulted with his doctor about a swelling on his abdomen. Exams and tests revealed pelvic lymphoma needing radiation treatments five times a week for three to five weeks. Charlotte wrote their immediate family with details, asking that they not share the news with anyone else, noting that Jack's principal symptom was lassitude. He was not in pain. She wrote that he was still organizing Stagecoach Press assets for sale and would then start selling his mailing list and reference collection. What Charlotte did not mention in her letter to the family was a huge project on which Jack had been happily collaborating with Tony Hillerman and which he was determined to help Tony finish.

In 1989 the Book of the Month Club pitched an idea to Hillerman for a book relating to the West with a "broad-ranging but highly personal collection of pieces on the region, and we very much hope that you will be interested in editing this collection." They were looking for a "diverse selection of fiction and nonfiction, from the earliest writings to the present. It could range from short stories to diaries and other factual accounts to travel writing to songs, circulars, and posters—in short any material you found pertinent and interesting."[9] The book would be titled *The Best of the West* and published first by HarperCollins, Tony's longstanding publisher, followed by the BMOC release to its membership a month or so later.

As soon as Hillerman read the letter from BMOC he asked Jack to help him with his new project. In their initial outline they agreed the

"West" was that part of the United States west of the hundredth meridian, a dividing line established in the nineteenth century by John Wesley Powell. The time span for selections would be fluid, and, at Tony's request, there would be no emphasis on cowboys, the Indian wars, Custer, or outlaws. *The Best of the West* began to take shape for Jack as soon as he returned home from his initial discussions with Tony. Leafing through Howard Lamar's *Reader's Encyclopedia of the American West*, he listed topics on a yellow pad. He then walked along his shelves, looking quickly at every title. He was familiar with each book on every shelf, many of which he had read in their entirety, some he had scanned, and others he had only "dipped into." Meanwhile, in the evenings Jack and Charlotte began watching the PBS Ken Burns series, *The Civil War*. As soon as the first episode unfolded, he realized that he and Tony were trying to tell the story of the West in a similar way with accounts experienced by individuals. When brought together they would form the mosaic of a large story.

Jack felt that his life with books had amply prepared him for this project. Each week he took Tony a sheaf of entries copied from the first editions surrounding him. He wrote, "Here are the first fifty suggested items. A couple of them can be edited drastically. A rough scan indicates this material would occupy about 181 printed pages, or about one-third of a 550-page book. . . . Please give back the sheets I have delivered previously, so we will always have one complete set at this end. . . . [The publishers] mentioned a book of 550 pages. I am lending a copy of Sonnichsen's *The Southwest in Life and Literature*. It is only a physical example of what a 550-page book may look like. I will pick it up on my next trip." Jack closed his letter by saying, "The farther I go, the more fun this is. And I am beginning to catch those items that give the book a flavor and personality, not just a textbook. For example, if you use the Mormon alphabet item, I want to follow it up with a few pages from the *Journal of Jacob Fowler*. He couldn't spell, so he wrote words as they sounded. I sold one copy to a man, and he complained he couldn't read it. I told him to read it aloud, and then all was clear. It also shows us exactly how those old trappers really spoke. Thanks, Jack."[10]

Two months later, after sending Tony more than 150 possible selections, Jack wrote with suggestions for a layout that grouped items under ten or fifteen headings such as "The Original Westerners," "The Navajos," "The Hispanos," "Frontier Life," "Characters," "Mines," "Women," "Travel," and more. Instead of a long table of contents, he recommended grouping authors, titles of individual pieces, and page numbers under the headings. With such a typographical layout, an index would not be necessary. Jack was considering all aspects of the book, from its contents and layout to the heft of a 550-page volume.

He also shared his ideas for an introduction with Tony.

> What this new Hillerman book deals with is what historians call a social history of the West. That is, it deals little or not at all with politics or wars. It deals with people, and with what people did and the legends of their deeds that have survived. Historians call such a treatment "popularizing," in that it attempts to interest a popular audience rather than to introduce new research or scholarly interpretation. Professional academic historians generally look down on "popularizers." Even such unaccredited historians as Bernard De Voto and David Lavender had difficulty in being tolerated by the gowned professionals, but Bernard and David laughed all the way to the bank. Each side has its place.[11]

He was having a grand time working on the project with his friend of almost thirty years. "I have enjoyed this research, because I have been amazed at the number of places I have visited in 49 years of wandering around every state you list for the book. I have in my library (or stock) about 9,000 volumes, and any good antiquarian bookseller should know the answer to most questions on 'do you have anything on . . . ?' All I need to start me off is a topic and each new topic suggests still another."[12]

Jack's contributions to the project reflected a massive amount of work among his books that over many years had provided him a remarkable and nuanced grasp of Western history and life. These books had occupied an integral part of his life and mind for nearly half a century, giving him insights into the landscape that kept drawing him back on the road for another journey through time, always heading west. Now nearing the end of his life, he drew upon all that he had learned from thousands of books he knew so well.

The more they worked on the book, the more Tony wanted Jack's name on the title page. Jack would not consider this possibility at all. His response was polite but firm. He had just looked at the press run of 850,000 copies for Tony's last paperback release and said to his friend the Hillerman name would sell the book; the Rittenhouse name would not. Tony then insisted on paying Jack outright and wrote him a check for ten thousand dollars. His recognition of Jack's role did not stop there. If he could not put Jack's name on the title page and the cover, he would take another approach—in the introduction he would praise at length Jack and his contributions to the book. "A two-line mention would please me most," Rittenhouse told him. "But I can't do it in two lines," Hillerman wrote. In the introduction to *The Best of the West*, Tony devoted nearly two pages to Jack. "This collection could be called 'A Sampler of the Jack Rittenhouse Personal Library.' Most of it came from the nine thousand or so volumes of Western Americana Rittenhouse has accumulated in a long career as a book lover, author, reviewer, publisher of the Stagecoach Press, editor of the Museum of New Mexico Press, Western Editor of the University of New Mexico Press and, for the past four decades, operator of his own antiquarian book dealership. Happily for this volume, Rittenhouse has read and remembered the contents of his library."

As *The Best of the West* moved into production, Jack continued working closely with Tony, even though his declining energy prevented him from devoting more than a few hours a day to the project. Still maintaining his keen-as-a-bird-dog ability to read galleys and proofs, he finished checking every line in the 528-page book in twenty-seven hours. He wrote Tony, "This is a remarkably good job of typesetting. . . . I found only seventy needed corrections, all marked. See the following pages. . . . Most are minor typographic changes, but four or five are major and would make author and publisher look ignorant or slovenly. . . . By the way, when you sent in your lead paragraphs, two sheets of corrections followed the next day. None of these changes were made by the publisher. I caught them all, but really you should not be charged for them as author's alterations."[13]

With *The Best of the West* in production and scheduled for release in October 1991, Jack turned once again to clearing out the press room that had once been the heart of Stagecoach Press. Eight years earlier he had given his Linotype machine to a young printer in Santa Fe. Still, he had a large assortment of type to sell. He must have mentioned this to Dick Weatherford in Port Orchard, Washington, because in a matter of days Dick introduced Jack to Dan Cronkhite, a California bookseller and printer with a deep interest in vintage type. Jack and Dan agreed on a price. Cronkhite drove to Albuquerque to start hauling type back home. He made two more trips to get it all. Cronkhite recalled that some of Jack's type was in California job cases but other historic fonts were in small 3 × 4 inch boxes stored in larger handmade wooden boxes. When the boxed sets of nineteenth-century type were loaded they weighed three hundred to four hundred pounds each.[14]

Early in 1991 Jack wrote a happy note at the beginning of Catalog 84:

> In this room, below a great old horse skull from Zuni, there is a large gong that once hung at the shaft head in a ghost town mine. Long ago it rang to signal for a hoist. Nowadays we ring it loudly perhaps eight or ten times a year to signal the completion of a major project, such as writing a catalog or doing the last paragraph of some essay or book.
>
> It rang in January to proclaim the departure of the printing equipment of our Stagecoach Press. Dan Cronkhite, who operates his Sagebrush Press at P.O. Box 87 in Morongo Valley, California 92256, acquired all of our type fonts as well as their cabinets. He also sells Western Ameriana books.

> We printed our last Stagecoach Press book in late 1967. Nothing beyond a Christmas card or bit of ephemera had been done since. It was time to put those glorious old type fonts in the hands of a craftsman who will keep them going in the same tradition.[15]

Catalog 84 was the last one Jack finished and mailed.

He sent an advance set of proofs for number 84 to Marilyn Myers, head of collection development, at Arizona State University, a valued customer for years who had already placed an order for part of Jack's reference collection worth five thousand dollars. His cordial letter to Myers reveals why there was a six-month lapse between catalogs:

> My health has been quite poor, and my energy down a great deal, but it is now coming back. I will continue to do catalogs, of course, but I will be surprised if I can stick at this business for more than another two years.
>
> Some time this fall, late August or beyond, there will be published a new book by Tony Hillerman, The Best of the West. It will also be a Book of the Month Club alternate selection. Take a look at the introduction for a surprise. I did ninety per cent of the research on this book, from my own collection, but I didn't write a word of the text. . . . Harper/Collins is the publisher. With my best wishes to all of your people, Jack R.[16]

With another catalog in the mail and the sale of his pressroom equipment concluded, Jack offered his mailing list for sale. His decades of experience selling books had taught him the value of a list like his, shaped with great care over time, dropping names only after numerous catalogs brought no orders, and adding others as potential clients contacted him. In the book trade such mailing lists are closely guarded by each bookseller, and no one offered an entire list for sale unless they were closing out their business. For the purposes of his offer, he divided more than 1,000 names and addresses into three categories. Number 1 was 525 private individuals, some of whom would buy from every catalog and others who bought less frequently but never hesitated to buy the more expensive books; number 2 was 425 booksellers specializing in Western Americana. "It is a major field for some and a minor specialty for others. Some sell only low-priced books; to a few 'low' means a book at $500. Most are antiquarian dealers; some are used-book dealers, many do handle some new Western books." List number 3 comprised 60 college and institutional libraries, recently active buyers of Western Americana. "Budget pressures cause library book buying to swing widely from year to year."[17]

Every bookseller interested in Western Americana either knew Jack personally or knew his name. After selling his mailing list to nearly a dozen booksellers, he polished up a list of his reference collection to offer it for sale more widely. He knew it would be his most difficult set of books to move because it was the most tightly focused and highly specialized part of his library, most likely of interest only to an academic library or a bookseller just starting their business. The list of 771 titles ran for more than thirty pages with a cover sheet noting categories and strengths of the collection. All the landmark bibliographies were present, from Wagner-Camp through the Graff collection at the Newberry, Farquhar's *Books of the Colorado River and the Grand Canyon*, Streeter's *Bibliography of Texas*, and Wheat's *Mapping the Trans-Mississippi West*. Other categories included guides to collections in different libraries around the country, resources for study on photography and photographers, books on maps and mapmakers, and printing history. Jack also held the early important catalogs of noted antiquarian booksellers such as Peter Decker and the Eberstadts. Books in all these categories sold well.[18]

While selling off his reference collection Jack also began selecting books from his stock for Catalog 85. He had already sold the landmark books fetching thousands of dollars, but scattered throughout the new catalog he listed a variety of unusual books not often found elsewhere, including George Hammond's book on Alexander Barclay, manager of Bent's Fort, 1838–1842, and builder of his own fort near present day Watrous, New Mexico, in 1848; Joseph O'Kane Foster's *The*

Great Montezuma, named by Lawrence Clark Powell as one of the most unusual books ever printed in New Mexico, and one of the best in a literary sense; and *Great Grandmother's Girls in New Mexico, 1670–1680*, a scarce novel of the Pueblo Revolt. Jack had only seen this novel four times in twenty years. As the summer wore on, work on the catalog slowed and then stopped. Jack succumbed to cancer at his home on August 10, 1991, with books selected to round out the next catalog resting on shelves in the fading shadows of a summer day. His advance copy of Hillerman's *Best of the West* had not yet arrived.

The two major newspapers in New Mexico carried his obituary, and several hundred people attended a celebration of his life on August 15. Dwight Myers helped Charlotte and her family organize the Saturday gathering at the First Unitarian Church in Albuquerque. Books that Jack had written and printed filled several tables. For the occasion he prepared a twelve-page booklet in paper wrappers with a frontispiece photograph of Jack standing in front of his bookshelves holding his pipe. The contents included a twenty-six-item list of Jack's jobs and awards over many years, Dwight's overview of his life, and a selection from one of Jack's Christmas letters titled "Books and I." Those familiar with *A Guide Book to Highway 66* recognized the cut on the cover of the booklet, a stagecoach pulled by a team of four horses with two riders sitting in the box. Jake Chernofsky wrote a long tribute to Jack in *AB Bookman's Weekly*, reaching booksellers around the world. It included a photograph of him with Charlotte, no doubt taken on one of Jake's visits to see his treasured friends in New Mexico. Marc Simmons, whose early work Jack had published in two different Stagecoach Press books, wrote about Jack's contributions to the Santa Fe Trail Association, his major bibliography on the Trail, and the gifting of the bibliography's introduction that allowed the SFTA to publish it as a separate booklet and thereby raise funds for the new organization.

Eduardo Garrigues, a diplomat serving at the time as consul general of Spain in Los Angeles, wrote one of the most eloquent tributes to Jack. They had met in the spring of 1987 during his first visit from

Spain. After traveling more than five thousand miles around Arizona, Colorado, and New Mexico and just before returning to Europe, Garrigues wanted to buy some books that would help him better understand the "human and natural landscape of one of the areas where the Spanish heritage is more deeply felt." On a list of Albuquerque booksellers he found Jack's name and called him. "Without any formal introduction" Jack invited him over to browse through "the volumes of his wonderful collection. That intellectual itinerary was, for me, as fascinating as my solitary ride behind the wheel of a rented car, in a cultural 'pony-express' of sorts, through some strange corners of this country." Over the next few years Jack had sent Garrigues, perhaps the only person in Europe on his mailing list, every new catalog he issued. From his London office where he was director of the Institute of Spain, Garrigues ordered books by phone, and gained Jack's "priceless advice, gradually building up a sizeable library." When he was posted to the Consulate of Spain in Los Angeles, he and his wife made a point of coming to visit Jack and Charlotte. "With a great sense of humor, Jack repeated the Spanish phrases which he had used in modest *fondas*, where no English was spoken to secure lodging and food." Before his departure, Jack presented Sr. Garrigues the gift of several books. "There was nothing in the relaxed and merry tone of our conversation which could lead me to believe that Jack would die of cancer a few weeks later." In closing his tribute, the ambassador wrote about Jack's brief history of Cabezón, saying, "This ghost town, which lies beyond the traditional tourist circuits, overlooked by present-day maps, would have vanished long ago from the history and geography of New Mexico, had it not been for those 100 pages masterfully written by Jack Rittenhouse with accuracy and imagination."[19]

Others in the book trade also held treasured memories, too few of which are preserved. However, the late Nicholas Potter in Santa Fe recalled his younger years as an antiquarian bookseller when he first met Jack. Nick had opened Nicholas Potter Books in 1975, and three years later Jack dropped by to introduce himself. Nick said, "It is a pleasure to meet you, Mr. Rittenhouse," to which he responded, "My father was Mr. Rittenhouse, but I'm Jack." Nick remembered him as the "most complete bookman" he ever knew, with a range of knowledge and skills for buying and selling both new and older books, setting type, printing with care and good taste, writing, editing, and lecturing about books for audiences of all ages. He admired Jack's practice of mentioning other booksellers when a customer did not find what they were looking for in his inventory.

Nick never forgot Jack's tutorial on the special points and historical significance of a rare book that he had not handled before, but which Jack knew well. Jack set the background for William Emory's major work, *Report on the United States and Mexican Boundary Survey*, published in 1857 and illustrated with many steel engravings, woodcuts, and color lithographs, along with fold-out maps bound in. A civil engineer trained at West Point, Emory was tasked with mapping the border between the United States and Mexico following the close of the Mexican-American War. His book is valued for information on biological and geological discoveries, anthropological studies of Mexican and Native American populations, and for beautiful landscape illustrations of the Southwest unknown to most US citizens at the time. Nineteenth-century books such as the Emory survey can be difficult to describe for sale in the antiquarian market because it is necessary to collate them carefully, but to do so one must know precisely what plates and maps were part of the original printing and where they should be located within the book. Jack covered all these points for Nick on the phone for more than half an hour.

Nick concluded his recollections of Jack by reflecting on how book people's constant desire to expand their horizons and learn more makes them so enjoyable to know. He felt this was especially so with Jack who would come to the sales desk with two books although he had only stopped by the shop to search for one. "He was happy with the one he was searching for and equally so with the book standing next to it that he did not know and which piqued his interest."[20] This ever-broadening range of interest was the quintessence of Jack D. Rittenhouse throughout his life with books.

Lew Buckingham also remembered Jack warmly from their association in the 1960s and later before Lew moved his own antiquarian book business from Texas to Pennsylvania.[21] When visiting Santa Fe he and Jack would walk the Plaza, talking about books and meeting writers along the way. Jack's introductions were cordial, revealing the mutual respect between the antiquarian bookman and authors. On one occasion they approached a dapper man in a white suit sitting on a park bench whom Jack knew well. He introduced Lew to Jack Schaefer, the author of *Shane*, and a fresh discussion of books and the West was immediately under way. In his nineties, Lew paid tribute for how much he had learned about Western Americana from Jack Rittenhouse and recalled one of their last visits when Jack flew to Dallas. Waiting at Love Field, Lew finally spotted Jack across the lobby in his seersucker suit, carrying his bags, wearing his favorite small, floppy hat. But something was missing. Where was that ever-present pipe? Then, as Jack shuffled closer, Lew spotted little spirals of smoke rising from his jacket pocket, testament to a habit of dropping his pipe in a pocket and then forgetting it for a moment too long. As they greeted one another and Lew drew Jack's attention to the smoking pocket, he lifted out the pipe, clamped it between his teeth, and began smoking once more. The scorched pocket went unnoticed; Jack Rittenhouse was with a friend once again, enjoying his pipe, and, best of all, talking about books.

APPENDIX 1

A Checklist of the Stagecoach Press

For his first two publications Jack D. Rittenhouse did not have a printing press or a name for his new publishing venture other than his own. Both books were printed off-site by commercial shops following his design specifications. Starting with *A Showing of Type Faces* (#3) he acquired two presses, began setting his own type, and named his small publishing imprint Stagecoach Press (referenced as S.P. in the list below.) Over the next seventeen years he formed a collection of historic type and printed most of the books listed below. He and Charlotte operated the Stagecoach Press from 1950 until its closing in 1967.

1. Rittenhouse, Jack D. *A Guide Book to Highway 66*. Los Angeles, Jack D. Rittenhouse, 1946.
2. Rittenhouse, Jack D. *American Horse-Drawn Vehicles*. Los Angeles, Jack D. Rittenhouse, 1948. Later reprinted by Clymer Publications.
3. Rittenhouse, Jack D. *A Showing of Type Faces*. Sierra Madre, S.P., 1950.
4. *Oil Humor in 1665*. Sierra Madre, S.P., 1950.
5. Kimsey, David (pseud.: Jack D. Rittenhouse). *Permian Pete and his Fabulous Projects*. Printed for Lane-Wells Company, Los Angeles, 1951.
6. Dodd, A. S. *Plans and Dimensions of U.S. Mail Wagon of 1880*. Sierra Madre, Jack D. Rittenhouse, 1951.

7. Rittenhouse, Jack D. *Dime Novels on Early Oil*. Sierra Madre, S.P., 1951.
8. Rittenhouse, Jack D. *The History of Drilling Mud*. Printed for Baroid Division, National Lead Company, Houston, 1954.
9. Rittenhouse, Jack D. *The Man Who Owned Too Much*. Houston, S.P., 1958.
10. McKee, Maj. James Cooper. *Narrative of the Surrender of Fort Fillmore, 1861*. Houston, S.P., 1960.
11. Storrs, Augustus. *Santa Fe Trail: First Reports, 1825*. Houston, S.P., 1960.
12. *Confederate Victories in the Southwest*. Printed for Horn and Wallace, Albuquerque, 1961.
13. Noel, Theophilus. *A Campaign from Santa Fe to the Mississippi*. Houston, S.P., 1961.
14. Powell, Lawrence Clark. *Act of Enchantment*. Houston, S.P., 1961.
15. Pratt, Wallace. *The Value of Business History in Oilfinding*. Printed for Texas Gulf Coast Historical Association, Houston, 1961.
16. Rittenhouse, Jack D. *Carriage Hundred: A Bibliography*. Houston, S.P., 1961.
17. Rittenhouse, Jack D. *New Mexico Civil War Bibliography*. Houston, S.P. 1961.
18. Stewart, Maco. *The Legend of Tok-Chock-Tow*. Christmas booklet printed for Maco Stewart, Houston, 1961.
19. Horn, Calvin P., and William S. Wallace, eds. *Union Army Operations in the Southwest*. Printed for Horn and Wallace, Albuquerque, 1961.
20. Beckett, V. B. *Baca's Battle*. Houston, S.P., 1962.
21. Davis, Edwin Adams. *Fallen Guidon*. Santa Fe, S.P., 1962.
22. Rittenhouse, Jack D. *Wendish Language Printing in Texas*. Printed for Dawson's Book Shop, Los Angeles, 1962.
23. Arrowsmith, Rex. *Mines of the Old Southwest*. Santa Fe, S.P., 1963.
24. Grisso, W. D. *From Where the Sun Now Stands*. Santa Fe, S.P., 1963.

25. Grisso, W. D. *From Where the Fun Now Stands*. Published in a smaller format with one less section. Santa Fe, S.P., 1963.
26. Schaefer, Jack. *The Great Endurance Horse Race*. Santa Fe, S.P. 1963.
27. Utley, Robert M. *Fort Union in Miniature*. Santa Fe, S.P., 1963. Miniature format book.
28. Greene, Capt. Jonathan H. *A Desperado in Arizona, 1858–1860*. Santa Fe, S.P., 1964.
29. Jones, Fayette. *Old Mining Camps of New Mexico, 1854–1904*. Santa Fe, S.P., 1964.
30. Napton, William B. *Over the Santa Fe Trail, 1857*. Santa Fe, S.P., 1964. Large format, extra illustrated, deluxe edition.
31. Napton, William B. *Over the Santa Fe Trail, 1857*. Santa Fe, S.P., 1964. Smaller format.
32. Rittenhouse, Jack D. *Outlaw Days at Cabezón*. Santa Fe, S.P., 1964.
33. Rittenhouse, Jack D. *Cabezón: A New Mexico Ghost Town*. Santa Fe, S.P., 1965.
34. Daniel, Price, Jr. *Texas and the West: Catalogue No. 32 Featuring Books Printed and Designed by Jack D. Rittenhouse of Stagecoach Press: A Bibliography*. Price Daniel Jr., Waco, Texas, 1965.
35. Fermín de Mendinueta, Pedro. *Indian and Mission Affairs in New Mexico, 1773*. Translated with notes by Marc Simmons. Santa Fe, S.P., 1965.
36. *Constitution of the State of New Mexico, 1850*. Santa Fe, S.P., 1965.
37. Hinkle, James F. *Early Days of a Cowboy on the Pecos*. Santa Fe, S.P., 1965.
38. Disturnell, John. *Disturnell's Treaty Map, 1847*. Santa Fe, S.P., 1965.
39. Carleton, Maj. James H. *Diary of an Excursion to the Ruins of Abo, Quarra and Gran Quivira in New Mexico in 1853*. Santa Fe, S.P., 1965.
40. Tice, Henry Allen. *Early Railroad Days in New Mexico, 1880*. Santa Fe, S.P., 1965.
41. Rittenhouse, Jack D. *Cartridge & Firearms Historical Album*. Santa Fe, S.P., 1966.

42. Hammond, John F. *A Surgeon's Report on Socorro, N.M., 1852*. Santa Fe, S.P., 1966.
43. *Map of Texas and Part of New Mexico, 1857*. Santa Fe, S.P., 1966.
44. Ryan, Andrew. *News From Fort Craig, N. M., 1863*. Santa Fe, S.P., 1966.
45. Wilson, Edward. *An Unwritten History: A Record from the Exciting Days of Early Arizona*. Santa Fe, S.P., 1966.
46. Arny, W. F. M. *Indian Agent in New Mexico, 1870*. Santa Fe, S.P., 1967.
47. Simmons, Marc. *Border Comanches: Seven Spanish Colonial Documents, 1785–1819*. Santa Fe, S.P., 1967.
48. Farmer, James E. *My Life With the Army in the West*. Edited by Dale F. Giese. Santa Fe, S.P., 1967.
49. Nims, Franklin A. *The Photographer and the River, 1889–1890*. Edited by Dwight L. Smith. Santa Fe, S.P., 1967.
50. Weber, David J. *The Extranjeros: Selected Documents from the Mexican Side of the Santa Fe Trail, 1825–1828*. Santa Fe, S.P., 1967.

APPENDIX 2

Notes on Key Research Collections Relating to Jack D. Rittenhouse

This book had its beginnings more than thirty-five years ago when I interviewed Jack D. Rittenhouse at length about his life and career with books. While Jack's interview was lively and filled with details, there was so much more needed for a biography by way of primary sources. This essential material is found in several locations but the most important is the Jack D. Rittenhouse Collection in the Archives and Special Collections at New Mexico State University Library in Las Cruces. The collection numbers more than sixty boxes of original correspondence, manuscripts for his essays and lectures, subject files supporting his research and writing, production records on Stagecoach Press books, and more. All material in the Rittenhouse Collection was recently organized and processed, with an online finding aid available to researchers worldwide. NMSU also holds records of the New Mexico Book League (NMBL), founded by Dwight and Carol Myers in 1971 and devoted to the promotion of books throughout the state for three decades. Jack's essays for the NMBL publication *Book Talk* are a delight to read and are documented in its archive. In Loraine Lavender's papers at NMSU are files relating to her tenure as president of the Historical Society of New Mexico. Rittenhouse served two terms as president of the HSNM before Lavender led the organization, and her papers include annual meeting minutes, bylaws, and printed materials relating to Jack's leadership years from 1967 to 1971.

In the Center for Southwest Research and Special Collections

(CSRSC), Zimmerman Library, UNM, there are several collections with documents relating to Rittenhouse, including the archival files from UNM Press where he worked from 1968 until his retirement ten years later. There are also files relating to his landmark book published by UNM Press, *The Santa Fe Trail: A Historical Bibliography* (1971), including page proofs, notes for the manuscript, and correspondence with archivists at Yale University and the Huntington Library. His unpublished essay on the research and writing of this bibliography tells us much about Jack's meticulous and thorough research techniques, which led to an award-winning book. CSRSC also holds archives of the *New Mexico Historical Review*, the scholarly journal published by the Historical Society of New Mexico. This collection includes substantial correspondence of the editors with contributors as well as with HSNM board members, including Rittenhouse.

The Fray Angélico Chávez History Library at the New Mexico History Museum holds significant material relating to Rittenhouse, including the Zang Wood Collection with all of Jack's Stagecoach Press books, many of the annual Christmas cards that he designed and printed, and his numerous contributions to the oil-field journals, *Baroid News Bulletin* and *Tomorrow's Tools Today* published by the Lane Wells Company. Jack's contributions to these journals, both for content and for design, are little known, and the Wood collection most likely includes the only complete set in any library in the country. The Chávez History Library also holds a copy of Jack's unpublished manuscript, "A Condensed History of the University of New Mexico Press," which he gave to Marta Weigle and can be found in her collection of papers. The Stagecoach Press Samples Collection at the Chávez History Library includes other examples of his privately printed Christmas cards not found in the Zang Wood Collection.

While conducting research for this book I kept hoping to locate a complete set of Jack's extensive Christmas letters, recollections of the major stages and events in his life, typed over many years and given only to his family. No archive or university special collections in the country listed any parts of these memoirs that Jack never intended for publication. The closest version to his extensive original Christmas letters can be found on the website Recollections Jack D. Rittenhouse, lovingly edited and maintained online by his son-in-law, Harry Briley. When I mentioned my quest to Dr. T. Lindsay Baker, historian and authority on Route 66, he suggested contacting the Special Collections in the library at Missouri State University, which conducted interviews and gathered a major collection of papers and printed material about Route 66. It was there I found the 371-page typescript in nine parts that Jack had given his son David. When David (born in 1938) was interviewed about Route 66, he gave the typescript to the library where it is uncatalogued and filed as "Reflections by Jack D. Rittenhouse" in the Route 66 Oral History Project (M67).

In November 1981, at Eastern New Mexico University in Portales, Mary Jo Walker and Cecil Clotfelter conducted an interview with Jack Rittenhouse that focused on antiquarian bookselling in New Mexico. An audio recording is available at the Golden Library, ENMU in materials gathered for their Oral History Project.

There are other collections from New York to Los Angeles with a Rittenhouse letter here and there, far too numerous for this overview of key resources for a study of Jack's life. Those leads can be found in my footnotes for anyone who enjoys the bibliographical chase.

NOTES

Chapter 1

1. Jack D. Rittenhouse, *Reflections*, "Books and I," Route 66 Oral History Project (M67), Special Collections and Archives, Missouri State University Libraries, Springfield.
2. Jack D. Rittenhouse, *Recollections*, © HBLT, chap. 1, "Life in Mid-West Twenties," https://brileyh.weebly.com/uploads/6/0/5/0/60501297/jr_chap01_life.pdf.
3. *Recollections*, (HBLT website), chap. 1.
4. *Recollections*, (HBLT website), chap. 1.
5. *Recollections*, (HBLT website), chap. 1.
6. *Recollections*, (HBLT website),chap. 1.
7. Not part of the Harvey Hotels developed along the AT&SF Railroad.
8. Rittenhouse, *Reflections*, "Books and I."
9. Rittenhouse, *Reflections*, "Books and I."
10. Rittenhouse, *Reflections*, "Books and I."
11. Rittenhouse, *Reflections*, "In the Boy Scouts."
12. Rittenhouse, *Reflections*, "In the Boy Scouts."
13. "Fort Wayne Boy Scout on European Trip Keeps Diary," Fort Wayne, Ind. *News-Sentinel*, July 27, 1929; "Diary of Jamboree Scout Received by Parents Here," *News-Sentinel*, August 19, 1929; "Jamboree Scouts Making Many Friends in England," *News-Sentinel*, August 24, 1929; "Final Days of Fort Wayne Scouts at Jamboree Happy," *News-Sentinel*, August 31, 1929.
14. Rittenhouse, *Reflections*, "In The Boy Scouts."
15. "C. H. S. Seniors Elect. Jack Rittenhouse named President of Class of 1930." Fort Wayne, Ind., *News-Sentinel*, September 24, 1929.
16. Rittenhouse, *Reflections*, "In the Boy Scouts."
17. Rittenhouse, *Reflections*, "The College Years."
18. Rittenhouse, *Reflections*, "The College Years."
19. Rittenhouse, *Reflections*, "The College Years."
20. Rittenhouse, *Reflections*, "The College Years."
21. Rittenhouse, *Reflections*, "The College Years."

22. Rittenhouse, *Reflections*, "The College Years."
23. Rittenhouse, *Reflections*, "The College Years."
24. Rittenhouse, *Reflections*, "The College Years."
25. Rittenhouse, *Reflections*, "The College Years."
26. Rittenhouse, *Reflections*, "The College Years."
27. Rittenhouse, *Reflections*, "The College Years."

Chapter 2

1. Jack D. Rittenhouse, *Reflections*, "Books and I" (typescript), Route 66 Oral History Project (M67), Special Collections and Archives, Missouri State University Libraries.
2. Rittenhouse, *Reflections*, "Books and I."
3. Rittenhouse, *Recollections*, "Wander Year." (HBLT website) https://brileyh.weebly.com/uploads/6/0/5/0/60501297/jr_chap06_wander.pdf.
4. Fort Wayne, Ind. *Journal-Gazette*, April 7, 1934, p. 12.
5. Rittenhouse, *Recollections*, "Wander Year." (HBLT website). Kingan and Company was a large meatpacking company established in Indianapolis from 1862 to 1966.
6. Rittenhouse, *Diary, Travel Notes*, vol. 1, 1934, Jack D. Rittenhouse Collection, NMSU Library Archives and Special Collections, Las Cruces.
7. Rittenhouse, *Diary, Travel Notes*, vol. 1, 1934.
8. Rittenhouse, *Diary, Travel Notes*, vol. 1, 1934.
9. Rittenhouse, *Diary, Travel Notes*, vol. 1, 1934.
10. Rittenhouse, *Diary, Travel Notes*, vol. 1, 1934.
11. Marvin Mondlin and Roy Meador, *Book Row: An Anecdotal and Pictorial History of the Antiquarian Book Trade* (New York: Carroll & Graf, 2005), xi.
12. Rittenhouse, *Diary, Travel Notes*, vol. 1, 1934.
13. Rittenhouse, *Diary, Travel Notes*, vol. 1, 1934.
14. Rittenhouse, *Diary, Travel Notes*, vol. 1, 1934.
15. Rittenhouse, *Diary, Travel Notes*, vol. 1, 1934.
16. Rittenhouse, *Diary, Travel Notes*, vol. 1, 1934.
17. Rittenhouse, *Diary, Travel Notes*, vol.1, 1934.
18. Rittenhouse, *Diary, Travel Notes*, vol. 1, 1934.
19. Rittenhouse, *Diary, Travel Notes*, vol. 1, 1934.
20. Rittenhouse, *Diary, Travel Notes*, vol. 1, 1934.
21. Rittenhouse, *Diary, Travel Notes*, vol. 1, 1934.
22. Rittenhouse, *Diary, Travel Notes*, vol. 1, 1934.
23. 1934 US Navy Fleet Review, New York City, Hudson River. YouTube, https://www.youtube.com/watch?app=desktop&v=HgPnJrngH1M.
24. Rittenhouse, *Reflections*, "Wanderyear."

25. "Fort Wayne Boy Barely Missed Disaster at Sea," Fort Wayne, Ind. *Journal-Gazette*, September 11, 1934. Beneath the headline is an editor's note: "Last spring Jack Rittenhouse, who had spent several months writing for The Journal-Gazette, decided to make a vagabond tour of Europe. He paused at New York and has remained there."
26. In the diary Jack meticulously kept in 1934, he noted leaving Park Row Books and Magazines on good terms with Harry Smolin. Fifty years later he recalled Smolin firing him for wanting an afternoon off to see the burning wreckage of the SS *Morro Castle*.
27. Jack D. Rittenhouse, *Reflections*, "Wanderyear."
28. Rittenhouse, *Reflections*, "Wanderyear."
29. Rittenhouse, *Reflections*, "Wanderyear."
30. Rittenhouse, *Reflections*, "Wanderyear."
31. Rittenhouse, *Reflections*, "Wanderyear."
32. Rittenhouse, *Reflections*, "Wanderyear."
33. Rittenhouse, *Reflections*, "Wanderyear."
34. Rittenhouse, *Reflections*, "Wanderyear."
35. Rittenhouse, *Reflections*, "Wanderyear."
36. Rittenhouse, *Reflections*, "Wanderyear."
37. "Bulls": hobo slang for railroad police, not always trained in law enforcement and excessively cruel at times.
38. Rittenhouse, *Reflections*, "Wanderyear."
39. Upon taking office on March 4, 1933, FDR immediately began planning relief programs to counteract effects of the Great Depression. One of the first acts passed by Congress was the Federal Emergency Relief Act (FERA) in April 1933, which provided funds to states to help those in need, including transients and homeless.
40. Rittenhouse, *Reflections*, "Wanderyear."
41. Rittenhouse, *Reflections*, "Wanderyear."
42. Rittenhouse, *Reflections*, "Wanderyear."
43. Rittenhouse, *Reflections*, "Wanderyear."
44. Rittenhouse, *Reflections*, "Wanderyear."
45. Rittenhouse, *Reflections*, "Wanderyear."
46. Rittenhouse, *Reflections*, "Wanderyear."
47. Rittenhouse, *Reflections*, "Wanderyear."
48. Rittenhouse, *Reflections*, "Wanderyear."
49. Rittenhouse, *Reflections*, "Wanderyear."
50. Rittenhouse, *Reflections*, "Wanderyear."
51. Rittenhouse, *Reflections*, "Wanderyear."
52. Rittenhouse, *Reflections*, "Wanderyear."
53. Rittenhouse, *Reflections*, "Wanderyear."

54. Rittenhouse, *Reflections*, "Wanderyear."
55. Rittenhouse, *Reflections*, "Wanderyear."
56. Rittenhouse, *Reflections*, "Wanderyear."
57. Rittenhouse, *Reflections*, "Wanderyear."
58. "Riding the Rails," PBS documentary on *American Experience*, 2011.
59. Rittenhouse, *Reflections*, "Wanderyear."
60. Author's interview with Jack Rittenhouse, Albuquerque, July 27, 1989. NMSU Library Special Collections.
61. Rittenhouse, *Reflections*, "Books and I."
62. Rittenhouse, *Reflections*, "Books and I."
63. Rittenhouse, *Reflections*, "Books and I."
64. Rittenhouse, *Reflections*, "Books and I."
65. Rittenhouse, *Reflections*, "Books and I."
66. Big Long Lake, a 365-acre lake located in LaGrange County, Indiana, near Kendallville, forty miles north of Fort Wayne. Jack and Beulah bought their cabin on this lake in 1936.
67. Rittenhouse's 1936 letter, duplicated and sent to NYC publishing houses. Rittenhouse Collection, NMSU.
68. Rittenhouse, *Reflections*, "Books and I."
69. Rittenhouse, *Reflections*, "Books and I."
70. Rittenhouse, *Reflections*, "Books and I."
71. Rittenhouse, *Reflections*, "Books and I."
72. Rittenhouse, *Reflections*, "Wanderyear." Macmillan sold 176,000 copies of *Gone with the Wind* when it was first published in 1936. It won the Pulitzer Prize in 1937, and by the end of the next year it had sold a million copies.

Chapter 3

1. Jack D. Rittenhouse, *Reflections*, "The Advertising Years," Route 66 Oral History Project (M67), Special Collections and Archives, Missouri State University Libraries.
2. Rittenhouse, *Reflections*, "The Advertising Years."
3. Rittenhouse, *Reflections*, "The Advertising Years."
4. Rittenhouse, *Reflections*, "Books and I." Ellis developed the concept for his plan over several years. See "Only Two Things Can Upset This System," Lynn Ellis Inc. advertisement, *Printers' Ink* 137 (November 25, 1920), 174.
5. Rittenhouse, *Reflections*, "Books and I."
6. Rittenhouse, *Reflections*, "The Advertising Years."
7. Rittenhouse, *Reflections*, "The Advertising Years."
8. Rittenhouse, *Reflections*, "The Advertising Years."
9. Rittenhouse, *Reflections*, "The Advertising Years."

10. Rittenhouse, *Reflections*, "The Advertising Years."
11. Rittenhouse, *Reflections*, "The Advertising Years."
12. Rittenhouse, *Reflections*, "The Advertising Years."
13. Rittenhouse, *Reflections*, "The War Years."
14. Rittenhouse, *Reflections*, "The War Years."
15. Rittenhouse, *Reflections*, "The War Years."
16. Rittenhouse, *Reflections*, "The War Years."
17. Rittenhouse, *Reflections*, "The War Years."
18. Rittenhouse, *Reflections*, "The War Years." Robert Briffault (1873–1948) was a prolific writer between the two world wars. After serving in World War I, he moved to England and gained international fame with his novel *Europa* (1935). In September 1935, the book was featured in a full front-page review in the *New York Times Book Review* at the same time Jack worked in the Alfred A. Knopf mailroom and was closely following the New York publishing scene. He included *Europa* in his year-end review of the best books of 1935. See Rittenhouse, "1935 Rich in Fine Books," Fort Wayne, *Journal-Gazette*, February 2, 1936, p. 21.
19. Rittenhouse, *Reflections*, "The War Years."
20. Rittenhouse, *Reflections*, "The War Years."
21. Rittenhouse, *Reflections*, "The David Years."
22. Ultimately, Jack was never drafted.
23. Rittenhouse, *Reflections*, "The David Years." Gasoline rationing began on the East Coast in mid-May and nationwide in December 1942.
24. Rittenhouse, *Reflections*, "The David Years."
25. Rittenhouse, *Reflections*, "The David Years."

Chapter 4

1. Tom Teague, *Searching for 66* (Springfield, IL: Samizdat House, 1991), 148.
2. Jack D. Rittenhouse, *Recollections*, "Settling on Route 66. Harry Briley, ed. https://brileyh.weebly.com/uploads/6/0/5/0/60501297/jr_chap05_settling.pdf.
3. Rittenhouse, *Reflections*, "The David Years," Route 66 Oral History Project (M67), Special Collections and Archives, Missouri State University Libraries. Mike Croteau made an impression on Jack who included him in the entry on Grants, *Route 66 Guide Book*, saying his trading post "is an interesting place, and Mike himself is full of unusual anecdotes for those who come to know him."
4. Rittenhouse, *Recollections*, "Settling on Route 66."
5. Rittenhouse, *Recollections*, "Settling on Route 66."
6. Radios were first installed in automobiles in 1928.

7. Rittenhouse, *Reflections*, "The David Years."
8. Rittenhouse, *Reflections*, "The David Years."
9. Teague, *Searching for 66*, 148.
10. Rittenhouse, *Reflections*, "The Advertising Years."
11. This would be the Bantam's last long trip before Jack sold it.
12. Michael Wallis, *Route 66: The Mother Road*, 75th Anniversary Edition (New York: St. Martin's Griffin, 2002), 21–22.
13. Rittenhouse, *Reflections*, "Books and I."
14. An exception would have been drivers lucky enough to tune in some of the Border radio stations from Mexico, especially at nighttime when they reached the farthest. These radio stations were beyond the reach of US regulators and boosted their signals with 50,000 to 500,000 watts, totally overpowering any competing broadcast frequencies.
15. Lacking funds to pay for ten thousand copies, Jack printed only three thousand.
16. Jack D. Rittenhouse Collection, Promotion file for *A Guide Book to Route 66*, New Mexico State University, Las Cruces, Library Archives and Special Collections.
17. Rittenhouse Collection, Promotion file, *A Guide Book to Route 66*.
18. Teague, *Searching for 66*, 148. The 1947 guide was titled *Highway 66*[,] *the Mainstreet of America through the Heart of the Nation* [,] *Chicago to Santa Monica*[,] *E-Z Way Travel Guide*. I am grateful to T. Lindsay Baker for information on this title.
19. Jack D. Rittenhouse, *A Guide Book to Highway 66* (Albuquerque: UNM Press, 2016, ii–iii). By 2024 the UNM Press facsimile of Rittenhouse's book on Highway 66 had gone through fourteen printings and sold fifty thousand copies.
20. Teague, *Searching for 66*, 148–49.
21. David Kimsey, "Introducing Permian Pete and His Fabulous Projects," *Tomorrow's Tools—Today!* 15, no. 1 (First Quarter 1949), 18.
22. Rittenhouse, *Reflections*, "The Advertising Years." See David Kimsey, *Permian Pete and His Fabulous Projects* (Los Angeles: Lane-Wells, 1951). Rittenhouse listed this book in "First Fifty, A Checklist of the Stagecoach Press." All of his Stagecoach Press books can be found in the Zang Wood Collection, Fray Angélico Chávez History Library at the New Mexico History Museum.
23. The topical files in Jack's papers at NMSU are vast, filled with clippings, tear sheets, and articles reflecting his wide range of interests and the scope of the periodicals he read from year to year throughout his life.
24. Victoria Dailey, "How L.A. Became a Destination on the Rare Book Trail," in *Paperback L.A.: A Casual Anthology*, ed. Susan LaTempa (Los Angeles: Prospect Park Books, 2018), 28.

25. Stephen R. Tabor, "The Antiquarian Book Trade in Los Angeles," *AB Bookman's Weekly*, February 4, 1980.
26. Rittenhouse, *Reflections*, "Books and I."
27. Rittenhouse, *Reflections*, "Books and I."
28. Rittenhouse, *Reflections*, "Books and I."
29. Rittenhouse, *Reflections*, "Books and I."
30. In addition to articles of interest to book collectors and the book trade, other pages of *AB* were filled with ads (short and long), for books people wanted to buy for building their own collections, or to stock their shops. For more than forty years it was essential reading for collectors, booksellers, librarians, and others interested in books. The Internet has now replaced *AB*.
31. Rittenhouse, *Reflections*, "Books and I."
32. Douglas died at age fifty-four in 2001, a decade after his father's death.
33. Rittenhouse, *Reflections*, "Books and I."
34. Rittenhouse, *Reflections*, "Books and I."
35. Jack D. Rittenhouse Collection, unpublished diary and account book titled "Personal," NMSU Library Special Collections.
36. "The Rounce & Coffin Club was a 20th-century fine press book and printing club that operated from 1931 to 2007. It was founded by four members, and at its peak had over fifty-five local members. The Club sponsored the Western Books Exhibition (a traveling exhibition of the best fine press printing from the Western United States) from 1938 to 2005." Description is from the Online Archive of California (OAC). The Rounce & Coffin Club archives are housed at UCLA's Clark Memorial Library.

Chapter 5

1. Jack D. Rittenhouse, *Reflections*, "Books and I," Route 66 Oral History Project (M67), Special Collections and Archives, Missouri State University Libraries.
2. Rittenhouse, *Reflections*, "Books and I."
3. Jack D. Rittenhouse, *Advance List No. 1* (Los Angeles, 1949). This was Rittenhouse's first bookseller catalog in a career that ran forty-two years until his death.
4. Jack D. Rittenhouse to Ivan L. Collins, November 25, 1949, Rittenhouse Collection.
5. Edwin V. Glaser, "The ABAA at Fifty: Notes Toward a History of the Antiquarian Booksellers' Association of America," https://web.archive.org/web/20090821223224/http://hq.abaa.org/books/antiquarian/abaapages/history.html.

6. Rittenhouse, *Reflections*, "Books and I."
7. Rittenhouse, *Reflections*, "Books and I."
8. Rittenhouse, *Reflections*, "Books and I."
9. Shortly before Rittenhouse bought a Gally's Universal press he had acquired a small table-top Kelsey press suitable for printing cards and envelopes but not books.
10. Rittenhouse, *Reflections*, "The Advertising Years."
11. This press is now part of a notable collection of printing equipment and type at the Press of the Palace of Governors in Santa Fe.
12. Rittenhouse, *Reflections*, "Books and I."
13. Water and Power Associates, website https://waterandpower.org/Museum2/Pickwick_Book_Shop.html#:~:text=Pickwick%20opened%20on%20Hollywood%20Blvd,for%20movie%20stars%2C%20among%20others.
14. Rittenhouse, *Reflections*, "Books and I."
15. Rittenhouse, *Reflections*, "Books and I."
16. For a detailed, illustrated biography of W. Everett Miller, see http://www.coachbuilt.com/des/m/miller/miller.htm.
17. Miller's library, now part of the Nethercutt Automotive Research Library and Archive in Sylmar, California, is considered one of the ten most comprehensive collections of its kind in the United States.
18. Rittenhouse, *Reflections*, "The David Years."
19. Jack D. Rittenhouse, "A History of the *Baroid News Bulletin*," unpublished typescript, Rittenhouse Collection, NMSU Library Archives and Special Collections. A complete set of Jack's contributions to this publication can be found in the Zang Wood Collection.
20. Rittenhouse, "A History of the *Baroid News Bulletin*."
21. Rittenhouse, "A History of the *Baroid News Bulletin*."
22. Rittenhouse, "A History of the *Baroid News Bulletin*."
23. Jack D. Rittenhouse to Paul Klosterman, May 24, 1949. Rittenhouse Collection.
24. Jack D. Rittenhouse to Tillie M. Loertsch, May 24, 1949, Rittenhouse Collection.
25. Tillie M. Loertsch to Jack D. Rittenhouse, May 9, 1949, Rittenhouse Collection. Coats made his pencil drawing on ruled paper torn out of a school notebook.
26. Jack D. Rittenhouse to Tillie M. Loertsch, May 24, 1949, Rittenhouse Collection.
27. Jack D. Rittenhouse, diary and account book titled "Personal," Rittenhouse Archive.
28. Rittenhouse, *Reflections*, "The David Years."
29. US Department of Commerce, 1950 Census of Population, September 28, 1950.

30. *Los Angeles Almanac*, Motor Vehicle Registrations, Los Angeles County, https://www.laalmanac.com/transport/tr02.php.
31. Rittenhouse, *Reflections*, "The David Years."
32. Rittenhouse, *Reflections*, "The David Years."
33. Rittenhouse, *Reflections*, "The David Years."
34. Rittenhouse, *Reflections*, "Books and I."
35. Rittenhouse, *Reflections*, "The David Years."
36. Rittenhouse bought the Mikita Shaded type from a collector in Loysville, Pennsylvania, after seeing an ad in *Popular Mechanics*. He only identified it later while perusing an old magazine from 1869 where a complete alphabet was shown. A foundry mark revealed it was cast by Bruce, New York. In 1960 he loaned his Mikita type to Charles Broad, Typefounder, in Phoenix to duplicate. In return for the favor, he asked for a font of 24 pt. Tuscan Ornate. T.L.S. Jack D. Rittenhouse to Charles Broad, Typefounders, March 20, 1960, Rittenhouse Collection.
37. "Local Collector Interested in Early Sierra Madre Printing," *Sierra Madre News*, February 1, 1951.
38. Jack D. Rittenhouse, "The Poor Man's Practical Collector," Rittenhouse Collection, NMSU.
39. Rittenhouse, "The Poor Man's Practical Collector."
40. Rittenhouse, *Reflections*, "The Advertising Years."
41. Rittenhouse, *Reflections*, "Books and I."

Chapter 6

1. Jack D. Rittenhouse, *Reflections*, "Books and I," Route 66 Oral History Project (M67), Special Collections and Archives, Missouri State University Library.
2. Carl Hertzog to Jack D. Rittenhouse, August 13, 1951. Rittenhouse Collection.
3. Jack D. Rittenhouse, "Diary" (small Golden West Notes notebook), 1949–1951. Rittenhouse Collection.
4. Jack D. Rittenhouse, *Reflections*, "The Advertising Years,"
5. Rittenhouse, *Reflections*, "Books and I."
6. Rittenhouse, *Reflections*, "The Advertising Years."
7. Rittenhouse, *Reflections*, "The David Years."
8. Rittenhouse, *Reflections*, "The Advertising Years."
9. Rittenhouse, *Reflections*, "The Advertising Years."
10. Jack D. Rittenhouse to William A. Marsteller, July 26, 1957. Rittenhouse Collection.
11. Rittenhouse, *Reflections*, "Wanderyear."
12. Vintage type was one of Rittenhouse's lifelong pursuits. In a pocket notebook

from 1946 to 1951, he recorded a suggestion from Roland L. Holford, publisher of the Hico, Texas, *News* to visit print shops in Garland and Meridian and inquire about old type. As long as he had presses, he mentioned vintage type in letters to friends with similar interests.

13. "Post Card by George Fuermann, Jack Rittenhouse Guest Columnist," *Houston Post*, August 22, 1955. In 2013 the Texas Historical Commission reported results from an archeological dig at San Felipe de Austin verifying the location of Cotton's printing establishment and unearthing several pieces of type, including an 18 pt. Great Primer shaded small cap K.
14. "POST CARD by George Fuermann, *Houston Post*, August 8, 1956.
15. "POST CARD by George Fuermann," *Houston Post*, August 8, 1956.
16. "Book Mart Adds New Touch for City's Culture Minded," *Victoria Advocate*. November 11, 1956.
17. Joe Petty and his wife, Lydia, moved to Victoria, Texas, late in 1956. It was there that Jack's good friend, Lawrence Clark Powell, visited and wrote about Petty as one of the premier Texas bookmen in the mid-twentieth century.
18. Rittenhouse, *Reflections*, "Books and I."
19. Ed Bartholomew, *The Houston Story: A Chronicle of the City of Houston and the Texas Frontier* (Houston: Frontier Press of Texas, 1951).
20. Rittenhouse, *Reflections*, "Books and I."
21. Rittenhouse, *Reflections*, "Books and I."
22. Texas State Historical Association, *Handbook of Texas* (online), https://www.tshaonline.org/handbook/entries/rose-noah-hamilton.
23. Jack's Oklahoma friend, W. D. Grisso, informed him about the interest at OU in buying the Rose photograph collection.
24. Rittenhouse, *Reflections*, "The David Years."
25. Rittenhouse, *Reflections*, "Books and I."
26. At the time William H. Hudson had a private press that could do this, but Rittenhouse was the only printer in Houston who collected the vintage type used for the program. A clipping, "Civil War Journalism Recalled," from *Publishers' Auxiliary*, May 13, 1961, gives some details on the event.
27. E. L. DeGolyer to Jack D. Rittenhouse, April 17, 1951. Rittenhouse Collection, NMSU Library Special Collections.
28. DeGolyer's library contained three major collections in one grand room—English literature, the history of science, and early voyages and travels including the history of Mexico and the Trans-Mississippi west. The first of these collections he gave to the University of Texas at Austin, the history of science formed the cornerstone for a noted collection now at the University of Oklahoma, and the Western Americana and early voyages formed the noted DeGolyer Library now at Southern Methodist University in Dallas.

29. Rittenhouse, *Reflections*, "Books and I."
30. Rittenhouse, *Reflections*, "Books and I."
31. Rittenhouse, *Reflections*, "Books and I."
32. Untitled and unpublished two-page typescript, Rittenhouse Collection, NMSU Library Special Collections. E. L. DeGolyer died December 14, 1956. For several years before his death DeGolyer had underwritten publication of the *Saturday Review of Literature*.
33. For information about the Cowboys' Christmas Ball see the *Handbook of Texas* online, https://www.tshaonline.org/handbook/entries/cowboys-christmas-ball.
34. Jack D. Rittenhouse to Carl Hertzog, August 18, 1952, Rittenhouse Collection.
35. Some of the cuts most likely came from a multi-drawer cabinet with 644 stock cuts Rittenhouse bought from the Dealy-Adey Company, a large printing and stationary company in Houston. He later sold the collection to the Harry Ransom Center at UT-Austin.
36. Rittenhouse, *Reflections*, "Books and I."
37. Rittenhouse, *Reflections*, "Books and I."
38. Rittenhouse, Proof sheets for *Wendish Language Printing in Texas*, Rittenhouse Collection.
39. Rittenhouse, *Reflections*, "Books and I."
40. Rittenhouse, *Reflections*, "Books and I."
41. Rittenhouse, *Reflections*, "Books and I."
42. Rittenhouse, *Reflections*, "Books and I."
43. Rittenhouse offered this book for sale through Stagecoach Press but not as a publication of the press.
44. Rittenhouse, *Reflections*, "Books and I."
45. Rittenhouse, *Reflections*, "Books and I."
46. For a good history of this legendary bookshop see Mary Carolyn Hollers George, *Rosengren's Books: An Oasis for Mind and Spirit* (San Antonio: Wings Press, 2015).
47. Rittenhouse, *Reflections*, "Books and I."
48. Twenty-five years later, when Rittenhouse was writing recollections for his family, he misremembered the press as LaGrange Steam Press; the titlepage in the book correctly identifies Sticker Steam Press.
49. Rittenhouse, *Reflections*, "Books and I."
50. Mrs. David W. Knepper to Jack D. Rittenhouse, November 4, 1958, Rittenhouse Collection. Mrs. Knepper, Director of the San Jacinto Monument, asked Rittenhouse if he could move the Hoe since they could no longer house it.
51. A metal stick used to set quoins for locking type in a chase. See Rittenhouse,

"Story of the Stagecoach Press–Continued," unpublished typescript, Rittenhouse Collection.

52. Rittenhouse, "Story of the Stagecoach Press."
53. Rittenhouse, *Reflections*, "Books and I."
54. Rittenhouse, *Reflections*, "The Advertising Years."
55. Rittenhouse, *Reflections*, "The Advertising Years."
56. Rittenhouse, *Reflections*, "The Advertising Years."
57. Rittenhouse, *Reflections*, "The Advertising Years."
58. A doggedly persistent researcher could order a photostat from the Library of Congress, but Jack knew collectors wanted more.
59. Jack D. Rittenhouse to William Holman, April 18, 1978, Rittenhouse Collection.
60. *Westways*, November 1960. The circulation of this magazine was around two hundred thousand at the end of 1960.
61. Lawrence Clark Powell, "50 Good Books About New Mexico," *New Mexico Magazine* 38, no. 1 (January 1960), 6–8, 26, 36–37.
62. "Books by Jack D. Rittenhouse," Typescript, November 9, 1990, author's collection.
63. Stagecoach Press flyer, Rittenhouse Collection.
64. Calvin Horn to Lawrence Clark Powell, December 20, 1960, Rittenhouse Collection.
65. Jack D. Rittenhouse to Lawrence Clark Powell, January 23, 1961, Rittenhouse Collection.
66. W. D. Grisso to Jack D. Rittenhouse, January 6, 1961, Rittenhouse Collection.
67. Al Shumate to Jack D. Rittenhouse, September 16, 1961, Rittenhouse Collection.
68. Howard R. Lamar, "Much to Celebrate: The Western History Association's Twenty-Fifth Birthday," *Western Historical Quarterly* 17, no. 4 (October 1986), 397–416.
69. Mission statement, The Westerners, www.westerners-international.org.
70. George Fuermann, "Post Card by George Fuermann," *Houston Post*, February 17, 1961.
71. George Fuermann, "Post Card by George Fuermann," *Houston Post*, April 26, 1961.
72. *The Stagecoach Press Waybill*, October 1960, Rittenhouse Collection. In 1960 Foley's was still the largest department store in downtown Houston, a time when many department stores maintained active, well-stocked book departments.
73. "Post Card by George Fuermann," *Houston Post*, December 18, 1961.
74. "Post Card by George Fuermann," *Houston Post*, May 18, 1962.

75. J. Frank Dobie sat next to Baca at a luncheon in Albuquerque and found him a politician with a "mediocre mind" and not to be trusted. J. Frank Dobie to Jack D. Rittenhouse, January 29, 1962, J. Frank Dobie papers, Harry Ransom Center, UT-Austin.
76. Rittenhouse, *Reflections*, "The Advertising Years."

Chapter 7

1. Johnson, Spud, "The Santa Fe Gadfly," *The New Mexican*, January 23, 1966, 2, 11.
2. Jack W. Rittenhouse to W. D. Grisso, April 12, 1962, Rittenhouse Collection.
3. Oral history interview with Samuel Lanham, Institute for Oral History, Baylor University, Institute for Oral History, https://digitalcollections-baylor.quartexcollections.com/oral-history-collections/oral-history-interviews. The Rittenhouse/Adams Cottage Press is now located at Schreiner University in Kerrville, Texas.
4. Jack D. Rittenhouse to William Holman, April 18, 1978, Rittenhouse Collection. The press had been used in a Waco shop to set type for a trade-union newspaper. While still in Houston Rittenhouse had access to a Linotype repairman on call; in Santa Fe he would be on his own for maintenance of his sixty-six-year-old typesetting machine.
5. Jack D. Rittenhouse to W. D. Grisso, May 12, 1962, Rittenhouse Collection.
6. Jack D. Rittenhouse to W. D. Grisso, May 24, 1962, Rittenhouse Collection.
7. Jack D. Rittenhouse to W. D. Grisso, May 24, 1962, Rittenhouse Collection.
8. Rittenhouse, "Story of the Stagecoach Press–continued," Rittenhouse Collection.
9. Rittenhouse, "Facts about the Stagecoach Press," Rittenhouse Collection.
10. Rittenhouse, "Story of the Stagecoach Press–continued," Rittenhouse Collection. Rittenhouse used numerous Dealy-Adey Company cuts to good effect in the sixteen issues of *La Gaceta: El Boletin del Corral de Santa Fe Westerners* that he edited and printed from 1963 to 1966.
11. Rittenhouse, "Story of the Stagecoach Press."
12. Jack D. Rittenhouse to R. Russo, September 28, 1962, Rittenhouse Collection.
13. Rittenhouse, "Story of the Stagecoach Press–continued," Rittenhouse Collection.
14. Rittenhouse, "Story of the Stagecoach Press–continued," Rittenhouse Collection.
15. Rittenhouse, "Story of the Stagecoach Press–continued," Rittenhouse Collection.
16. Rittenhouse, "Story of the Stagecoach Press–continued," Rittenhouse Collection.

17. William S. Wallace, *Rogers Library Notes*, October 1962, New Mexico Highlands University, Las Vegas.
18. Jack D. Rittenhouse to W. D. Grisso, October 27, 1962, Rittenhouse Collection. Lottinville was the long-time, highly respected director of OU Press who moved it into the top ranks of university presses publishing Western history.
19. Rittenhouse closed the Stagecoach Press before reprinting the Rideing book.
20. The Beinecke Library still holds one of the most comprehensive collections of books and manuscripts on the American West.
21. Jack D. Rittenhouse to W. D. Grisso, October 27, 1962, Rittenhouse Collection.
22. Jack D. Rittenhouse, "Book Notes," *La Gaceta: El Boletin del Corral de Santa Fe Westerners*, 1, no. 1 (October 1963).
23. *La Gaceta*, 1, no. 2 (December 1963).
24. Publicity file for *New Mexico Book News*, Rittenhouse Collection.
25. Publicity file, *NMBN*, Rittenhouse Collection.
26. Publicity file, *NMBN*, Rittenhouse Collection.
27. *New Mexico Book News* 2, no. 2 (November 1965).
28. *New Mexico Book News* 1, no. 10 (July 1965).
29. See David Farmer, "The Fred Harvey Company, Bookseller to the Southwest," *Book Talk* 24, no. 2 (March 1995): 1–3.
30. Spud Johnson, "The Santa Fe Gadfly," *Santa Fe New Mexican*, January 23, 1966.
31. Col. John M. Virden to W. D. Grisso, July 29, 1960, Rittenhouse Collection.
32. W. D. Grisso to Jack D. Rittenhouse, January 6, 1961, Rittenhouse Collection.
33. Jack D. Rittenhouse to W. D. Grisso, January 9, 1961, Rittenhouse Collection.
34. Jack D. Rittenhouse to W. D. Grisso, March 26, 1962, Rittenhouse Collection.
35. W. D. Grisso to Jack D. Rittenhouse, May 30, 1962, Rittenhouse Collection.
36. Jack D. Rittenhouse to W. D. Grisso, May 31, 1962, Rittenhouse Collection.
37. Jack D. Rittenhouse to W. D. Grisso, June 1, 1962, Rittenhouse Collection.
38. Jack D. Rittenhouse to W. D. Grisso, February 2, 1963, Rittenhouse Collection.
39. Jack D. Rittenhouse to W. D. Grisso, February 2, 1963, Rittenhouse Collection.
40. Jack D. Rittenhouse to W. D. Grisso, April 25, 1963, Rittenhouse Collection.
41. Rittenhouse was no doubt referring to Alfred Bush, remembered for his careful and dedicated stewardship of the Western collections at Princeton's Firestone Library.

42. Jack D. Rittenhouse to W. D. Grisso, November 6, 1963, Rittenhouse Collection.
43. Jack D. Rittenhouse to W. D. Grisso, February 17, 1964, Rittenhouse Collection.
44. Jack D. Rittenhouse to Beth Grisso, August 3, 1965, Rittenhouse Collection.
45. Jack D. Rittenhouse to Carl Hertzog, July 31, 1966, Hertzog Collection, University of Texas, El Paso Library Special Collections.
46. Rittenhouse, *Reflections*, "Books and I."
47. Rittenhouse, *Reflections*, "Books and I." "Stone" is a printer's term for the hard and perfectly flat surface on which type is imposed and locked up in the chase before going on the press.
48. "Robert G. Ferris Quits Museum Job," *Santa Fe New Mexican*, January 5, 1964.
49. Janice Guercio, "Vast Reorganization Planned by Museum of New Mexico," *Santa Fe New Mexican*, August 23, 1963.
50. Rittenhouse, *Reflections*, "Books and I."
51. Rittenhouse, *Reflections*, "Books and I."
52. Jack D. Rittenhouse, "Methods of Financing a Publications Program," Rittenhouse Collection.
53. Rittenhouse, *Reflections*, "Books and I."
54. David J. Weber to Jack D. Rittenhouse, September 19 and December 19, 1966, Rittenhouse Collection.
55. Pamela Smith, *Passions in Print: Private Press Artistry in New Mexico* (Santa Fe: Museum of New Mexico Press, 2008), 110.

Chapter 8

1. Jack D. Rittenhouse, "The Bibliographic Quest," Rittenhouse Papers, Center for Southwest Research and Special Collections, UNM Library.
2. "UNM Press Readers' Reports," Rittenhouse Collection, NMSU Library Special Collections.
3. "UNM Press Readers' Reports," Rittenhouse Collection.
4. *Signature of the Sun: Southwest Verse, 1900–1950* was edited by Mabel Major and T. M. Pearce, distinguished professors at UNM.
5. J. Frank Dobie, *Guide to Life and Literature of the Southwest* (Dallas: SMU Press, 1952).
6. Jack D. Rittenhouse to Orlan Sawey, December 7, 1976, Rittenhouse Collection, NMSU Library Special Collections.
7. John Houghton Allen to "The Editor," n.d., Rittenhouse Collection.
8. Jack D. Rittenhouse to John Houghton Allen, February 7, 1977, Rittenhouse Collection.

9. Jack D. Rittenhouse to Edward Abbey, November 4, 1976, Rittenhouse Collection.
10. See *Gus Blaisdell Collected*, edited by William Peterson and Nicole Blaisdell Ivey (Albuquerque: UNM Press, 1912).
11. Jack D. Rittenhouse to Don Congdon, November 8, 1976, Rittenhouse Collection.
12. At the time of this writing, only one copy of the first edition of *The Brave Cowboy* was offered for sale in the United States, listed for $5,500. It belonged to T. M. Pearce, a well-respected author and professor of English at UNM for more than thirty-five years. He annotated this book extensively in pencil and wrote on the front flyleaf some of his recollections of Abbey. He also included a newspaper clipping about Kirk Douglas who bought the film rights, engaged Dalton Trumbo to write the script, and starred in the 1962 film, *Lonely Are the Brave*, based on Abbey's book.
13. Everett L. Cooley to Jack D. Rittenhouse, November 3, 1971, Rittenhouse Collection.
14. Jack D. Rittenhouse, "President's Report–1968, Historical Society of New Mexico," Rittenhouse Collection.
15. Jack D. Rittenhouse, "President's Report–1968."
16. Beatrice Chauvenet, *Hewett and Friends: A Biography of Santa Fe's Vibrant Era* (Santa Fe: Museum of New Mexico Press, 1983), 80.
17. "Meeting of the Board of Directors, Historical Society of New Mexico," Minutes, September 25, 1969. Rittenhouse Collection.
18. Michael Stevenson, "The Museum and Collections of the Historical Society of New Mexico, 1859–1977," in *Telling New Mexico: A New History*, edited by Marta Weigle, Frances Levine, and Louise Stiver (Santa Fe: Museum of New Mexico Press, 2009). See also Bill Garland, "Museum Catalogs Gifts from New Mexico's Past," *Santa Fe New Mexican*, July 11, 1977. Garland quotes Arthur Olivas, photographic archivist, who noted some sixty thousand photographic prints came from the Historical Society collections.
19. "'Let's Talk More' Road Meet Theme," *Las Cruces Sun News*, April 4, 1968, p. 1. Unsigned article.
20. "National Historic Preservation Act of 1966," National Park Service website, https://www.nps.gov/subjects/archeology/national-historic-preservation-act.htm.
21. Jack D. Rittenhouse, "Project: Photo Census of New Mexico, 1970," May 29, 1969, Rittenhouse Collection.
22. Jack D. Rittenhouse, "Proposed Photographic Inventory of New Mexico Historic Places," Rittenhouse Collection.
23. Jack D. Rittenhouse, "Save Those 'Old West' Photographs," Rittenhouse Collection.

24. "New Mexico History Day Saturday in Silver City," *Deming Graphic* (Demming, NM), November 9, 1970.
25. "Day to Spotlight State History," *Albuquerque Journal*, May 30, 1971. It is very likely Jack wrote the press release resulting in newspaper coverage of this event in the *Albuquerque Journal*, the *Santa Fe New Mexican*, and the *Las Cruces Sun News*. The stories are carefully organized, tightly written, and historically sound—just the kind of news releases Jack wrote with ease and newspaper editors recognized as ready to run without any rewriting.
26. Rittenhouse, "The Bibliographic Quest."
27. As part of a national survey, William E. Brown worked with historian Ray Mattison to produce the 1963 *National Survey of Historic Sites and Buildings: The Santa Fe Trail.*
28. Jack D. Rittenhouse, "Notes on the Writing of *The Santa Fe Trail: a Historical Bibliography*," Rittenhouse Collection, NMSU Library Special Collection.
29. Rittenhouse, "Notes on the Writing."
30. Rittenhouse, "The Bibliographic Quest."
31. Rittenhouse, "The Bibliographic Quest."
32. Rittenhouse, "The Bibliographic Quest."
33. Rittenhouse, "Notes on the Writing."
34. Jack D. Rittenhouse, "Some Facts and Observations on the Fort Wayne Book Market," Rittenhouse Collection. In a single page Rittenhouse presented statistics on the number of bookstores in the United States; gross sales across the country for different categories, from textbooks and Bibles, to fiction, and more; library statistics; and a list of the four bookstores in Fort Wayne.
35. Jack D. Rittenhouse, "The Bibliographic Quest."
36. George Wilkins Kendall, *Narrative of the Texan Santa Fe Expedition*, 2 vols. (New York: Harper and Bros., 1844); and Josiah Gregg, *Commerce of the Prairies: or the Journal of a Santa Fe Trader, during Eight Expeditions across the Great Western Prairies, and a Residence of nearly Nine Years in Northern Mexico*, 2 vols. (New York: Henry G. Langley, 1844). Rittenhouse cited these two books as the cornerstones for study of the Santa Fe Trail. They were rare and expensive during his lifetime and are even more so today.
37. Rittenhouse, "The Bibliographic Quest."
38. Jack D. Rittenhouse to Roger W. Shugg, August 28, 1970, Rittenhouse Collection.
39. Michael D. Heaston to Jack D. Rittenhouse, July 13, 1971, Rittenhouse Collection.
40. Dick Mohr to Jack D. Rittenhouse, July 19, 1971, Rittenhouse Collection.
41. Ray A. Billington to Jack D. Rittenhouse, July 29, 1971, Rittenhouse Collection.

42. David J. Weber, "Book Review: The Santa Fe Trail, A Historical Bibliography, by Jack D. Rittenhouse," *New Mexico Historical Review* 47, 1 (1972) 69–70.
43. See *Montana: The Magazine of Western History* (Winter 1972), 73, for Moorehead review and *The Colorado Magazine* 48, no. 4 (1971), for Bannon review.
44. Shelah-Bell Cragin to Jack D. Rittenhouse, October 27, 1971, Rittenhouse Collection, NMSU Library. See also, UNM News Release, November 17, 1972, Rittenhouse Collection.
45. James McGrath Morris, *Tony Hillerman: A Life* (Norman: University of Oklahoma Press, 2021), 159.
46. Jack D. Rittenhouse, *Trail of Commerce and Conquest: A Brief History of the Road to Santa Fe* (Woodston, KS: Santa Fe Trail Council, 1987).
47. Jack D. Rittenhouse to Marc Simmons, June 15, 1987, Rittenhouse Collection. As of this writing, the Santa Fe Trail Association is still offering copies for sale.
48. Marc Simmons, "Jack D. Rittenhouse, 1912–1991," *Wagon Tracks* 6, no. 1, (November 1991): 5.
49. Jack D. Rittenhouse, "History of UNM Press," (working notes), UNM Press Archive, Center for Southwest Studies and Special Collections.
50. Subscription fulfillment remained in Santa Fe, which later became a logistical challenge.
51. Jack D. Rittenhouse, "A Condensed History of the University of New Mexico Press," Marta Weigle Collection, Fray Angelico Chavez History Library, New Mexico History Museum.
52. Rittenhouse, "A Condensed History of UNM Press."
53. Rittenhouse, "A Condensed History of UNM Press."
54. "UNM Press Books to be Presented by Columbia Press," *Albuquerque Journal*, January 9, 1972.
55. Jack D. Rittenhouse, "The Canadian Book Market for Books of the University of New Mexico Press—A Report," Rittenhouse Collection.
56. Jack D. Rittenhouse to Professor Hoyt Trowbridge, November 30, 1972, Rittenhouse Collection.
57. Jack D. Rittenhouse, *Recollections*, © HBLT. Chapter 12 "University of New Mexico," https://brileyh.weebly.com/uploads/6/0/5/0/60501297/jr_chap12_unm.pdf.
58. Jack D. Rittenhouse, "Books Needed in Every State—A Checklist," Rittenhouse Collection.
59. *New Mexico Historic Documents* was number 57 on Rittenhouse's checklist of books needed in every state.
60. Book review by Alice Bulloch *Santa Fe New Mexican*, November 23, 1975.
61. Jack Janowski, "Writers' Visions Handful of Gems," *Albuquerque Journal*, January 30, 1977.

62. Bruce Gentry worked with Walter Goodwin at Rydal Press, Santa Fe, in the late 1930s before moving to New York to work for H. Wolff and Company. He returned to Santa Fe in the late 1960s and was soon hired as book designer for UNM Press. John G. H. Scoon, assistant director at the Press, gained university press editorial experience at Princeton, Chicago, and OU. See Jack D. Rittenhouse, "Books and I," unpublished typescript, "Reflections, Route 66 Oral History Project (M67), Special Collections and Archives, Missouri State University Libraries; also, Roger W. Shugg, "Report of the University of New Mexico Press," typescript photocopy, June 1968, NMSU Library.
63. Rittenhouse, *Reflections*, "Books and I."
64. Courtesy of Harry Briley, personal collection.
65. Frank H. Wardlaw to Jack D. Rittenhouse, June 28, 1978. Courtesy of Harry Briley.
66. Claire Morrill and Genevieve Janssen to Jack D. Rittenhouse, n.d. Courtesy of Harry Briley.
67. Carl Hertzog to Jack D. Rittenhouse, June 17, 1978. Courtesy of Harry Briley.
68. Bruce Gentry to Jack D. Rittenhouse, June 25, 1978. Courtesy of Harry Briley.
69. Tony Hillerman to Jack D. Rittenhouse, June 13, 1978. Courtesy of Harry Briley.

Chapter 9

1. Jack D. Rittenhouse, "The Poor Man's Practical Collector," Rittenhouse Collection, NMSU.
2. Jack D. Rittenhouse to Carl Hertzog, January 23, 1978, Rittenhouse Collection, NMSU Library.
3. Other travel-oriented magazines in the 1940s included *Sample Case Magazine*, *Tourist Court Journal*, *Sunset*, *The Desert Spotlight*, and *The Desert Magazine*. Jack's ads for *A Guide Book to Highway 66* appeared in all of these.
4. Jack D. Rittenhouse, untitled summary of book business, 1949, Rittenhouse Collection.
5. Jack D. Rittenhouse to Robert Greenwood, December 6, 1960, Rittenhouse Collection.
6. Jack D. Rittenhouse, Bookseller, Catalog 82, *Old, New & Rare Books on the American West*, (Albuquerque, New Mexico, 1990). At the time Jack issued this catalog, I was the first buyer to call about his set of the first twenty-five *AB Yearbooks* for sale. They are now on the shelves at DeGolyer Library, Southern Methodist University.

7. Jack D. Rittenhouse to Bob Hesler, August 22, 1978, Rittenhouse Collection.
8. Jack D. Rittenhouse to Marshall Townsend, August 21, 1979, Rittenhouse Collection.
9. Jack D. Rittenhouse to Jerry Keenan, May 7, 1981, Rittenhouse Collection.
10. Jack D. Rittenhouse, "The Millionth Book," unpublished typescript, Rittenhouse Collection.
11. Rittenhouse, "The Millionth Book."
12. Rittenhouse, "The Millionth Book."
13. Jack D. Rittenhouse, "The Millionth Book." See also *A Million Stars, The Millionth Acquisition for the University of New Mexico General Library* (Albuquerque, University of New Mexico General Library, 1981), with contributions by Rudolfo Anaya, Donald Farren, et al.
14. Jack D. Rittenhouse to David Nevin, June 3, 1984, Rittenhouse Collection.
15. J. L. Perry Jr. to Jack D. Rittenhouse, September 20, 1981, Rittenhouse Collection.
16. Jack D. Rittenhouse to J. L. Perry Jr., October 26, 1981, Rittenhouse Collection.
17. Jack D. Rittenhouse to J. L. Perry Jr., December 31, 1982, Rittenhouse Collection.
18. Jack D. Rittenhouse to J. L. Perry Jr., March 22, 1989, Rittenhouse Collection.
19. Jack D. Rittenhouse to J. L. Perry Jr., October 6, 1978, Rittenhouse Collection.
20. A. B. Guthrie to Rittenhouse, March 18, 1979, Rittenhouse Collection.
21. Jack D. Rittenhouse to William S. Wallace, December 6, 1958, Rittenhouse Collection.
22. Jack D. Rittenhouse to William S. Wallace, March 25, 1961, Rittenhouse Collection; William S. Wallace, "Introduction to Book Collecting," *New Mexico Magazine* 39, no. 4 (April 1961), 22–23, 34–35.
23. The two books were *Confederate Victories in the Southwest* (Albuquerque: Horn and Wallace, 1961); and *Union Army Operations in the Southwest* (Albuquerque: Horn and Wallace, 1961).
24. Jack D. Rittenhouse, "Hallmarks of Fine Printing," *Rogers Library Notes* 12, no. 1 (October 1962), 1–2.
25. Jack D. Rittenhouse to Donna R. Bratton, December 17, 1985, Rittenhouse Collection.
26. Jack D. Rittenhouse, "Putting Out a Bookseller Catalogue," *AB Yearbook, 1987* (Clifton, NJ).
27. Jack D. Rittenhouse, Bookseller, Catalog 51, *Old, New & Rare Books on the American West*. Albuquerque, n.d.
28. Rittenhouse, Bookseller, Catalog 82, *Old, New & Rare Books on the American West*. Albuquerque, 1990.

29. Rittenhouse, Catalog 82.
30. Rittenhouse, Catalog 59.
31. Rittenhouse, Catalog 78.
32. Rittenhouse, Catalog 57.
33. Rittenhouse, Catalog 52. Rittenhouse's catalog notes quoted above were drawn from the two best holdings of his catalogs that I could locate. One is in the Zang Wood Collection, Fray Angélico Chávez History Library at the New Mexico History Museum in Santa Fe; the other is held by DeGolyer Library, Southern Methodist University.
34. Jack D. Rittenhouse, "Putting Out a Bookseller Catalogue."
35. Rittenhouse, "Putting Out a Bookseller Catalogue."
36. Jack D. Rittenhouse to Dennis McDonnell, January 9, 1988, Rittenhouse Collection.
37. Jack D. Rittenhouse to Kim Whalg, Rockland Books, August 17, 1987, Rittenhouse Collection.
38. Jack D. Rittenhouse to Darla Beckman, November 2, 1984, Rittenhouse Collection.
39. Jack D. Rittenhouse to Lynn Bevill, November 16, 1984, Rittenhouse Collection.
40. Jack D. Rittenhouse to Marshall Townsend, August 21, 1979, Rittenhouse Collection.
41. Jack D. Rittenhouse to Ernest L. Olson, November 29, 1980, Rittenhouse Collection.
42. Rittenhouse to Olson.
43. Rittenhouse to Olson.
44. Jack D. Rittenhouse to Richard L. Wentworth, November 27, 1984, Rittenhouse Collection.
45. Jack D. Rittenhouse to Fred Rochlin, April 5, 1984, Rittenhouse Collection. Rochlin was a decorated World War II pilot and LA architect who collected Western Jewish Americana. In retirement he became a spellbinding monolinguist who performed in theaters around the country with his show, "Old Man in a Baseball Cap: A Memoir of World War II."
46. Jack D. Rittenhouse to James P. Dyke, September 13, 1977, Rittenhouse Collection.
47. In those years, John Jenkins' father, "Mr. J.," lived on the premises to oversee Johnnie's large metal building and maintain nighttime security. With a comfortable suite of rooms and kitchen inside the building, Jenkins invited select, serious book buyers like Jack to spend the night and continue finding books long after the doors were locked at the end of a regular workday. Mr. J. always made sure coffee was brewed first thing in the morning.

48. When Jenkins purchased the remaining stock of the Eberstadt booksellers after they closed their legendary New York book business in 1975, he installed the collection in a lighted, air conditioned, concrete bunker inside his building entered only through a bank vault door.
49. Rittenhouse, *Recollections*, chap. 12, “University of New Mexico.”
50. Jack D. Rittenhouse to Tal Luther, September 22, 1977, Rittenhouse Collection. Stories still circulate about how Bat Masterson always found a way, year after year, to sell “his” Colt .45” to the next collector who knocked on the door. It was easy. He either bought another one from the Colt Manufacturing Company or walked down the street to the nearest pawn shop.
51. Jack D. Rittenhouse, “Southwest Imprints–Writers’ Editions,” *Book Talk* 4, no. 5 (December 1974), 3–4.
52. Jack D. Rittenhouse, “The Bookseller, the Library, and the Collector,” *Book Talk* 5, no. 4 (September 1976), 1–2.
53. Jack D. Rittenhouse, “The West is Wider Than You Think,” *AB Bookman’s Weekly* 72, no. 15 (October 10, 1983), 2226–34.
54. Jack D. Rittenhouse to Jerry Wise, September 13, 1980, Rittenhouse Collection. Richard Hicks (1922–2012) crafted thirty-one wooden presses based on his extensive research on the Medieval and the common press. Examples of his presses can be seen in the Center for the Book at the Albuquerque Public Library.
55. Calla Hay, “Paso por aqui,” *Santa Fe New Mexican*, July 13, 1978.
56. Newspaper ad, *Santa Fe New Mexican*, September 23, 1979.
57. “Western Author to Speak,” *Farmington Daily Times*, November 30, 1981.
58. Notes from the proceedings of the Rio Grande Historical Collections meeting, November 30, 1982, NMSU Library.
59. Memo headed “CONFIDENTIAL,” November 12, 1987, Rittenhouse Collection.
60. Jack D. Rittenhouse, *A Guide Book to Highway 66*, “Preface to Facsimile Edition,” (Albuquerque: UNM Press, 1989).
61. Rittenhouse, *Recollections*, chap. 18, “Closing Shop,” https://brileyh.weebly.com/uploads/6/0/5/0/60501297/jr_chap18_closing.pdf.

Chapter 10

1. Jack D. Rittenhouse, *Reflections*, “Books and I,” Route 66 Oral History Project (M67), Special Collections and Archives, Missouri State University Libraries.
2. Jack D. Rittenhouse, Bookseller, Catalog 80, *Old, New, & Rare Tooks on the American West*, Albuquerque, NM.
3. Jack D. Rittenhouse to Allan Floersheim, January 8, 1988, Rittenhouse

Collection. Floersheim ran a printing shop in Roy, New Mexico, where Jack contracted for the production of many of his catalogs. There is no record of how they met, but Jack's pattern of driving the "Blue highways" all over the West suggests he may have been passing through Roy on his way to see the nearby Santa Fe Trail ruts, spotted the sign for Floersheim's shop, and stopped to introduce himself and talk about printing.

4. Jack D. Rittenhouse, Bookseller, Catalog 83, *Old, New & Rare Books on the American West* (Albuquerque, NM), November 1990, 2.
5. "A Special Note," n.d., author's correspondence with Rittenhouse.
6. Jack D. Rittenhouse, "Foundations for Castles in the Air" (typescript), Rittenhouse Collection. Jake Chernofsky arranged for Jack's keynote address to be published early the following year with a new title, "Antiquarian Bookselling: The Dream and the Reality," *AB Bookman's Weekly*, February 25, 1991, pp. 748–51.
7. Rittenhouse, "Foundations for Castles in the Air," pp. 7–8.
8. Rittenhouse, "Foundations for Castles in the Air," pp. 9–10.
9. Maroon Waxman to Tony Hillerman, September 28, 1989, Rittenhouse Collection. Waxman was the executive director of book development at Book of the Month Club in New York.
10. Jack D. Rittenhouse to Tony Hillerman, January 24, 1990, Rittenhouse Collection.
11. Jack D. Rittenhouse to Tony Hillerman, March 15, 1990, Rittenhouse Collection.
12. Jack D. Rittenhouse to Tony Hillerman, March 15, 1990, Rittenhouse Collection.
13. Jack D. Rittenhouse to Tony Hillerman, June 16, 1991, Rittenhouse Collection.
14. Telephone interview with Dan Cronkhite, Yucca Valley, California, August 4, 2020.
15. Jack D. Rittenhouse, Bookseller, Catalog 84, *Old, New & Rare Books on the American West*, Albuquerque, March 1991, p. 4.
16. Jack D. Rittenhouse to Marilyn Myers, March 13, 1991, Rittenhouse Collection.
17. Jack D. Rittenhouse, "Suggestions on Best Use of These Mailing Lists," Rittenhouse Collection.
18. Jack D. Rittenhouse to Marilyn Myers, December 28, 1990, Rittenhouse Collection. In the process of interviewing Jack in July 1989 for an article on him in *AB Bookman's Weekly* and seeking his suggestions for a lecture I was preparing for the Santa Fe Trail Association, he told me about the reference collection he was selling and sent a list. For my personal collection I bought 175 books from Jack, which he and Charlotte delivered by car. We

were living in Southlake, Texas, not far from their daughter Susan, whom they visited after we unloaded boxes of books. That was likely his last visit with his daughter and the last driving trip he made anywhere in the West. Charlotte wrote my wife and me at the end of July that Jack was ill with terminal lymph node cancer. He died August 10 in Albuquerque.

19. Eduardo Garrigues, "*Pasó por aquí* Jack Rittenhouse, the Author," *Santa Fe New Mexican*, August 29, 1991.
20. Author's interview with Nicholas Potter, Santa Fe, February 15, 2024.
21. Telephone interview with Lew Buckingham, December 2023.

INDEX

Page numbers in italic text indicate images.